BUSINESS
PLANS
MADE EASY

Additional Titles in Entrepreneur's *Made Easy Series*

▶ *Accounting and Finance for Small Business Made Easy: Secrets You Wish Your CPA Had Told You* by Robert Low

▶ *Managing a Small Business Made Easy* by Martin E. Davis

▶ *Meetings Made Easy: The Ultimate Fix-It Guide* by Frances Micale

▶ *Strategic Planning Made Easy* by Fred L. Fry, Charles R. Stoner, and Laurence G. Weinzimmer

▶ *Advertising Without an Agency Made Easy* by Kathy J. Kobliski

Entrepreneur® MADE EASY *Series*

Business Plans Made Easy

THIRD EDITION

DAVID H. BANGS JR.

EP
Entrepreneur®
Press

Editorial Director: Jere L. Calmes
Cover Design: Beth Hansen-Winter
Editorial and Production Services: Eliot House Productions

This publication is designed to provide accurate and authoritative information in regard to
the subject matter covered. It is sold with the understanding that the publisher is not
engaged in rendering legal, accounting, or other professional services. If legal advice or
other expert assistance is required, the services of a competent professional person should
be sought.

> —From a Declaration of Principles jointly adopted by
> a Committee of the American Bar Association and
> a Committee of Publishers and Associations

Library of Congress Cataloging-in-Publication Data
Bangs, David H.
   Business plans made easy/by David H. Bangs.—3rd ed.
     p. cm.—(Entrepreneur made easy series)
   Rev. ed. of: Business plans made easy/Mark Henricks and John Riddle. 2nd ed. 2002.
   Includes index.
   ISBN 1-932531-70-X (alk. paper)
   1. Business planning. I. Henricks, Mark. Business plans made easy. II. Title. III. Series.
   HD30.28.H474 2005
   658.4'012—dc22

                                    2005005167

Printed in Canada

10 09 08 07 06   10 9 8 7 6 5 4 3 2

Contents

SECTION TWO

Writing Your Business Plan

Preface

For the revised Third Edition of
Business Plans Made Easy

Over the past 30 years I have noticed that the most difficult part of writing a business plan is simply getting started. Some people need to know what a business plan is and why it's a good idea to have one. Others are unsure of where to begin, what to put in or leave out, who to aim the plan at, how to put it all together, and how to package it. Mark Henricks and John Riddle (authors of the earlier editions of *Business Plans Made Easy*) did a fine job addressing these concerns. I have tried to maintain their reasoning and structure while adding a few thoughts of my own.

Business Plans Made Easy is divided into three sections:

1. Before Writing Your Plan
2. Writing Your Business Plan
3. Enhancing Your Business Plan

You don't want to write a business plan in a vacuum. Before writing your plan, you need to have an idea of how you want to use it—usually, but not always, this will be to test your business ideas and/or to raise capital to put those ideas to work. This prewriting phase won't lock you into a single use, but it will simplify the writing process if you know at whom your plan is aimed. Is it for your own use? Is it for a banker or other investor?

Writing a business plan is not a linear activity but rather an organic process. Much of the value of a plan lies in the process. As you think, write, and revise your plan, you will get to know more about your business and how it works, which almost always leads to improvements, new insights, and increased profitability. A bright idea in the marketing section may lead to changes in staffing, management, and financial areas. Accordingly, I urge people who are writing their first business plan to buy and use a thick three-ring binder and to set up a business plan document on their computer. Both the binder and the document will have subheads that vary according to the nature of the business. (More on this below.) The binder becomes a useful repository of early thoughts; ideas that are not beneficial today may be useful tomorrow. Although it is easy to keep early drafts on the computer, it is more helpful to print them out and store them in the binder so you can refer back to them. You will be surprised how useful these early drafts are when you assemble the final draft of your business plan (or financing proposal if that is its use). Some of the most valuable information will be the assumptions you make in your financial projections: What were you thinking? Why did you pick this value rather than some other?

The headings are pretty much the same no matter what your business. All business plans have to describe what the business sells (product or service), how it produces that product or service (operations, personnel, management, equipment, and capital), how it identifies and serves a market (who the customers are, why they will buy from this business instead of a competitor), how it will attract and retain those customers (marketing and promotion), and how all the numbers add up to a profit (financial statements and projections). A manufacturing company will have detailed information on operations and production processes. A retailer will be more concerned with location and selling practices, including training and appearance of sales staff. You choose your subheads—but be sure to include the four Cs:

1. *Concept.* What is the business about? What is its history and future?
2. *Customers.* Who are they? Why will they buy?
3. *Competition.* All business is competitive.
4. *Cash.* No business can run without cash, and only financial discipline as embodied in the financial statements can make sure you don't run out of cash!

If you have followed along so far and have jotted down a few subheads, you've accomplished the most difficult part of writing a business plan. You've gotten started.

One common misapprehension about business plans is that the hardest part is dealing with the financial statements. Bear in mind that help is more readily available for the financial part of the plan than for the narrative part. The financial statements and projections express the thinking and research of the first parts of the plan, those parts in which you lay out how the business will use its assets to attract and retain a customer base sufficient to make a profit over the long haul. Bankers, accountants, and other experts are more than capable of helping you create a model of your business and how it works in standard financial terminology and formats. If you are not comfortable with this aspect of the plan, by all means avail yourself of expert advice. The financial model you create in your business plan will repay your efforts a thousand fold. You can use the model to create what-if scenarios, to convince investors to put their money in your venture, to test ideas, and to create budgets to control cash.

What should be the focus of your business planning efforts? That's easy—on marketing. All good business plans contain a good marketing plan. Think about it. The purpose of your business is to make money. Without customers who are able and willing to buy your product or service at a price that affords you a decent profit, you won't be in business for long, no matter how much capital you begin with. Shrewd investors (you included) want to make sure that every effort has been or will be taken to identify, reach, and retain that invaluable customer base. Everything in your business—its organization, its operations, and its staffing and financing—revolves around the customer. Therefore, it makes sense to focus your planning efforts on this central issue. The rest then follows.

Good luck with your business plan!

—Andy Bangs
Portsmouth, NH

Introduction

EACH CHAPTER IN THIS BOOK IS DEVOTED TO ANALYZING, EXPLAINING, and wherever and whenever possible, making entertaining an important concept relating to business plans. The chapter topics range from why you even need a plan to what to do with it when you're finished. You'll learn techniques for figuring your break-even ratio and tips for approaching potential investors. You'll hear stories about the business plans of famous entrepreneurs and even learn about a few entrepreneurs who admit that they don't write plans—willingly, at least.

Along the way, you'll find definitions of important terms, contact information for useful resources, warnings of especially common or serious mistakes, and pointers to steer you in the right direction. When you've finished, you'll be prepared to write a sound, comprehensive, convincing plan for almost any business, whether it's a brand-new start-up or an existing company. More important, however, you'll be the owner of a thoroughly prepared mind and need just the slightest nod from good fortune to proceed.

Following is a chapter-by-chapter summary of the book. The chapters are intended to be read in sequence, with exercises, worksheets, and samples to be studied, completed, and examined along the way. If after finishing you need more help with a particular section, the chapters can be reviewed as self-contained tutorials on their particular topics.

Section One: Before Writing Your Plan

Prepare to write your plan before starting to write it. This section will prevent false starts (which are very discouraging) and help you focus on what information you need to get, where to get it, to whom to address the plan, and more.

Chapter 1: Plan to Prosper: Business Plan Basics

This chapter shows that there are many compelling answers to the question, Why write a business plan? It explores the basic definition of a business plan and when and why to write one, and it lays out what a business plan cannot do for you.

Chapter 2: Digging for Dollars

Writing a business plan is often closely tied to raising money for a start-up business. This chapter examines sources of funding and explains how business plans can be used to help entrepreneurs obtain financing from the most commonly used sources.

Chapter 3: Put Your Plan to Work

One of the most important purposes of a business plan is to evaluate a business proposition's chances for success. You can also sell, comfort suppliers and customers, even manage your business with your plan.

Chapter 4: Before Beginning Your Plan

No two plans are the same, but they all follow similar routes to creation. This chapter tells how to navigate the major steps, including determining your personal goals and objectives and understanding how they figure in planning.

Chapter 5: One Plan Does Not Fit All

Plans differ among industries, and they also have different purposes. You will want to pick the general type of plan that fits your needs and your company. This chapter explains how to do that, and describes the major types of plans, such as working plans, miniplans, and presentations.

Section Two: Writing Your Business Plan

This is where the effort you put into preplanning pays off.

Chapter 6: Executive Summaries Sell Ideas

The executive summary is the most important part of your plan. This chapter tells you why and details exactly what should go into a well-conceived summary.

Chapter 7: Management Makes Money

The section of your business plan describing your management team is likely to be one of the first readers turn to. You'll need to explain what each team member does, how you plan to grow it if necessary, and who your advisors are. This chapter explains the techniques and underlying import of these tasks.

Chapter 8: What You Are Really Selling

Most entrepreneurs really enjoy describing the product or service that is their business's reason for being. This chapter tells how to channel that enthusiasm into answering the questions investors and other plan readers most often ask.

Chapter 9: Riding Industry Trends

Every business plan has to understand the industry in which it will operate. In this chapter, you'll describe the state of your industry using market research, trend analysis, and competitive factors. You'll explain why you picked this industry, whether it's growing or shrinking, and what makes you better.

Chapter 10: Marketing: The Plan Within Your Plan

No matter how great your products or services, if you don't know how to persuade someone to buy them, or can't show you know how in your business plan, your plan will get short shrift. This primer in marketing strategy will tell how to employ the four Ps of traditional marketing as well as how to prepare a follow-up marketing plan for the next generation of products.

Chapter 11: How Does Your Business Work?

Operations is an area few entrepreneurs have trouble mustering enthusiasm for. As usual, however, the entrepreneurial enthusiasm has to be directed at the right targets if the plan is to achieve maximum impact on its readers. This chapter tells how to write operations sections for service firms, retailers, and manufacturers and to take into account special considerations for each.

Chapter 12: Expressing Your Ideas in Financial Terms

The most intimidating part of a business plan for many entrepreneurs is the required financial statements, including historical and projected balance sheets, income statements, and cash flow statements. This chapter dispels fears by clearly presenting explanations of the major financial statements and analytical ratios, along with instructions on how to prepare them and how to avoid common pitfalls.

Section Three: Enhancing Your Business Plan

Now that the plan itself has been completed (insofar as any plan is ever complete), there may be material that didn't fit in but would help make your case more compelling to a particular audience. There are also format and presentation issues to consider.

Chapter 13: Enlightening Extras: Appendices

Many plans have important information that doesn't fit into the major sections. This chapter tells you what to consider for a plan's appendix, including employee resumes, product samples, press clippings, and the like.

Chapter 14: You Only Make a First Impression Once

Good presentation can make a good plan even better. This chapter provides straightforward tips for doing that, along with hints on multimedia presentations and other elements of a plan package, such as cover sheets and cover letters. You need to pick the proper stationery, printing, and design for your plan. You need to make sure that you use charts, graphs, and tables when appropriate, without overdoing it.

Chapter 15: Information Creates Capital

The internet has leveled the playing field for business owners in the new millennium. In the old days, it was difficult or even impossible to find business information that would help your business succeed. Not any longer. The internet has a wealth of information that is there for the picking. Learn how you can take advantage of the internet to help your business succeed.

There is as much information and assistance available on business plan writing as any entrepreneur could hope for. This chapter describes some of it, including software for writing business plans, books and how-to manuals, web sites, trade groups and associations, business plan consultants, and even business plan competitions.

Appendices: Sample Business Plans

Here you will find sample business plans for six very different types of businesses. Everything from A to Z can be found in these plans, which can be used in part or in whole as models for your own business plan.

The Government Listings appendix provides contact information for Small Business Development Centers, Small Business Administration district offices, and state economic development departments across the country.

Tips

Scattered throughout the book you'll find various tip boxes. Each will provide useful information of a different type.

Plan of Action

Here you are directed to sources for more information and guidance.

Plan Pitfall

This box warns you of common errors made by plan writers.

Fact or Fiction?

Get straight answers to common business plan questions.

Plan Pointer

This box offers advice on ways to improve your plan.

BUZZWORD

This box offers brief definitions of terms you'll run into when writing your plan.

Section One

Before Writing Your Plan

Chapter 1

Plan to Prosper: Business Plan Basics

A BUSINESS PLAN IS A WRITTEN DESCRIPTION OF YOUR BUSINESS'S future, a document that tells what you plan to do and how you plan to do it. If you jot down a paragraph on the back of an envelope describing your business strategy, you've written a plan, or at least the germ of a plan.

Business plans are inherently strategic. You start here, today, with certain resources and abilities. You want to get to a there, a point in the future (usually three to five years out) at which time your business will have a different set of resources and abilities as well as greater profitability and increased assets. Your plan shows how you will get from here to there.

There are some generally accepted conventions about what a full-blown business plan should include and how it should be presented. A plan should cover all the important matters that will contribute to making your business a success. These include the following:

1. *Your basic business concept.* This is where you discuss the industry, your business structure, your particular product or service, and how you plan to make your business a success.

2. *Your strategy and the specific actions you plan to take to implement it.* What goals do you have for your business? When and how will you reach your goals?

3. *Your products and services and their competitive advantages.* Here is your chance to dazzle the readers with good, solid information about your products or services and why customers will want to purchase your products and services and not your competitors'.

4. *The markets you'll pursue.* Now you have to lay out what your marketing plan is. Who will your customers be? How will you attract and retain enough customers to make a profit? What sets your business apart from its competition?

5. *The background of your management and key employees.* Having information about key personnel is an important but often overlooked portion of a business plan.

6. *Your financing needs.* These will be based on your projected financial statements. These statements provide a model of how your ideas about the company, its markets, and its strategies will play out.

As you write your buisness plan, stick to facts instead of feelings, projections instead of hopes, and realistic expectations of profit instead of unrealistic dreams of wealth. Facts, checkable demonstrable facts, will invest your plan with the most important component of all—credibility.

How Long Should Your Plan Be?

A useful business plan can be any length, from that scrawl on the back of an envelope to more than 100 pages for an especially detailed plan describing a complex enterprise. A typical business plan runs 15 to 20 pages, but there is room for wide variation from that norm.

The size will depend on the nature of your business. If you have a simple concept, you may be able to express it in very few words. On the other hand, if you are proposing a new kind of business or even a new industry, it may require quite a bit of explanation to get the message across. If you are writing a plan for a division of a large organization, you will probably have a set format and prescribed length.

The purpose of your plan also determines its length. If you are looking for millions of dollars in seed capital to start a risky venture, you will have to do a lot of explaining and convincing. If you're just going to use your plan

4

Cocktail Napkin Business Plan

Business plans don't have to be complicated, lengthy documents. They just have to capture the essence of what the business will do, and why it will be a success.

The business plan for one of the most successful start-ups ever began with a triangle scrawled on a cocktail napkin. The year was 1971, and Herb Kelleher and Rollin King were formulating their idea for an airline serving Houston, Dallas, and San Antonio. The triangle connecting the cities was their route map—and the basis of the business plan for Southwest Airlines.

The two entrepreneurs soon expressed their vision for Southwest Airlines more fully in a full-fledged business plan and raised millions in start-up capital to get off the ground. Eventually they went public. Along the way, the airline expanded beyond the three cities to include other Texas destinations, and now it serves 59 cities in 30 states with 2,800 flights daily and revenues of $6.53 billion. It's the nation's fifth-largest airline and the only major airline that specializes in low-cost, no-frills, high-frequency service, which, if you just add some lines to the original triangle, is the same strategy mapped out on that cocktail napkin.

for internal purposes to manage an ongoing business, a much more abbreviated version should do fine.

When Should You Write It?

The fact that you're reading this book means you suspect it's about time to write a business plan. Odds are you are at or near one of the many occasions when a business plan will prove useful.

▶ A business plan is a good way to explore the feasibility of a new business without actually having to start it and run it. A good plan can help you see serious flaws in your business concept. You may uncover tough competition when researching the market section, or you may find that your financial projections simply aren't realistic. On the other hand, a careful business plan that doesn't predict failure can be a rare comfort and motivator to proceed.

▶ Any venture that faces a major change needs a business plan. If the demographics of your market are rapidly changing, strong new competitive products challenge your profitability, you expect your business to grow or shrink dramatically, or the economic climate is improving or slipping rapidly, you'll need a business plan. If you are contemplating buying or selling a business, a business plan can provide you with a handy tool to establish a value—and to support that value if challenged.

▶ You will need a business plan if you are seeking financing. Your business plan is the backbone of your financing proposal. Bankers, venture capitalists, and other financiers rarely provide money without seeing a plan. Less sophisticated or less unbiased investors, such as friends and family, may not require a business plan, but they deserve one. Even if you're funding the business with your own savings, you owe it to yourself to plan how you'll expend the resources you're committing.

Writing a business plan is not a one-time exercise. Just because you wrote a plan when you were starting out or raising money to get under way doesn't mean you are finished. A business plan should be rewritten or revised regularly to get maximum benefit from it. Commonly, business plans are revised yearly, more frequently if conditions have changed enough to make the previous plan unrealistic.

Pumping Up a Puny Plan

Jay Valentine doesn't like business plans, doesn't believe in them, and doesn't write them for start-ups he's involved in. "It's ridiculous for a start-up to make these plans and projections," he says. Valentine prefers to wait until he's conferred with a number of customers and booked a few sales. Then he knows how he'll sell his product and what revenues are likely to be.

But as CEO of InfoGlide Inc., a database technology start-up, Valentine was responsible for coming up with a plan that would please the venture capitalists InfoGlide was asking for several million dollars to bring the technology to market. So he wrote one. "It was maybe 15 pages," says Valentine. "Just me writing about the company and what we were trying to do."

That wouldn't please number-crunching venture capitalists, Valentine knew. So he hired a consultant to prepare a five-year financial forecast. Then he sent it in, sight unseen. "I never even looked at the financials," he says. "But it was thick—and that's what the venture capitalists like to see." Crazy? Maybe. But the pumped-up plan landed $3 million from a big venture capital firm.

Who Needs a Business Plan?

About the only person who doesn't need a business plan is one who's not going into business. You don't need a plan to start a hobby or to moonlight from your regular job. But anybody beginning or extending a venture that will consume significant resources of money, energy, or time and that is expected to return a profit should take the time to draft some kind of plan.

Start-Ups

The classic business plan writer is an entrepreneur seeking funds to help start a new venture. Many, many great companies had their starts on paper, in the form of a plan that was used to convince investors to put up the capital necessary to get them under way.

However, it's a mistake to think that only cash-starved start-ups need business plans. Companies and managers find plans useful at all stages of their existence, whether they're seeking financing or trying to figure out how to invest a surplus.

Fact or Fiction?

The typical image of a business planner is an entrepreneur seeking to lure investors to a hot start-up. But most plans are not written by entrepreneurs or even business owners. Nor are they always seen by anyone outside the company involved. They're often written by corporate managers for corporate managers and are used for internal planning and control.

No Plan, No Problem

When six Stanford University students started calling on venture capitalists looking for money to fund an internet start-up called Architext, they had only a rough outline for a company that would help people find information on the World Wide Web.

Yet the six were able to convince seasoned Silicon Valley venture capitalists that the idea was sound. So sound, in fact, that co-founder Joe Kraus reports, "We raised our first $3 million without a written business plan."

Kraus' company went on to be renamed Excite Inc. and to become one of the most successful of all internet start-ups. Excite garnered more financing and went public in 1996, raising $34 million and making instant millionaires out of the six co-founders.

This experience shows that there is an exception to every rule and also that if your idea is strong enough, you don't need a lot of complicated spreadsheets and market analyses to get help to start your company. However, we can't stress enough, you do need some sort of business plan.

Corporate Managers

If you've ever held a managerial position of any stature in a large corporation, you know well the rounds of five-year, three-year, annual, quarterly, and even monthly budgets, forecasts, reports, analyses, and plans you are expected to draft. Many large companies employ sizable staffs who do nothing but plan and assist others in planning, and sometimes one round of planning seems to lead directly into the next, with precious little time for actually implementing all the schemes.

Some people enjoy all this corporate paperwork; others consider it a good argument for entrepreneurship. Either way, it's hard to imagine running an organization that employs tens of thousands without careful documentation and controls. Plans serve this purpose in big companies, which is why most business plans are written by employees, not entrepreneurs.

Established Firms Seeking Help

Many business plans are written by and for companies that are long past the start-up stage but also well short of large-corporation status.

These middle-stage enterprises may draft plans to help them find funding for growth just as the start-ups do, although the amounts they seek may be larger and the investors more willing. They may feel the need for a written plan to help manage an already rapidly growing business. A business plan may be seen as a valuable tool to convey the mission and prospects of the business to customers, suppliers, or other interested parties.

Fact or Fiction?

Legend says FedEx founder Fred Smith wrote the company's business plan as a term paper while he was a student at Yale. Not so, says Smith. His Yale paper outlined some possibilities of a centralized package distribution system but was far from a full-fledged business plan.

Preselli, An Unproven Concept

Walker Group/Designs, for instance, was already well established as a designer of stores for major retailers when founder Ken Walker got the idea of trademarking and licensing to apparel makers and others the symbols 01-01-00 as a sort of numeric shorthand for the approaching millennium. Before beginning the arduous and costly task of trademarking it worldwide, Walker used a business plan complete with sales forecasts to convince big retailers that promising to carry the 01-01-00 goods would be a good idea. It helped make the new venture a winner long before the big day arrived. "As a result of the retail support up front," Walker says, "we had over 45 licensees running the gamut of product lines almost from the beginning."

Focus on Value

Kodiak Venture Partners, a venture capital firm that invests in high-tech, early-stage companies focusing on communications, semiconductors, and software, believes that a business plan is important. "The business plan is an important tool in keeping an early-stage company focused, but the key is to use it in this way and not treat it as a static item: produced once, polished, and set on the shelf," says Luciana Castro, marketing director.

For the early-stage company, the business plan is often viewed solely as a key part of obtaining financing. A business plan that effectively helps the company obtain financing will clearly communicate the company's value, the customer problems solved by the company's product, and the important investments required to bring those products to market. Focus on these items is critical to the growth of a strong company, so a plan that clearly articulates these items should also be used in the management of the growing company.

Why Should You Write a Business Plan?

Business plans are cheap insurance. Just as many people don't buy fire insurance on their homes and rely on good fortune to protect their investment, many successful business owners do not rely on written business plans but trust their own instincts. However, your business plan reflects your ideas, intuitions, instincts, and insights about your business and its future—and provides the cheap insurance of testing them out before you are committed to a course of action.

Where Are You Going?

You need to think of what you want and whether your plan's findings suggest you'll get it. For instance, say you desire above all else freedom from control by other people. If your plan shows that you'll have to take on several equity partners, each of whom will desire a chunk of ownership, you may need to come up with a business whose capital needs are not so intensive.

Or say you really want a company that will let you do your work and get home at a reasonable hour. The only problem is your business plan requires you to squeeze your labor costs down so much, you're going to be doing the work of two people (and possibly getting paid for less than one, but that's another story). Again, whether or not this business survives and

Plan Pointer
Check with your local Small Business Development Center (www.sba.gov) if you need help developing your business plan. Many colleges and universities also have small-business experts available to lend a hand.

prospers, it may not be a winner for you if the plan shows it won't take you where you want to go.

What Your Business Plan Can't Do

The author of a book on business plans is likely to dream up a lot of benefits to writing one. And a business plan can do a lot for you. But it would be a disservice to claim that a good business plan is all you need to succeed. Even a perfectly planned business can fail if fortune fails to smile on it.

Predict the Future

Stay alert to events that may change the odds, and adjust your expectations accordingly.

It may seem dishonest to say that a business plan can't predict the future What are all those projections and forecasts if not attempts to predict the future? There is a subtle difference.

The fact is no projection or forecast is really a hard-and-fast prediction of the future. It's simply an attempt to show what will happen if a particular scenario occurs. That scenario has been determined by your research and analysis to be the most likely one of the many that may occur. But it's still just a probability, not a guarantee.

While you're running your business during the future period that is covered by your plan, you'll need to keep in mind that your sales forecasts, market trends, and other projections are merely likely, not certain, to occur. Stay alert to events that may change the odds, and adjust your expectations accordingly. If the scenario starts looking as if it will probably play out a lot differently than you expected, you may need to go back and rework your plan to figure out a way to deal with it.

Guarantee Funding

There are all kinds of reasons why a venture capitalist, banker, or other investor may refuse to fund your company. It may be that there's no money to give out at the moment. It may be that the investor just backed a company very similar to your own and now wants something different. Perhaps the investor has just promised to back her brother-in-law's firm or is merely having a bad day and saying no to everything that crosses her desk. The point is the quality of your plan may have little or nothing to do with your prospects for getting funded by a particular investor.

But what about the investment community as a whole? Surely if you show a well-prepared plan to a lot of people, someone will be willing to back you. Again, not necessarily. Communities, as well as people, are subject to fads, and your idea may be yesterday's fad. Conversely, it may be too far ahead of its time.

The same is true of the availability of funds. At times, banks everywhere seem to clamp down on lending, refusing to back even clearly superior borrowers. In many countries, there is no network of venture capitalists to back fledgling companies. Even in the United States, where the VC community is large and active, that was true not too many years ago.

By all means, do the best job you can on your plan. And send it to prospective investors with confidence. But don't consider it a guarantee of funding. There is many a slip twixt cup and lip when it comes to getting backing for a venture. As a rule, you can only count on funding when the money has been deposited to your account.

Raise All the Money You'll Need

Even if you are successful in finding an investor, odds are good that you won't get quite what you asked for. There may be a big difference in what you have to give up, such as majority ownership or control, to get the funds. Or you may simply find you can't snare as large a chunk of cash as you want.

In a sense, a business plan used for seeking funding is part of a negotiation taking place between you and your prospective financial backers. The part of the plan where you describe your financial needs can be considered your opening bid in this negotiation. The other information it contains, from market research to management bios, can be considered supporting arguments. If you look at it in that way, a business plan is an excellent opening bid. It's definite, comprehensive, and clear.

A business plan used for seeking funding is part of a negotiation taking place between you and your prospective financial backers.

But it's still just a bid, and you know what happens to bids in negotiations. They get whittled away, the terms get changed, and, sometimes, the whole negotiation breaks down under the force of an ultimatum from one of the parties involved. Does this mean you should ask for a good deal more than you need in your plan? Should you, for example, expect to follow some sort of halve-the-difference strategy with financiers who don't want to pony up all you're asking for?

Actually, that may not be the best strategy either. Investors who see a lot of plans are going to notice if you're asking for way too much. That may make you appear greedy, ill-informed, or simply naive. Such a move stands a good chance of alienating those who might otherwise be enthusiastic backers of your plan. It's probably a better idea to ask for a little more than you think you can live with, plus slightly better terms than you really expect. That will recognize the fact that you aren't likely to get everything you want, while maintaining your credibility and giving you some negotiating room.

Fool People

A professional financier such as a bank loan officer or a venture capitalist will see literally hundreds of business plans in the course of a year. After this has gone on for several years, and the financier has backed some percentage of those plans and seen how events have turned out, he or she becomes very good at rooting out inconsistencies, deflating overblown projections, and zeroing in on weaknesses, including some you'd probably rather not see highlighted.

In short, most financiers are expert plan analyzers. You have little chance of fooling one of them with an overly optimistic or even downright dishonest plan. That doesn't mean you shouldn't make the best case you honestly can for your business. But the key word is "honestly."

You certainly shouldn't play down your strengths in a plan, but don't try to hide your weaknesses either.

You certainly shouldn't play down your strengths in a plan, but don't try to hide your weaknesses either. Intelligent, experienced financiers will see them anyway. Let's say you propose to open a small bookstore at an address directly across the street from a book superstore. An investor who knows this fact but doesn't see any mention of it in your plan may suspect you've lost your senses—and who could blame her?

Now think about the effect if your plan notes the existence of that big bookstore. That gives you a chance to differentiate yourself explicitly, pointing out that you'll be dealing only in rare antiquarian titles—which the superstore doesn't carry, but many of its customers may want. Suddenly that high-volume operator becomes a helpful traffic builder, not a dangerous competitor.

So recognize and deal appropriately with the weaknesses in your plan. If you do it right, this troubleshooting can become one of the strongest parts of the whole plan.

Business Planning Risks

There are risks associated with writing a business plan. That's right, while one of the main purposes of a business plan is to help you avoid risk, the act of creating one does create a few risks as well. The risks include:

- ▶ *The possible disclosure of confidential material.* Although most of the people you show your plan to will respect its confidentiality, a few may (either deliberately or by mistake) disclose proprietary information.

- ▶ *Leading yourself astray.* You may come to believe too strongly in the many forecasts and projects it contains.

- ▶ *Ruining your reputation or worse.* You fill the plan with purposely overly-optimistic prognostication, exaggeration, or even falsehoods. Some plans prepared for the purpose of seeking funds may run afoul of securities laws if they appear to be serving as prospectuses unblessed by the regulators.

- ▶ *Spending too much effort planning.* You then may not have enough energy or time to actually run your business. Some call it "analysis paralysis." It's a syndrome that occurs when you spend so much time planning that you never do anything. For a lot of businesspeople, this is a non-issue—they detest planning so much that there's no chance at all they'd forgo actually doing business and merely plan it.

But business planning can take on a life of its own. It's possible to spend so much time planning a start-up that you miss your window of opportunity or to schedule such frequent updates of a plan for an established business that it becomes difficult to administer its other details. Big corporations have large staffs, which can be devoted to year-round planning. As a small-business person, you have to be more selective.

Your planning may be approaching the paralysis stage if you find yourself soothing your nerves about starting a business by delaying the start-up date so you can plan more. If you notice yourself putting off crucial meetings so you can dig up more information for a plan update, suspect that planning has become overly important.

- ▶ *Diluting the effectiveness of your plan.* If you put too much detail into your plan, you run the risk of overburdening anybody who reads it with irrelevant, obscuring detail. A plan isn't supposed to be a pot-boiler, but it should tell a story—the story of your business. Therefore, it should be as easy as possible to read. That means keeping technical jargon under control.

Explain any terms that may be unfamiliar to a reader who's not an expert on your industry. And never make the mistake of trying to overawe a reader with your expertise. There's a good chance someone reading your

If you put too much detail into your plan, you run the risk of overburdening anybody who reads it with irrelevant, obscuring detail.

13

plan will know more than you do. If you come across as an overblown pretender, you can bet your plan will get short shrift.

It's easy to believe that a longer, more detailed plan is always better than a short, concise one. But financiers and others to whom you may send your plan are busy people. They do not have time to plow through an inches-thick plan and may in fact be put off by its imposing appearance. Better to keep it to a couple dozen pages and stick to the truly important material.

After considering all these risks, is writing a business plan worth it? Think of vaccines to protect children against chickenpox. A certain number of children are going to become ill from the vaccine. However, far more children would suffer much worse from complications of chickenpox if they weren't vaccinated.

You'll probably want several versions of your business plan.

Some parents are more concerned about the risk posed by the vaccine and opt not to have their children inoculated. But most children do take the shots, and the overall result is positive. Will you inoculate your business against risk with a plan? The choice is yours.

⋆ EXPERT ADVICE ⋆

Kaye Vivian, an expert in writing business plans, offers this advice on how you can improve your content and presentation:

Content

- ▶ *Know your competition.* Be prepared to name them and tell what makes you different from (and better than) each of them.
- ▶ *Know your audience.* You'll probably want several versions of your business plan—one for bankers or venture capitalists, one for individual investors, one for companies that may want to do a joint venture with you rather than fund you, etc.
- ▶ *Have proof to back up every claim you make.* If you expect to be the leader in your field in six months, you have to say why you think so. If you say your product will take the market by storm, you have to support it with facts. If you say your management team is fully qualified to make the business a success, be sure their resumes demonstrate the experience needed.

▶ *Be conservative in all financial estimates and projections.* If you feel certain you will capture 50 percent of the market in the first year, you can say why you think so and hint at what those numbers may be. But make your financial projections more conservative—for example, 10 percent market share is much more credible.

▶ *Be realistic with time and resources available.* If you are working with a big company now, you may think things will happen faster than they will once you have to buy the supplies and drive to the post office and write the checks and answer the phones yourself. Over-optimism with time and resources is a common error entrepreneurs make. Being realistic is important because it lends credibility to your presentation.

Include all the variables that can have an impact on the result or outcome of your idea.

▶ *Be logical.* Think like a banker and write what he/she would want to see, in an order that makes it easy to find the information.

▶ *Have a strong management team.* Make sure it has good credentials and expertise. Your team members don't have to have worked in the field, but you do need to draw parallels between what they have done and the skills needed to make your venture succeed. Don't have all the skills you need? Consider adding an advisory board of people skilled in your field, and use their resumes. Or discuss the shortcomings factually in the business plan, showing how and when you will address getting the right people on board to fill in the gaps in your management team.

▶ *Document why your idea will work.* Have others done something similar that was successful? Have you made a prototype? Include all the variables that can have an impact on the result or outcome of your idea. Show why they don't apply to your situation or explain how you intend to overcome them or make them better.

▶ *Describe your facilities and location for performing the work.* If you will need to expand, discuss when, where, and why.

▶ *Discuss payout options for the investors.* Some investors want a hands-on role; some want to put associates on your board of directors; some don't want to be involved in the day-to-day. All investors want to know when they can get their money back and at what rate of return. Most want out within three to five years. Provide a brief description of options for investors, or at least mention that you are ready to discuss options with any serious prospect.

Presentation

▶ *Appearance counts.* If you are in a technology business, don't use a typewriter. If you are pushing an artistic or imaginative idea, show some creativity (but not at the cost of keeping the document easy to skim and find facts).

▶ *Use informative headings in the document.* Use lots of subtitles, and let them sell your idea. Think of *USA Today*, with its short paragraphs and headlines that convey information even if you don't read the article. Make it easy for your readers to find what they want to know. They won't read it from start to finish.

▶ *Answer the five Ws.* Good journalists tell who, what, where, when, why, and how in their articles. Be sure your business plan does the same.

▶ *Keep it short.* No matter how complex your technology or how abstract your concept, you need to get all the information the investor needs into 20 to 25 pages or less—including the financial projections.

▶ *Package it nicely.* Two-column documents are easier to read than full pages of text. Use charts or tables or graphics or illustrations to break up long passages of words. Add a spot of color on the pages if you have the option—a colored line on the pages or a colored logo or other "spot" color. Readability studies say that adding a second color increases retention of the information.

What Not to Include in a Business Plan

▶ *Form over substance.* If it looks good but doesn't have a solid basis in fact and research, you might as well save your energy.

▶ *Empty claims.* If you say something is so, back it up in the next sentence with a statistic or fact or quote from a knowledgeable source that supports the claim.

▶ *Rumors about the competition.* If you know for sure one is going out of business, you can allude to it, but avoid listing its weaknesses or hearsay. Stick to facts.

▶ *Superlatives and strong adjectives.* Words like "major," "incredible," "amazing," "outstanding," "unbelievable," "terrific," "great," "most," "best," and "fabulous" don't have a place in a business plan. Avoid "unique" unless you can demonstrate with facts that the product or service is truly one of a kind. Your opportunity is probably not unique.

- *Long documents.* Keep it under 25 pages total. Write whatever else you want to write, but keep it at home. If they want details, they will ask.

- *Overestimating on your financial projections.* Sure you want to look good, but resist optimism here. Use half what you think is reasonable. Better to underestimate than set expectations that aren't fulfilled.

- *Overly optimistic time frames.* Ask around or do research on the internet. If it takes most companies 6 to 12 months to get up and running, that is what it will take yours. If you think it will take three months to develop your prototype, double it. You will face delays you don't know about yet—ones you can't control.

- *Gimmicks.* Serious investors want facts, not hype. They may eat the chocolate rose that accompanies the business plan for your new florist shop, but it won't make them any more interested in investing in the venture.

- *Typos and misspelled words.* Use your spell checker, hire an editor, or have four people read the document from back to front, but get those errors out of there if you want to be taken seriously.

- *Amateurish financial projections.* Spend some money and get an accountant to do these for you. They'll help you think through the financial side of your venture, plus put the numbers into a standard business format that a businessperson expects.

(Above sections © Kaye Vivian.)

And if you follow these conventions, you're going to need an awfully big envelope to fit it all on the back. Maybe that's not all bad. Jay Valentine, CEO of software start-up InfoGlide Inc., says that when it comes to plans, the bigger, the better. "Venture capitalists only look at one thing," he says. "And that is, how thick is it?"

Chapter 2

Digging for Dollars

A BUSINESS PLAN IS ALMOST ESSENTIAL FOR ENTREPRENEURS SEEKING to raise money to help fund their companies. In fact, business plans are so closely tied to fundraising that many entrepreneurs look at them as only suited for presenting to investors and overlook the management benefits of planning. "We don't have a formalized business plan, mainly because we aren't seeking capital," says Jeff Musa, president and founder of Cutting Edge Software Inc. "You're not going to refer to your business plan when you're going to make some microdecision about the way your company's running," he adds. "In a three-person company, we sit down at a roundtable with a couple of beers and make decisions."

But for those entrepreneurs who are seeking funding, a business plan accomplishes several things. First, it helps convince potential sources of funding that the entrepreneur has thought the idea through. It also gives any actual investors a set of financial benchmarks for which the entrepreneur can be held accountable.

In a sense, a business plan is a ticket to enter the financial dance. It would be overly simplistic to say that you must have a plan to get funding. But it's

Tips to Help You Win Funding

Keep these tips in mind to help you win the funding you are searching for:

- *Don't use hype.* Most entrepreneurs are very excited when it comes time to talk about their business and their plans for the future. Remember that most financial experts are likely to go by the book and follow basic business analyses and guidelines when determining if you will get the funding you are looking for.
- *Spend extra time working on the executive summary.* (See Chapter 6.) Because bankers and professional investors receive so many business plans, they sometimes go right to the executive summary for an overall view of what your plan is all about. If you can't seize their interest in your executive summary, go back to the drawing board and try again.
- *Make sure your business plan is complete.* You would be surprised at how many business plans are submitted with important data missing. You need to double and triple check to make sure all of the important components are included. Leave nothing to chance. A well-written and complete business plan gives you a higher chance of success and better odds of getting the financing you are looking for.

BUZZWORD

Direct Funding Sources *invest directly in your business, whether at start-up or later on. These include funds from individuals, banks, government agencies, and various levels of professional investors.* Indirect Funding Sources *provide trade credit and financing mechanisms such as extended terms on purchases. These are important sources of working capital, but they do not put funds directly into your business.*

not too simplistic to say that a good plan will help you to raise your funds more quickly, more easily, and more completely than you could without it.

Direct Funding Sources

When you're looking for money, it may seem that investors are as scarce as hen's teeth. But the real problem may be that you're not looking in enough places for potential financiers. You may find investors as close as your immediate family and as far away as professional venture capitalists on the other side of the world.

Investors come in many shapes and sizes, as well as with various needs and intentions. Odds are you can find someone to help you with your business's financing needs if you cast your net wide enough.

Your Own Resources

Your own resources, savings, investments, and other valuable assets are the beginning of your financing efforts. One reason to write a business plan is to provide reassurance that you are making a sensible investment. Note that you will be investing serious nonfinancial assets in your business: your time, effort, hopes, and reputation.

Family and Friends

The most likely source of financing are the people closest to you. Spouses, parents, grandparents, aunts, uncles, and in-laws, as well as friends and colleagues, have reasons to help you that arm's-length financiers lack. For that reason, they may back you when no one else will.

One seldom-noticed aspect of asking family and friends to invest in your venture is that other investors (especially bankers and venture capitalists) often ask if you have approached family and friends to raise initial capital. If you say no, you haven't, they'll then ask why not. If your deal is so appealing, why wouldn't you let your family and friends in on the ground floor? If you say yes, but they couldn't come through for you, at least the banker or VC will know you tried.

Willingness to take a risk doesn't make family and friends foolish investors. Money from family and friends has backed many a successful business venture. Here are a few:

▶ *Albertson's Inc.* Co-founder Joe Albertson borrowed $7,500 from his aunt to make his $12,500 contribution to the partnership that began the grocery store that grew to sales of more than $2 billion a year.

▶ *Pizza Hut Inc.* Co-founders Frank and Dan Carney borrowed $600 from an insurance fund left by their late father to start the pizza chain.

▶ *Eckerd Corporation.* Jack Eckerd raised $150,000 from family members to purchase three failing Florida drugstores, the cornerstone of a company whose sales would one day top $9 billion a year.

Family and friends may not be able to raise millions of dollars, but they can provide long-term financing to highly speculative endeavors that more mainstream financiers wouldn't touch.

Even Families Need a Plan. If you're financing your venture with family money, you may think all you need is a smile and a polite request to raise what you need. In the short term, that may work and produce the funds you need. But over the long term, even family-financed enterprises will benefit from having a business plan.

A business plan shows family members who are putting up the money what they can expect for their contribution. And it helps keep the entrepreneur—

Fact or Fiction? ???

Think Daddy's money is no way to start a business? Consider that Eddie Bauer had to have his father cosign a $500 loan to open his first tennis shop in Seattle. Spiegel purchased Bauer's catalog operation in 1988 for $260 million.

21

you—mindful of responsibilities to family members who backed you and on track to fulfill your obligations.

Banks

Most successful businesses are financed by banks. Banks can provide small to moderate amounts of capital at market costs. They don't want control—at least beyond the control exerted in the covenants of a loan document. And they don't want ownership. Bankers make loans, not investments, and as a general rule they don't want to wind up owning your company.

Bankers primarily provide debt financing. That is, you take out a loan and pay it back, perhaps in installments consisting of principal and interest, perhaps in payments of interest only, followed by a balloon payment of the principal. One of the nice things about debt financing is that the entrepreneur doesn't have to give up ownership of his or her company to get it. The cost is clearly stated.

Bankers can usually be counted on to want minimal, if any, input into how the business is run. Most of the time, as long as you're current on payments, you can do as you like. Get behind the payment schedule, and you're likely to find a host of covenants buried in your loan documentation.

Loan covenants may require you to do all sorts of things, from setting a minimum amount of working capital you must maintain to prohibiting you from making certain purchases or signing leases without approval from the bank. In fact, most bank loans contain so many covenants that it's difficult for a borrower to avoid being technically in default on one or more of them at a given time.

Your loan officer is likely to ignore many covenant violations unless you stop, or seem likely to stop, making timely payments. Even then you'll probably get a chance to work out the problem. But if you remain in violation, you may find yourself declared in default in short order, and the bank may demand all of its money immediately, perhaps seizing your collateral and even forcing you to protect yourself by declaring bankruptcy.

What Bankers Want. A banker's first concern is getting the bank's money back plus a reasonable return. To increase the odds of this, bankers look for certain things in the businesses they lend to. Those include everything from a solid explanation of why you need the money and what you're going to use it for to details about any other borrowing or leasing deals you've entered into.

22

Bank loan applications can be voluminous, almost as long and complete as a full-fledged business plan. Plans and loan applications aren't interchangeable, however. A banker may not be too interested in your rosy projections of future growth. In fact, when confronted with the kind of growth projection required to interest a venture capitalist, a banker may be turned off. On the other hand, a banker is likely to be quite interested in seeing a contingency plan that will let you pay back the loan, even in the event of a worst-case scenario. The things a banker will look for you to address are:

▶ *Cash flow.* One of the most convincing things you can show a banker is the existence of a strong, well-documented flow of cash that will be more than adequate to repay a loan's scheduled principal and interest. Basically, you're going to have to show where you're going to get the money to pay back what you're borrowing.

You'll need more than a projection of future cash flow, by the way. Most bankers will want to see cash flow statements as well as balance sheets and income statements for the past three or so years. And don't forget your tax returns for the same period.

▶ *Collateral.* If you're just starting out in business or if you're dealing with a banker you don't know well, you're unlikely to be able to borrow from a bank without collateral. (That's doubly true if, as is the case with many entrepreneurs, both descriptions apply to you.) Collateral is just something the banker can seize and sell to get back some or all of the money you've borrowed in the event that everything goes wrong and you can't pay it back with profits from operations. It may consist of machinery, equipment, inventory, or all too often, the equity you own in your home.

But it's a good idea to take the initiative here and propose something that will be used if you suspect a banker will require it. Often the collateral will consist of whatever you're borrowing money to buy—production equipment, computers, a building, etc.

Why do bankers seek collateral? They have no desire to own second-hand equipment or your house. Experience has taught them entrepreneurs who have their own assets at risk are more likely to stick to a business than those who have none of their own assets at risk.

▶ *Cosigners.* They provide an added layer of protection for lenders. If your own capacity for taking on additional debt is shaky, a cosigner

23

(who is essentially lending you his or her creditworthiness) may make the difference.

▶ *Marketing plans.* Bankers are taking a closer look at the marketing plans embedded in business plans than ever before. Strong competitors, price wars, me-too products, the fickle habits of the buying public, and other market-related risks must be addressed. Your banker (and most other investors) have to know that you recognize these risks and have well-thought out ways to deal with them. Besides, it's the cash flow from operations that pays off bank loans.

▶ *Management.* Bankers these days like to stress the personal aspect of their services. Many state that they are interested in making loans based on a borrower's character as well as his or her financial strength. And in fact, the borrower's track record and management ability are concerns for bankers evaluating a loan application. If you can show you've run one or more other companies successfully, it will increase your chances of landing a loan to get a start-up going.

When Bank Financing Is Appropriate. Bank financing is most appropriate for up-and-running enterprises that can show adequate cash flow and collateral to service and secure the loan. Bankers are less likely to provide start-up money to turn a concept, even a well-proven one, into a business, and they are even less likely to put up seed money to prove a concept.

Bankers are sensitive to the term or length of a loan. Most bank loans are short to intermediate term, meaning they are due in anywhere from less than a year to five years. A short-term loan may be for 90 days, to finance receivables so you can get a big order out the door. A longer-term loan, up to 20 years, may be used to purchase a piece of long-lasting capital equipment.

Borrowing When You Really Need It. The old saw about bankers only lending to people who don't need to borrow is almost true. Bankers prefer to lend to companies that are almost, but not quite, financially robust enough to pursue their objective without the loan. Bankers are lenders, not investors. Unlike a venture capitalist who takes an equity position, bankers don't get a higher return on their loan if you happen to be more successful than expected. Their natural tendency is to be conservative.

This is important to understand because it affects how and when you will borrow. You should try to foresee times you'll need to borrow money and arrange a line of credit or other loan before you need it. That will make it easier and, in many cases, cheaper in terms of interest rates than if you wait until you're a needier and, in bankers' eyes, less attractive borrower.

Small Business Administration and Other Government Agencies

Sometimes the government really does want to help. The Small Business Administration (SBA) is devoted to helping small-business people. One of its most valuable offerings is a set of financial assistance programs that aim to help you raise the money you need to get started and keep going.

There are more than a dozen SBA loan programs, each with unique characteristics. The primary SBA financing program is the 7(a) Loan Guaranty Program. The SBA, using the full faith and credit of the U.S. government, guarantees a lender will get back most—but not all—of the money lent out, even if the borrower can't pay. A typical loan guarantee covers 80 percent of the loan. You will find it easier to borrow money and usually get a lower finance rate if you can get an SBA guarantee.

Some examples of specialized 7(a) programs:

▶ The Specialized Pollution Control Program provides small businesses with loan guarantees to fund the planning, design, or installation of pollution control equipment.

▶ A microloan program helps businesses get loans for as little as $100.

▶ Special loan programs exist for minority and women-owned businesses, exporters, and veterans.

The SBA sometimes lends money directly to small businesses, but most of its financing help is in the form of loan guarantees. To avail yourself of these programs, you need to meet the SBA's definition of a small business and put up pretty much all the business's assets as collateral. Most banks handle SBA-backed loans and can tell you more about the programs. Their "low-doc" program, with minimal paperwork, is particularly helpful for businesses seeking loans under $150,000. Call your local SBA office for information (see Appendix G for a state-by-state listing of district offices).

Angel Investors

If you are having trouble getting funding for your venture under the right terms, or under any terms at all, you'll be glad to know about the existence of angels in the investment world. Angels are individuals who invest their

Plan Pointer THIS WAY

Lenders look for borrowers exhibiting the four Cs of credit: 1) Character: What's your reputation and record? 2) Capacity or cash flow: Do you have sufficient cash flow to repay principal and interest? 3) Capital: Does your business have enough capital to keep going if you can't pay the debt from earnings? and 4) Collateral: Do you own something valuable the banker can take if you can't pay the loan back?

Small Business Investment Company Program

The SBA has a program that bridges the capital gap in which loans (direct or guaranteed) and equity investments are most difficult to find. Most banks are unwilling to offer very long term loans (sometimes called "quasi-capital") and most venture capital firms are unwilling to invest under $3,000,000 in businesses that are unlikely to go public or be acquired for a fancy multiple within three to five years. Enter the SBICs.

Congress created the Small Business Investment Company (SBIC) Program in 1958 to fill the gap between the availability of venture capital and the needs of small businesses in start-up and growth situations. SBICs, licensed and regulated by the SBA, are privately owned and managed investment firms that use their own capital plus funds borrowed at favorable rates with an SBA guarantee to make venture capital investments in small businesses.

Virtually all SBICs are profit-motivated businesses. They provide equity capital, long-term loans, debt-equity investments, and management assistance to qualifying small businesses. Their incentive is the chance to share in the success of the small business as it grows and prospers.

There are two types of SBICs: regular SBICs and specialized SBICs, also known as 301(d) SBICs. Specialized SBICs invest in small businesses owned by entrepreneurs who are socially or economically disadvantaged, mainly members of minority groups.

The program makes funding available to all types of manufacturing and service industries. Many investment companies seek out small businesses with new products or services because of the strong growth potential of such firms. Some SBICs specialize in the field in which their management has special knowledge or competency. Most, however, consider a wide variety of investment opportunities.

Go to www.sba.gov/INV/liclink.html for a listing of SBICs.

own money as opposed to institutions or professional money managers, who invest other people's money. Many angels are well-off professionals, such as doctors and lawyers. Others are successful small-business owners who have made a bundle with their own entrepreneurial efforts and are now interested in letting their money work for them in someone else's venture.

Because angels invest their own money, you might think they are the most discriminating, difficult-to-please investors. In fact, they are as a rule much more willing to take a flier on a risky, unproven idea than are professional investors and lenders.

Another common characteristic of angels is that they usually are friends, acquaintances, colleagues, relatives, or in some other way are allied to you in an informal, personal way. One reason for that is that angels don't generally advertise their existence, certainly not in the way a bank might with a newspaper ad or billboard on the freeway offering loans. Another reason is that angels are usually swayed more by personal concerns than by financial ones. They may hope to make a killing, but they're really investing in your enterprise because they like and believe in you.

The angel investment community has become more sophisticated in recent years. ACE-Net is an electronic network of angel investors sponsored by the SBA. It helps angel investors and small businesses seeking capital meet online, turning the informal angel investment community into a 21st century internet-based securities listing service. To learn more about ACE-Net, call the SBA at (800) 8-ASK-SBA or visit the ACE-Net web site at www.sba.gov/services/acenet.html.

If you have a valid business concept, you may be an appropriate vehicle for angel investors even if you have been unsuccessful at finding financing elsewhere. Angels are, above all else, unconventional. If 20 banks turn you down, chances are the 21st will, too. That's because all bankers have pretty much the same training and use the same formulas and requirements

Plan Pointer

If you're after angels, it's in your interest to guard their interests. Unsophisticated angels may, for instance, give you money without specifying exactly what, such as percentage of ownership, they're buying. Such angels can be taken advantage of. But you may want more help someday, and angels tend to talk with each other. So make it legal, make terms clear, and take care of their interests as well as your own.

A Pie-Eyed Plan

Gordon Weinberger of Londonderry, New Hampshire, likes to call himself the 6-foot, 9-inch Pie Guy. A better name for the founder and CEO of Top of the Tree Baking Co. might be the dollar-at-a-time guy.

Weinberger started his company as a bakery, making and marketing all-natural apple and other pies. After a few years, he decided he needed to concentrate on the marketing alone, and he contracted out the manufacturing of the pies to larger commercial bakeries. The only problem was, it would take money to reposition his company from being a manufacturer to being a marketer of already-cooked pies. So he took to the road in a gaudily painted school bus. He traveled to spots as disparate as Aspen, Colorado, and wealthy Connecticut suburbs in search of the haunts of the rich and investment-minded. When he rolled up, he presented his business plan and asked for backers.

By the time he pulled out his thumb, Weinberger had raised several hundred thousand dollars, primarily in small amounts. And he was well on the way to a successful restructuring of his ten-person company.

to evaluate loans. Most angels, on the other hand, have little training in evaluating business ideas. If 20 angels turn you down, it doesn't mean a thing.
Until you've gone through the last name in your Rolodex, you still have a
chance of landing an angel backer.

You may also fit angel guidelines if you don't need a whole lot of money.
Institutional venture capitalists can, by pooling the funds of several different
groups, raise vast sums. It's not unheard of for venture capitalists to invest
nine-figure sums—more than $100 million—in relatively new, unproven
ventures. Even Bill Gates or Warren Buffett is unlikely to feel comfortable
sinking that kind of money into anything uncertain. Your angel's capacity
will vary, of course, but few angels can come up with more than a few tens
of thousands of dollars, at least at the outset. If you need more, you may
need more than one angel.

Venture Capitalists

Venture capitalists represent the most glamorous and appealing form of
financing to many entrepreneurs. They are known for backing high-risk
companies in the early stages, and a lot of the best-known entrepreneurial
success stories owe their early financing to venture capitalists.

When many entrepreneurs write a business plan, obtaining venture capital backing is what they have in mind. That's understandable. Venture capitalists are associated with business success. They can provide large sums of
money, valuable advice, priceless contacts, and considerable prestige by their
mere presence. Just the fact that you've obtained venture capital backing
means your business has, in their eyes at least, considerable potential for
rapid and profitable growth.

When Venture Capital Is an Option

Venture capital is most often used to finance companies that are young without being babies and that are established without being mature. But it can also
help struggling firms as well as those that are on the edge of breaking into the
big time.

Following are the major types and sources of capital, along with distinguishing characteristics of each:

- *Seed money.* Seed money is the initial capital required to transform a business from an idea into an enterprise. Venture capitalists are not as likely
  to provide seed money as some other, less tough-minded financing

sources, such as family investors. However, venture capitalists will back seedlings if the idea is strong enough and the prospects promising enough.

VCs are less likely to provide equity capital to a seed-money-stage entrepreneur than they are to provide debt financing. This may come in the form of a straight loan, usually some kind of subordinated debt. It may also involve a purchase of bonds issued by the company. Frequently these will be convertible bonds that can be exchanged for shares of stock. Venture capitalists may also purchase shares of preferred stock in a start-up. Holders of preferred shares receive dividends before common stockholders and also get paid before other shareholders if the company is dissolved.

Seed money is usually a relatively small amount of cash, up to $250,000 or so, that is used to prove a business concept has merit. It may be earmarked for producing working prototypes, doing market research, or otherwise testing the waters before committing to a full-scale endeavor.

- *Start-up capital.* Start-up capital is financing used to get a business with a proven idea up and running. For example, a manufacturer might use start-up capital to get production under way, set up marketing, and create some actual sales. This amount may reach $1 million.

  Venture capitalists frequently are enthusiastic financiers of start-ups because they carry less risk than companies at the seed-money stage but still offer the prospect of the high return on investment that VCs require.

- *Later-round financing.* Venture capitalists may also come in on some later rounds of financing. First-stage financing is usually used to set up full-scale production and market development. Second-stage financing is used to expand the operations of an already up-and-running enterprise, often through financing receivables, adding production capacity, or boosting marketing. Mezzanine financing, an even later stage, may be required for a major expansion of profitable and robust enterprises. Bridge financing is often the last stage before a company goes public. It may be used to sustain a growing company during the often lengthy process of preparing and completing a public offering of stock.

Venture capitalists even invest in companies that are in trouble. These turn-around investments are riskier than start-ups and therefore even more expensive to the entrepreneurs involved.

VCs aren't for everybody, but they provide a very important financing option for some young firms. When you're writing a business plan to raise money, you may want to consider venture capitalists and their unique needs.

Plan Pitfall

Management control—Many VCs insist on placing one or more directors on the boards of companies they finance. And these directors are rarely there merely to observe. They take an active role in running the company.

VCs are also reluctant to provide financing without obtaining majority or controlling interest in the companies they back. This can make them just as influential as if they had a majority of the directors on the board, or more so.

Turnaround *is the term used to describe a reversal in a company's fortunes that takes it from near death to robust health. For example, in the 1970s, Chrysler had to be bailed out by the federal government. Then in the 1990s, Daimler-Benz bought the turned-around Chrysler in what was at the time history's biggest industrial buyout. Some turn-arounds are faster, taking months or weeks. Some never happen at all.*

Venture capitalists both lend to and make equity investments in young companies. The loans are often expensive, carrying rates of up to 20 percent. They sometimes also provide what may seem like very cheap capital. That means you don't have to pay out hard-to-get cash in the form of interest and principal installments. Instead, you give a portion of your or other owners' interest in the company in exchange for the VC's backing.

What Venture Capitalists Want. While venture capitalists come in many forms, they have similar goals. They want their money back, and they want it back with a lot of interest or capital growth.

VCs typically invest in companies that they foresee being sold either to the public or to larger firms within the next several years. As part owners of the firm, they'll get their rewards when that sale goes through. Of course, if there's no sale or if the company goes bankrupt, they don't even get their initial money back.

VCs aren't quite the plungers they may seem. They're willing to assume risk, but they want to minimize it as much as possible. Therefore, they typically look for certain features in companies they are going to invest in. Those include:

- Rapid sales growth
- A proprietary new technology or dominant position in an emerging market
- A sound management team
- The potential to be acquired by a larger company or be taken public in a stock offering within three to five years
- High rates of return on their investment

Rate of return *is the income or profit earned by an investor on capital invested in a company. It's usually expressed as an annual percentage.*

Rates of Return. Like most financiers, venture capitalists want the return of any funds they lend or use to purchase equity interest in companies. But VCs have some very special requirements when it comes to the terms they want and, especially, the rates of return they demand.

Venture capitalists require that their investments have the likelihood of generating very high rates of return. A 30 percent to 50 percent annual rate of return is a benchmark many venture capitalists seek. That means if a venture capitalist invested $1 million in your firm and expected to sell out in three years with a 35 percent annual gain, he or she would have to be able to sell the stake for approximately $2.5 million.

These are high rates of return compared with the 6 percent or so usually offered by U.S. Treasury instruments and the 10 percent historically returned by the U.S. stock market. Venture capitalists justify their desires for such high rates of return by the fact that their investments are high-risk.

Most venture capital-based companies, in fact, are not successful and generate losses for their investors. Venture capitalists hedge their bets by taking a portfolio approach: If one out of ten of their investments takes off, and six do OK, then the three that stutter or fail will be a minor nuisance rather than an economic cold bath.

Cashing Out Options. One key concern of venture capitalists is a way to cash out their investment. This is typically done through a sale of all or part of the company, either to a larger firm through an acquisition or to the public through an initial offering of stock.

In effect, this need for cashing out options means that if your company isn't seen as a likely candidate for a buyout or an initial public offering (IPO) in the next five years or so, VCs aren't going to be interested.

Being Acquired. A common way for venture capitalists to cash out is for the company to be acquired, usually by a larger firm. An acquisition can occur through a merger or by means of a payment of cash, stock, debt, or some combination.

Mergers and acquisitions don't have to meet the strict regulatory requirements of public stock offerings, so they can be completed much more quickly, easily, and cheaply than in an IPO. Buyers will want to see audited financials, but you—or the financiers who may wind up controlling your company—can literally strike a deal to sell the company over lunch or a game of golf. About the only roadblocks that could be thrown up would be if you couldn't finalize the terms of the deal, if it turned out that your company wasn't what it seemed, or rarely, if the buyout resulted in a monopoly that generated resistance from regulators.

Venture capitalists assessing your firm's acquisition chances are going to look for characteristics such as proprietary technology, distribution systems, or product lines that other companies might want to possess. They also like to see larger, preferably acquisition-minded, firms in your industry. For instance, Microsoft®, the world's largest software firm, frequently acquires small personal-computer-software firms with talented personnel or unique technology. Venture capitalists looking at funding a software company are

Plan Pitfall

Some VCs specialize in a field, such as retail, biotechnology, or high-tech. Others have a regional focus. But whatever his or her special interests, almost any venture capitalist will admit to desiring the three basic characteristics of steady growth, market dominance, sound management, and potential for going public in an investment.

31

Plan of Action

The National Association of Certified Valuation Analysts is the trade group for people whose business is deciding what businesses are worth. It can help you find a valuation analyst as well as learn the basics of figuring a business's worth. Contact NACVA at 1111 Brickyard Rd., Suite 200, Salt Lake City, UT, 84106, (801) 486-0600.

almost certain to include an assessment of whether Microsoft might be interested in buying the company out someday.

Going Public: Initial Public Offerings

Some fantastic fortunes have been created in recent years by venture-funded start-ups that went public. Initial public offerings of their stock have made multimillionaires, seemingly overnight, of entrepreneurs such as Marc Andreessen of Netscape Communications. Larry Page and Sergey Brin took Google public in late 2004 and became overnight billionaires. Less obvious but equally, if not more, important is the fact that the same IPOs have made many millions for the venture investors who provided early-stage financing.

The stringent requirements for IPOs leave out most companies, including those that don't have audited financials for the past several years as well as those who operate in slow-growing or obscure industries such as car detailing or paper-clip manufacturing. And IPOs take lots of time. You'll need to add outside directors to your board and clean up the terms of any sweetheart deals with managers, family, or board members as well as have a major accounting firm audit your operations for several years before going

EZ VC

When you have a hot business concept that promises big things, sometimes you can dictate terms to venture capitalists instead of them dictating to you. Before Yahoo! went public in 1996, the co-founders of the internet directory service provider sold 30 percent of the company to giant Japanese publishing conglomerate, Softbank.

Yet even though Yahoo! founders Jerry Yang and David Filo—who at the time were Stanford University graduate students—were running a brand-new business concept in an unproven industry, they were able to strike a favorable deal with their Japanese financiers. That was especially true, Yahoo! COO Dan Rosenweig says, when it came to the matter of control.

Softbank came on board the Yahoo! train just a month before an IPO raised $35 million for the start-up. Yet despite Softbank's sizable ownership share and the inexperience of the co-founders, Softbank pretty much lets them run the company the way they want to, Rosenweig says.

"They have no hands on [our] operation, save one board seat," says Rosenweig. "We have lots of discussions with Softbank, but at the end of the day, they give us the reins to run our own company."

public. If you need money today, in other words, an IPO isn't going to provide it.

An IPO is also probably the most expensive way to raise money in terms of the amount you have to lay out up front. The bills for accountants, lawyers, printing, and miscellaneous fees for even a modest IPO will easily reach six figures. For this reason, IPOs are best used to raise amounts at least equal to millions of dollars in equity capital. Venture capitalists keep all these requirements in mind when assessing an investment's potential for going public.

Bonds

There are two kinds of debt financing: straight loans, corresponding to those you get from a bank, and bonds. Bonds give you a way to borrow from a number of people without having to do separate deals with each of them. If you need to borrow $500,000, for instance, you can issue 500 bonds in $1,000 denominations. Then you can sell those bonds to anyone who'll buy them, including family, friends, venture capitalists, and other investors subject to stringent legal constraints.

Corporations use a bewildering variety of bonds for financing, but the most common type simply calls for you to pay a stated amount of interest on the face amount for a certain period. After that time, usually five years, you pay back the face amount to the buyer.

Bonds give you the great advantage of being able to set the interest rate and terms and amount you're trying to raise instead of having to take whatever a lender offers. The problem with bonds is that they are regulated similarly to public stock offerings. So although they're widely used by big companies, very few small companies issue them.

There is an exception to this general rule. Some states pool together long-term loans in state-guaranteed industrial bonds for industrial (read: job creating) businesses. This has the advantage of lowering the issuing costs for the companies involved while providing the patient quasi-capital they need to succeed. Check with your state's economic development department.

Indirect Funding Sources

Direct funding sources put money into your business. Indirect funding sources postpone taking money out of the business, thus conserving working capital. Trade credit is far and away the most important indirect source of funding.

Fact or Fiction? ??

Many entrepreneurs dream of going public. But IPOs are not for every firm. The ideal IPO candidate has a record of rapidly growing sales and earnings and operates in a high-profile industry. Some have a lot of one and not much of the other. Low earnings but lots of interest characterizes many biotech and internet-related IPOs.

Trade Credit

You don't need a loan application, permission from the Securities and Exchange Commission, or even a note from your mother to take advantage of one of the most useful and popular forms of financing around. Trade credit, the credit extended to you by suppliers who let you buy now and pay later, can make a substantial difference to your cash flow.

You can measure the amount of trade credit you have outstanding by simply adding up all your accounts payable, or the amount of unpaid bills on your desk. Any time you take delivery of materials, equipment, or other valuables without paying cash on the spot, you're using trade credit.

For many businesses, trade credit is an essential form of financing. For instance, the owner of a clothing store who receives a shipment of bathing suits in April may not have to pay for them until June. By that time she can hope to have sold enough of the suits to pay for the shipment. Without the trade credit, she'd have to look to a bank or another source for financing.

✳ EXPERT ADVICE ✳

Clayton Associates, LLC (CA), is an investment and financial advisory firm located in Nashville, Tennessee. Formed in January 1996 by R. Clayton McWhorter and managed by his son Stuart McWhorter, CA invests primarily in health-care companies during the start-up and early stages of the venture capital and private equity investment cycle. Strategically located in the "Silicon Valley" of health-care, it enjoys a very favorable environment for new business development. Its incubator approach enables the firm to analyze the management capabilities of its portfolio companies and draw upon the McWhorters' extensive network of relationships throughout the health-care community.

The company assisted in the creation in 1997 of FCA Venture Partners I, L.P., which provided individual investors co-investment opportunities and provided additional capital to portfolio companies. Clayton Associates and FCA Venture Partners I have invested in approximately 25 companies, many in Tennessee and others in Georgia, Mississippi, and South Carolina.

In August 1998, the company helped to form FCA Venture Partners II, L.P., in which it has both limited and general partnership interests. It has invested with the same strategic approach as Clayton Associates and FCA I, primarily in start-up and early-stage companies in the health-care field. FCA

II has invested in 17 companies, including ten follow-on investments from FCA I and seven investments with new companies.

Though health-care is its primary focus, Clayton Associates is also affiliated with a real estate development and management company, an insurance and financial planning company, a third-party reimbursement consulting firm, and a publicly traded telecommunications provider.

Q: *Clayton Associates receives as many three to five business plans a week. How do you review so many documents and still have time to run the firm?*

A: Like most venture capital firms, we have a review team. An incoming plan will be reviewed by one team member, then reported on to the group in a weekly meeting. If a plan shows promise—if it's a strong idea, has good people behind it, and fits well into our portfolio—then other team members will review it and the dialogue will continue. If the plan is a bust from the first read, whether it's a weak idea or shows poor preparation, then the research ends there.

There was a time not so long ago that people could pitch ideas over coffee and croissants and get funding for a start-up. That approach never worked at Clayton Associates, and most all investors are back to the "old economy" way of making business decisions.

Q: *Even being part of a team, you must have a screening process or system by which you review plans?*

A: There are a few key elements I look for right away to get a sense for the idea and the plan. First, I read the executive summary—probably anyone reviewing a plan starts here. Next, I go straight to the biographies: I want to know who the individuals are behind the idea, what kind of experience they've had, what kind of people and firms they've worked with. Knowing that someone has experience in a specific field or company can be a strong endorsement to their qualifications. I particularly look for past entrepreneurial experience. Usually, it's only after I've checked out these two areas that I move on to the financials.

One element that always gets my attention and sends a positive message to investors is if the company's founders have made their own investment in the company. Lots of ideas look good on paper, but when an entrepreneur has put his or her own money into a deal, you know that their stake in the success of the company is greater than someone who has just developed an idea and written a business plan.

Q: Weighting the bios so heavily is probably not good news for young entrepreneurs.

A: Not necessarily. Sure, it is harder for young entrepreneurs because they simply don't have the experience that a more seasoned professional has acquired, which makes them a riskier investment from our perspective. We're looking for people who know their industry and have some history in it, but younger people can help compensate for lesser experience by surrounding themselves with mentors and talented people who are willing to advise them. The vast majority of our deals originate out of personal relationships—we know the principals or they have references from people we trust. There is most often a personal connection back to our firm. That elevates our comfort level and helps open dialogue for us. So connecting to your industry and knowing the key players, no matter what your age, is a sound business practice that will serve an entrepreneur in any field.

Q: You mentioned the importance of a strong executive summary. What do you consider key characteristics?

A: This is a proposer's best chance to state his or her case and get someone's attention. This part of the plan is where a business should really invest its time and make the most of its efforts. Make every word and every sentence count—touch on the hot buttons of business and show your industry knowledge and preparedness. If you have any concerns about the writing style or content, get feedback from seasoned professionals and mentors who are willing to preview your plan before you meet with investors. And evaluate the feedback you get after making presentations to potential investors; incorporate their ideas and make improvements if appropriate.

Q: What characteristics of a business plan do you consider least important?

A: For starters, I'm not necessarily impressed by bulk. Some folks clearly think that bigger is better when it comes to a business plan when in fact the exact opposite is true for many people reviewing plans. Very few investors—whether it's a VC fund, a bank, an angel investor, the SBA— have the time or inclination to pore over 100 pages of narrative and graphs. So respect your audience and assume that they have the intelligence and insight to grasp your ideas without reiterating 10 or 15 times.

Lengthy SWOT (strengths, weaknesses, opportunities, threats) reports or market analyses are also sections I skim pretty quickly. By approaching us for funding, you're asking us to analyze your situation and endorse your idea—that's our job. Most investors will do their own analysis and will already have a pretty keen idea about your market.

Q: *What advice can you give to someone writing and presenting a plan?*

A: It's important for entrepreneurs to remember that one size may not fit all. When possible, tailor a plan to a specific audience. For instance, I notice when a business plan or a PowerPoint presentation references a vendor or strategic partner that is one of our portfolio companies. It's flattering to know someone has done his or her homework and made the effort to communicate to my firm directly.

It's also important to remember that very, very few investors will decide to work with a company just on a business plan. Personal relationships and professional acquaintances are much more likely to give a businessperson the entree needed to present his or her ideas. I'm sure that countless great ideas have died from lack of funding because an entrepreneur hoped a cold call would do the trick with investors.

Lastly, I advise entrepreneurs to remember that a business plan should be a dynamic document. None of the businesses we've invested in reflect their exact original plan. As a company grows or a concept evolves, the business plan needs to be flexible enough to adapt to those changes. Even as a company get its legs and has less of a need to present its business plan, the actual document should be updated and developed into a strategic plan.

The frequent end result of venture capitalist management activism is that the entrepreneurs lose control of the company. This appears unfortunate to outside observers and may be plain heartbreaking to an entrepreneur who's worked hard for years to get an idea off the ground, only to see the controls snatched away just as it's about to take off.

It's also important to remember that very, very few investors will decide to work with a company just on a business plan.

37

Chapter 3

Put Your
Plan to Work

T HE PROCESS OF WRITING THE PLAN HELPS YOU TAKE A THOROUGH, careful, and comprehensive look at the most important facets of your business, including the contexts in which it operates. Just raising questions can sometimes lead to a solution, or at least ensure that if conditions change you won't be forced to make decisions hastily. The ongoing "what if this or that happens?" inherent in the planning process keeps you alert. In other words, the planning process itself makes you a far more capable manager than you would be without it. For many, this is a more valuable result than securing funding.

In many ways, writing a business plan is an end in itself. The process will teach you a lot about your business that you are unlikely to learn by any other process. You'll spot future trouble areas, identify opportunities, and help your organization run smoothly, simply through the act of writing a plan.

Evaluating a New Venture

Lisa Angowski Rogak is an entrepreneur who started several newsletters in much the same way. She devised a plan focusing on marketing strategy and cash flow projections to see if she could come up with a way to sell the 39 newsletters while keeping her bills paid. She then prepared a sample issue to be used in a direct mail and publicity campaign. "Planning is the key to the success of your newsletter," says Rogak, whose latest venture is Williams Hill Publishing. "It's the single most important thing you can do to ensure the success of your newsletter."

That's the kind of encouragement that helps entrepreneurs persevere, whether they have an existing concern that's hitting a rough spot or a start-up concept that nobody else seems to believe in. Numbers can lie, of course, and nobody can create a spreadsheet that really tells the future. But evaluating financial data is to entrepreneurship what evaluating lab results is to a medical doctor. If your vital signs are good, odds are your future will be as well.

But what if the odds don't look so favorable? What if the first pass through your cash flow projection or income *pro formas* contains more red than a fire station paint locker? Sure, you can go back and look for an error or an overly pessimistic or conservative assumption. You can even try altering a few of the inevitable numbers that you really have no way of estimating accurately to see where the pressure points are, if nothing else.

Business planning is a powerful tool for evaluating the feasibility of business ventures. Use it.

But what if you do that, even pushing your alterations past the point of credibility, and your plan still doesn't make sense? Well, in that case, you've probably done yourself the really big favor of finding out something isn't going to work before you sink your money into it. Nobody knows exactly how often this happens, but it's safe to say that a lot of businesses are never attempted because the plan convincingly says that they shouldn't be.

Is that bad? Well, it may feel bad. But think how much worse you would feel if you went ahead with the venture, and things turned out as the plan forecast. Business planning is a powerful tool for evaluating the feasibility of business ventures. Use it.

It would be a shame to keep the benefits of a well-done plan to yourself. And you shouldn't. You can use your plan to find funding. But a good plan can also help sell your products, services, and your whole company to prospects and suppliers. Furthermore, a plan is a valuable tool for communicating your visions, goals, and objectives to other managers and key employees in your firm.

Selling with Your Plan

As a rule, your business plan is only likely to be required in the later stages of being selected as a supplier. Let the customer's process decide when or if you'll present your plan. As an added benefit, working your way through the early stages of vendor selection will give you a chance to rework your plan, if necessary, to stress the areas that you have learned are more important to your potential customer.

Informing Suppliers and Customers

Increasingly, companies large and small have been trying to trim the number of suppliers and customers they deal with and develop deeper and stronger relationships with the ones they keep. An essential part of this is getting to know more about existing and prospective vendors and clients. So don't be surprised if one day, when you're trying to set up a new supplier relationship or pitch a deal to a big company, the person you're negotiating with asks to see your business plan.

Why do suppliers care about business plans? Suppliers only want to sell to people who can pay, which is one important reason a new supplier is likely to want to see your business plan before taking a big order. Remember, if a supplier is selling to you on credit—letting you take delivery of goods and pay for them later—that supplier is, in effect, your creditor. Suppliers who sell for other than cash on delivery have the same legitimate interest in your business's strategy and soundness as does a banker.

Say a supplier's analysis of customer records shows it has a knack for developing long-term profitable relationships with moderate-sized companies that emphasize excellent service, price at a premium level, and provide only the best merchandise. Business plans provide all the information such a company will need to find and clone its best customers. So if a supplier asks to see your plan, be willing to share it. It could be the start of a long and mutually beneficial relationship.

Customers are likely to be concerned about how well your respective strategies fit with theirs. For instance, say your mission statement says that you intend to produce the best-in-the-world example of your product no matter what the cost. Your customer, meanwhile, is a high-volume, low-price reseller of the type of products you make. Even if your offering fits the customer's need this time, odds are good that the relationship won't work out over the long haul. If, on the other hand, a look at your business plan reveals that your companies share the same kind of strategies and have similar objectives in type if not scope, it's an encouraging sign.

Plan Pointer THIS WAY

A confidentiality statement helps control the spread of proprietary information. It should say something like: "This document contains privileged information. Please don't show it to anybody else, and return to International Widgets when you're through." Get your attorney to help with the wording.

Managing with Your Plan

The spread of the open-book management theory means a lot more employees are seeing their companies' business plans than ever before. When employees get the key information managers are using to make decisions, they understand management better and make better decisions themselves, and efficiency and profitability often increase as a result.

Many companies hold annual meetings at which they present and discuss an edited version of their business plan to all employees. Others provide new hires with their business plan—type information as part of their indoctrination in company culture. Both are effective approaches. You can also use bulletin boards or company newsletters to publish smaller sections of your plan, such as your mission statement or some details of financial objectives and how you're progressing.

One drawback to using a plan to help inform and manage your employees is that many won't understand it.

One drawback to using a plan to help inform and manage your employees is that many won't understand it. Some firms provide employees with rudimentary training in such matters as how to read a financial report before they hand out the company's plans. Often this training is done by the CEO and can take considerable time. But don't be afraid to share details of your business plan with employees. They may turn out to understand it better than you.

Monitoring Your Business's Performance

Using a business plan to monitor your performance has many benefits. If your cash flow is running much shorter than projected at the moment, even though you're not currently in trouble, that information may help you to spot disaster before it occurs. By comparing plan projections with actual results, you gain a deeper understanding of your business's pressure points or the components of your operation that have the most effect on results.

Spotting Trouble Early

A teenager taking driver's education is told to look through the rear window of the car in front to try to see the brake lights on the vehicle ahead of that one. The idea is that if the novice driver waits until the car immediately ahead slams on the brakes, it may be too late to stop. Looking forward, past the immediate future, helps traffic move more smoothly and averts countless accidents.

The same principle applies in business planning. You don't have to be a wizard to get some solid hints about the future beyond tomorrow, especially when it comes to the operations of your own business. You can look at virtually any page of your business plan and find an important concept or number describing some expected future event that, if it turns out to be diverging from reality, may hint at future trouble.

Say your profit margins are shrinking slowly but steadily and seemingly irreversibly. If you can see that within a few months your declining margins will push your break-even point too high to live with, you can take action now to fix the problem. You may need to add a new, higher-margin product, get rid of an old one, or begin stressing marketing to a more profitable clientele. All these moves, and many more you could take, have a good chance of working if your careful comparison of plan projections with actual results warns you of impending danger. Wait until the last minute, and you could be peeling yourself off the windshield.

Understanding Pressure Points

Not all tips that come from comparing plans with results have to do with avoiding danger. Some help you to identify profit opportunities. Others may show how seemingly minor tweaks can produce outsized improvements in sales or profitability. For example, the plan for a one-person professional service business indicated that rising sales were not, in general, accompanied by rising costs. Fixed items such as office rent and insurance stayed the same, and even semivariable costs such as phone bills went up only slightly. The bulk of any extra business went straight to the bottom line, showing up as profit improvement. But one cost that didn't seem especially variable went up sharply as business volume climbed. That was the number of transactions.

Ordinarily this would be a given and not necessarily a matter of grave concern. A large enterprise would simply hire a few more modestly paid customer service reps, credit department staff members, or bookkeepers to handle the added order forms, invoices, and the like. For this single professional, however, added paperwork came at a very high cost—her own time.

Somehow in her projections of steadily rising sales volume, she'd neglected to note that more business meant more invoices to be sent out, more account statements to be mailed, more slow payers to be reminded, and more deposit slips to be filled out, checks to be endorsed, and trips to be taken to the bank. All this work, while not necessarily unpleasant (especially the check-cashing part), was taking up more and more of her time.

Plan of Action

The Futurist is a monthly magazine featuring ideas, theories, techniques, and commentaries from people whose job it is to try to figure out the future. For more information, contact the World Future Society, 7910 Woodmont Ave., #450, Bethesda, MD 20814, (800) 989-8274 or (301) 656-8274, fax: (301) 951-0394, e-mail: info@wfs.org.

As a part of checking her plan against results, she noticed this unexpected increase in transactions and figured out what it meant. Calculating that, when taking all paperwork into account, she spent around an hour on each transaction no matter how large or small. She realized that one of the most important pressure points in her business was related to the size of a transaction. By refusing small engagements and seeking clients who could offer big jobs, she would reduce the amount of time spent on otherwise unproductive paperwork and increase the time she could spend completing client requirements.

Ultimately, she was able to trim what had been 100 annual transactions down to 75, while increasing the amount of her dollar revenue. The result was a free 25 hours to spend working on more business or just vacationing. If you can see and relieve a pressure point like that, you can really keep your business from boiling over.

There are few things to equal the sensation of filling in all the numbers on a cash flow projection, hitting the recalculate button, and scrolling to the bottom of your spreadsheet to see what the future holds. If the news is good and you see a steady string of positive cash balances across the bottom row, you know that, assuming your data is good and your assumptions reasonable, your business has a good chance of making it.

Do the Numbers Add Up?

Many businesses fail because of events that are impossible to foresee. If you'd begun a car dealership specializing in yacht-sized gas guzzlers right before the Arab oil embargo in the 1970s, you would be in the same position as a driver heading at 100 miles per hour into a brick wall—through no fault of your own. The same might go for a software start-up that comes out with a new program just before Microsoft unveils a top-secret, long-term development effort to create something that does the same job for a lot less money.

It's probably not a bad idea, as part of your business planning process, to try to include some information in your business plan about the activities or intentions of the potential embargos and Microsofts. If nothing else, crafting a scenario in which the unthinkably awful occurs may help you to deal with it if it does. But some things are just wild cards and can't be predicted. For these you just have to trust the luck of the draw.

So what numbers have to add up? Certainly you have to be selling your products and services at a profit that will let you sustain the business long-term. You'll also have to have a financial structure, including payables and

Plan Pitfall

Caveat time. The fact that your business is unlikely to perform exactly as planned is no reason to skip planning! A plan isn't worthless just because it doesn't present the future with perfect accuracy. At worst it can help you monitor how reality is stacking up to your plan. If your plan seems way off base, you may need a fix—or another plan.

44

receivables systems and financing, that will keep you from running out of cash even once. If you have investors who want to sell the company someday, you may need a plan with a big number in the field for shareholders' equity on the projected balance sheet.

When you're asking yourself whether the numbers add up, keep the needs of your business and your business partners, if you have any, in mind. Even if it looks like it'll take an air strike to keep your business from getting started, you don't want to do it if the numbers say that long-term it's headed nowhere.

Attracting Good People

It takes money to make money, sure, but it also takes people to make a company, that is, unless you're a one-person company. Sometimes even then a

Plan of Action

The Employee Benefit Research Institute (EBRI) conducts regular studies and surveys to find out what employees want and what employers are giving them. To learn more about what benefits you should offer to attract the best, contact EBRI at 2121 K St. NW, #600, Washington, DC 20037, (202) 659-0670.

Fitting with Ford

The automobile industry provides one of the clearest examples of the extent to which big companies are trying to cut the number of suppliers they do business with. Ford Motor Co. has gone especially far in reducing the number of its suppliers. "In one of our vehicles, we now have one overall supplier, plus four other suppliers, for a total of five," says C. W. Graning, procurement strategy manager for purchasing and supply development and strategy at Ford. "In the past, we had a total of 27."

When you look at the bigger picture, it's even more startling. In 1983, Ford had more than 1,800 suppliers. By 1993, it had 825. By 1998, the number had shrunk to 600. What that means for the losing suppliers, of course, is that they had to replace the sales to the Dearborn, Michigan, giant or perish.

But for those who made the cut, they got even more business from Ford than before. How did they pass Ford's muster? The answer is by fitting into Ford's management system. That means lots of reports, lots of analysis, and lots of planning. In fact, a comprehensive business plan describing how the supplier will work with Ford in every aspect of the supplier-customer relationship, is one of the key criteria of the automaker in selecting companies to become its long-term bosom buddies.

It's not exactly going with the low bid, but for those who have the ability to prepare convincing plans, seeking business from big companies that are cutting the number of their suppliers can be rewarding indeed.

plan can be an important part of your effort to attract the best partners, employees, suppliers, and customers to you.

Prospective Partners

Partners are like any other investors, and it would be a rare one who would come on board without some kind of plan. Partners want to know your basic business concept, the market, and your strategy for attacking it; who else is on your team; what your financial performance, strengths, and needs are; and what's in it for them. Luckily, these are exactly the same questions a business plan is designed to address, so you're likely to please even a demanding prospective partner by simply showing him or her a well-prepared plan. The one difference is a plan probably won't contain the details of a partnership agreement. And you'll need one of these to spell out the conditions of your partnership, no matter how well you and your prospective partner know, understand, and trust one another.

Prospective Employees

Although employees may not be making cash contributions to your business, they're making an investment of something equally important—their own irreplaceable time. The kinds of employees you probably want are careful, thorough, good at assessing problems and risks, and unwilling to leap into hazardous waters. As it happens, these are just the kind of people who are going to want to see a written plan of your business before they come on board.

Fact or Fiction?

Every business is different, so every plan should be different, right? Not necessarily. Ken Olsen raised money to start Digital Equipment Corporation with the help of a plan copied out of a textbook; he just changed the name and a few numbers and other facts.

Is Success Easy?

Can you succeed as planned? A study of 150 start-ups found:

- 48 percent didn't achieve expected first-year revenues.
- 53 percent needed more capital than expected.
- 53 percent underestimated time spent on payroll, taxes, paperwork, recruiting, and training.
- 55 percent weren't as successful overall as expected.
- 63 percent progressed more slowly than projected.
- 74 percent of owners earned a lower-than-expected standard of living.

Now, it's not going to be necessary, if you're running a restaurant, to show your full business plan to every waitperson or assistant dishwasher who fills out a job application. It's the most desirable employees—the talented technologists, the well-connected salespeople, the inspired creative types, and the grizzled, seen-it-all managers—who are most likely to feel they can and should demand to see details of your plan before they cast their lot with you. So even if you don't show your plan to more than a few prospective employees, when you need it, you may really need it bad. Make sure you're ready when a promising but inquisitive job candidate shows up at your doorstep.

Another thing, as we've pointed out, not all businesses have plans. So by having one, you'll be making yourself a more desirable employer.

Plan for the Possibility of Failure

There's no point in planning for failure, but there is a point in writing a business plan that is willing to admit the possibility of failure. It's only natural to create a plan that will describe a roaring success, but you have to be careful not to present an overly optimistic view, especially of such elements as sales, costs, and profit margins.

If your plan indicates that the business idea isn't sound, by all means look for errors.

It's tempting to noodle around with the numbers until you come up with the desired result. And if you only make small changes here and there, it may seem all right. What difference does it make? Say you increase your projected market share by 1 percent here, reduce expected costs by 2 percent there, and lower your estimate of required start-up capital by a few percentage points as well.

A number of similarly small changes, in sum, can make a big difference in the bottom line of your plan and turn what otherwise looks like a loser into a projected winner. But don't be seduced. You may be asking for investments from friends and family you care about as well as putting your own life savings into the enterprise. Arm's-length investors' feelings may not be so important, but if you mislead them in your plan, you may open yourself up to accusation of misrepresentation.

Looking at things in your plan through rose-colored glasses may even doom your business to failure if it causes you to seek insufficient start-up capital, underprice your product or service, or expect unrealistically rapid growth. Temper your enthusiasm. If your plan indicates that the business idea isn't sound, by all means look for errors. But don't make the mistake of skewing your plan to fit an idea that isn't sound.

Update Your Plan

Writing a business plan is one of those skills that improves with practice. The first one or two times you create one, you may feel a little unsure of yourself and even less certain that what you're doing has value.

If you go on to start several ventures during your career, you'll naturally write several business plans, and each one will be better than the last. It's likely as well that with better planning skills will come improved business skills, boosting the odds that each successive company you start will do better than the one before.

But there's no reason that only serial entrepreneurs should get the benefit of regular business planning sessions. If you start just one company or even if you never start a company at all, you can and should be constantly honing your business planning skills by updating and rewriting your business plan.

Updating a plan is normally easier than starting from scratch.

Updating a plan is normally easier than starting from scratch. Instead of trying to figure out what your basic business concept is, you only have to decide whether it's changing. Instead of wondering where you'll find the current market research you need, you just have to go back to the original source for updated figures. You'll usually be able to reuse the financial formulas, spreadsheets, management biographies, and other more or less evergreen contents of your plan.

It's important, however, that a plan update not be a mechanical task, limited to plugging in the most recent sales figures. Take the time to challenge some of the core assumptions of your prior plan to see if they still hold up. Have profit margins been higher than you expected? Then start planning how to make the most of any extra cash you generate. Is your new retail store unit not performing as well as others or you expected? Then now's the time to figure out why. Has competition for your new product arisen sooner than you guessed? Take a look at other products with an eye to seeing if they are also more vulnerable than you think.

In large corporations with strict planning routines requiring annual, semiannual, and quarterly plans and plan updates, managers spend at least part of their time working on or thinking about a new plan or plan update. All that information flowing up to senior managers in the form of plans helps keep the brass informed. It helps those in the trenches, too. It's a fact that everybody is judged by past performance. And the best way to ensure that a year from now you'll be looking back on your performance with satisfaction and pride is to plan now and often.

Do You Need to Update Your Plan?

Here are eight reasons to think about updating your plan. If one applies to you, it's time for an update.

1. A new financial period is about to begin. You may update your plan annually, quarterly, or even monthly if your industry is fast changing.
2. You need financing, or additional financing. Lenders and other financiers need an updated plan to make financing decisions.
3. Significant markets change. Shifting client tastes, consolidation trends among customers, and altered regulatory climates can trigger a need for plan updates.
4. New or stronger competitors are looking to your customers for their growth.
5. Your firm develops or is about to develop a new product, technology, service, or skill. If your business has changed a lot since you wrote your plan, it's time for an update.
6. You have had a change in management. New managers should get fresh information.
7. Your company has crossed a threshold, such as moving out of your home office, reaching $1 million in sales, or employing 100 people.
8. Your old plan doesn't seem to reflect reality anymore. Maybe you did a poor job last time; maybe things have just changed faster than you expected. But if your plan seems irrelevant, redo it.

⋆ EXPERT ADVICE ⋆

What are the most important parts of a business plan?

"This changes with the stage of the company," says Robert Roeper, managing director of Venture Capital firm VIMAC. "In a very early-stage company, the key components are the definition of the need/projected market, the buyer, and the product/technology that will be used to fulfill the need. Next comes the business model that speculates on the cost to acquire a customer and the anticipated revenue from that customer."

"Then comes a rational review of potential competition. Finally is a presentation of the management team that will get you to the next stage of growth. The reason for this order is that, in general, if the potential market isn't big enough, all the other things don't matter, and if the market's big enough but you can't identify the buying chain then you don't know enough yet to position the product/technology, etc. Bad positioning is epidemic in early stage companies, but it can be corrected."

Donna Maria Coles Johnson, founder and president of Handmade Toiletries Network, thinks it depends on for whom the plan is prepared. "If it's for a venture capitalist, the most important part would be the financials because they want to know how they will make money and how quickly they will make money," she says. "Same if you are seeking a bank loan or investors. Also important, no matter who the audience is, is the executive summary because it's often the first thing people read. If the executive summary does not succinctly and enthusiastically convey the business concept, the reader will move on quickly to something else."

"Attention has to be captured quickly and held in order to obtain funding. If the plan is geared toward attracting top management to become part of the team, the financials are important. But the executive summary is also important because it's the part of the plan that demonstrates the idea that the management team will be part of a new, exciting, innovative venture with maximum chances of success. Everyone wants to be a part of success!"

"Overall, there really is no 'most important part.' A business plan has to tell a story. It has to flow with a fluidity and consistency throughout. If it does not, and even one section falls flat, the entire story can be called into question. Each section should build on the other and refer specifically to the other when appropriate. There must be no inconsistencies that would call your planning and management expertise into question. A business plan should create a synergy, where the whole is greater and more credible than the mere sum of its parts."

Scott Simpson, an associate with Battery Ventures Associates, thinks there are three important parts of a business plan: the problem statement, the explanation of your solution to the problem, and the explanation of your differentiation from your competitors. "The best plans clearly explain the reason for the proposed product or service's existence," he says. For example, "My software will allow large manufacturers to integrate with their suppliers, which is something that they cannot do today and is necessary for them going forward." The explanation of a product or solution should clearly explain exactly what the product, service, or business is going to produce or sell. The best plans are as specific as possible.

"Finally, explanation of a company's differentiation usually focuses on the competition that will be encountered, the barriers to entry for potential competitors, and the sustainable long-term advantage of the business over other competitors. Some other very important components of a plan include market data and description of the management team. It is crucial to understand exactly what skills each member of your team will bring to the business."

Ronald Peterson of Three Arrows Capital thinks that the most important part of your business plan is the very first paragraph. "Often that is the only part that most people will ever read, and of that, the opening sentence is the most important portion," he says. "At Three Arrows Capital we wrestle with that opening for days, and once we have it right, the rest comes far easier. The competition section is extremely important since not only does it demonstrate and give assurance that you have done your homework, it also alerts you to other business models and solutions in your chosen industry that you need to read and consider."

Chapter 4

Before Beginning Your Plan

Y OU'VE DECIDED TO WRITE A BUSINESS PLAN, AND YOU'RE READY TO get started. Congratulations. You've just greatly increased the chances that your business venture will succeed. But before you start drafting your plan, you need to plan your draft. Is planning a plan going too far? Not really, for a couple of reasons. Planning your plan will make it easier to write—and easier to live by.

One of the most important reasons to plan your plan is that you are accountable for the projections and proposals it contains. That's especially true if you use your plan to raise money to finance your company. Let's say you forecast opening four new locations in the second year of your retail operation. An investor may have a beef if, due to circumstances you could have foreseen, you only open two. Thinking a little about what you want to include in your plan is no more than common prudence.

Business plans can be complicated documents. You'll be making lots of decisions as you draft your plan, on serious matters such as what strategy you'll pursue as well as less important ones like what color paper to print it on. Thinking about these decisions in advance is an important way to minimize the time you spend planning and to maximize the time you spend generating income.

Raise Your Goals

When Stratus Computer founder William Foster was writing the plan for the computer manufacturer, he projected sales in the fifth year would hit $75 million. When, five years later, Stratus hit that total almost to the dollar, Foster was left to wonder what would have happened if he'd planned for $125 million. "I don't think we would have made $125 million," he says, "but I bet we would have done more than $75 million."

To sum up, planning your plan will help control your degree of accountability and reduce time-wasting indecision. To plan your plan, you'll first need to decide what your goals and objectives in business are. As part of that, you'll assess the business you've chosen to start, or are already running, to see what the chances are that it will actually achieve those ends.

Determine Your Goals and Objectives

Close your eyes. Imagine that it's five years from now. Where do you want to be? What will the business look like? Will you be running a business that hasn't increased significantly in size? Will you command a rapidly growing empire? Will you have already cashed out and be relaxing on a beach somewhere, enjoying your hard-won gains?

Your plan may look beautiful, but without a solid understanding of your own intentions in business, it is likely to lack coherence and, ultimately, prove ineffective.

Now is a good time to free-associate a little bit—let your mind roam, exploring every avenue that you would like your business to go down. Try writing a personal essay on your business goals. It could take the form of a letter to yourself, written from five years in the future, describing all you have accomplished and how it came about.

As you read such a document, you may make a surprising discovery, such as that you don't really want to own a large, fast-growing enterprise but would be content with a stable small business. Even if you don't learn anything new, though, getting a firm handle on your goals and objectives is a big help in deciding how you'll plan your business. Answering the questions in Figure 4–1 is an important part of building a successful business plan. If you don't have a destination in mind, it's not possible to plan at all.

Your plan may look beautiful, but without a solid understanding of your own intentions in business, it is likely to lack coherence and, ultimately, prove ineffective. Let's say in one section you describe a mushrooming enterprise on a fast-growth track, then elsewhere endorse a strategy of slow and steady

54

expansion. Any business plan reader worth his or her salt is going to be bothered by inconsistencies like these. They suggest that you haven't thought through your intentions. Avoid inconsistency by deciding in advance what your goals and objectives will be, and sticking to them.

Goals and Objectives Worksheet

If you're having trouble deciding what your goals and objectives are, here are some questions to ask yourself.

1. How determined am I to see this venture succeed?

   _____

   _____

2. Am I willing to invest my own money and to work long hours for no pay, sacrificing personal time and lifestyle, maybe for years?

   _____

   _____

3. What's going to happen to me if this venture doesn't work out?

   _____

   _____

4. If it does succeed, how many employees will this company eventually have?

   _____

   _____

5. What will be its annual sales in a year? Five years?

   _____

   _____

6. What will be its market share in that time frame?

   _____

   _____

7. Will it be a niche marketer, or will it sell a broad spectrum of good and services?

   _____

   _____

8. What are the plans for geographic expansion? Local? National? Global?

   _____

   _____

Figure 4-1. Goals and Objectives Worksheet

9. Am I going to be a hands-on manager, or will I delegate a large proportion of tasks to others?

_____

_____

10. If I delegate, what sorts of tasks will I share? Sales? Technical? Others?

_____

_____

11. How comfortable am I taking direction from others? Could I work with partners or investors who demand input into the company's management?

_____

_____

12. Is this venture going to remain independent and privately owned, or will it eventually be acquired or go public?

_____

_____

Figure 4-1. Goals and Objectives Worksheet, continued

Business Planning without a Net

When former Lotus Development CEO Jim Manzi joined a young company called Industry Net Corporation, he had big plans. He helped raise $25 million for the Pittsburgh-based online seller of industrial products, promising to turn it into the leader in internet marketing.

But the company, renamed Nets Inc., wasn't able to fulfill its projections. Employment doubled to 300 as Manzi simultaneously tried to develop a market and the technology to handle complex online transactions. Soon the company was running through its investors' stake at the rate of $3 million a month. Meanwhile, revenues were less than $10 million a month.

After less than two years, Nets Inc. still hadn't developed either its technology or its market in the way its plans had forecast. And investors had tired of waiting. They refused to provide more funding, and Nets Inc. had to file for bankruptcy protection in 1997. The experience illustrates the importance of coming up with a plan that not only offers promise but can fulfill that promise as well.

Dream a Little Dream

Don't count out any source of guidance when it comes to pinning down what you want. Even the dreams you dream at night can help boost self-awareness.

Marte Sheeran was a graduate student working on her goal of becoming a history teacher when she began to have doubts about her career choice. She even had doubts about the doubts. "It was a very difficult situation for me, trying to figure out what I was going to do," recalls Sheeran. The answer came, oddly enough, while she was asleep, in a series of vivid dreams.

"I was sinking into a bog, going down and down," Sheeran recalls. "And there was an enormous sense of being very afraid. That put me in touch with feelings that I was not really happy going into academia."

The feeling stirred by the dreams motivated Sheeran to change career plans. She got an MBA and went into business, working as a consultant and manager in several small companies. In 1992, she became an entrepreneur herself, beginning ShopFocus Inc., developer of employee-training products.

Now Sheeran says that without the dreams, she might be a frustrated history educator. She says, "The dreams released all these emotions and gave me the courage to finish my master's degree and stop there."

BUZZWORD

Objectives *are long-term aims. They frequently represent the ultimate level to which you aspire. For instance, you may have an objective to retire at 50, or to become the leading supplier in your industry. Neither of these will happen fast, but they help to guide the creation of shorter-term aims.*

Financing

It doesn't necessarily take a lot of money to make a lot of money, but it does take some. That's especially true if, as part of examining your goals and objectives, you envision very rapid growth.

Energetic, optimistic entrepreneurs tend to believe that sales growth will take care of everything, that they will be able to fund their own growth by generating profits. However, this is rarely the case, for one simple reason: You usually have to pay your own suppliers before your customers pay you. This cash flow conundrum is the reason so many fast-growing companies have to seek bank financing or sell equity to finance their growth. They are growing faster than they can afford.

Sometimes the cash flow gap is very large. Pharmaceutical companies may spend hundreds of millions of dollars in a multiyear project to develop and bring to market a new drug. These companies must have large cash flows from other products to fill the gap or seek loans or other forms of financing to avoid running out of money before having a market-ready product.

Plan of Action

Many enterprises can be started with the help of modest amounts of cash, no more than the contents of a small savings account. You'll find suggestions for hundreds of businesses you can start for amounts as little as nothing plus general start-up suggestions in the Ultimate Start-Up Directory *(Entrepreneur Press) by James Stephenson, or* Start Your Own Business *(Entrepreneur Press) by Rieva Lesonsky.*

From Usher to Tycoon

From an early age, David Geffen knew he wanted to be part of Hollywood. This simple, uncomplicated desire was the spur that helped him create a billion-dollar entertainment empire built around music and movies. In fact, it's hard to identify any other advantages that the young Geffen possessed when he traveled from his New York City hometown to Los Angeles. He had only a high school education, no money, and no contacts. His first job in Hollywood was as a studio usher.

But Geffen's pursuit of Hollywood success was unswerving. He went so far as to falsify his resume; he indicated he had a college degree to get a job at the William Morris talent agency. After working his way up to a position as an agent, he started his own record company and later sold it. Then he started Geffen Records, which he sold in 1990 for more than $550 million.

David Geffen's plan was nowhere near as sophisticated as even a modest business plan. But backed by almost total certainty with regard to his ultimate objective, he succeeded on an incredible scale. Today Geffen is a billionaire and one of the three visionaries, along with Steven Spielberg and Jeffrey Katzenberg, behind DreamWorks SKG.

Other companies require much smaller amounts of capital to finance their ongoing operations. Small service firms such as exterminators or carpet cleaners frequently operate on a cash basis, getting paid with cash, check, or credit card at the time they perform their services after making only small outlays for supplies in advance. But as a general rule, your business will most likely have to consider some kind of financing. Now is the time to think about some of the issues that will surface.

Start by asking yourself what kinds of financing you are likely to need—and what you'd be willing to accept. It's easy when you're short of cash, or expect to be short of cash, to take the attitude that almost any source of funding is just fine. But each kind of financing has different characteristics that you should take into consideration when planning your plan. These characteristics take three primary forms:

First, there's the amount of control you'll have to surrender. An equal-equity partner may, quite naturally, demand approximately equal control. Venture capitalists often demand significant input into management decisions by placing one or more people on your board of directors. The wealthy individuals known as angel investors may be very involved or not involved at all, depending on personal style. Bankers, at the other end of the scale, are

Financing Source	Control Issues	Funds Available	Cost
Bank loan	Little	Varies	Varies
Partner	Large	Varies	Low
Government-backed loan	Little	Usually small	Low
Venture capital	Large	Moderate to large	Low
Angel investor	Varies	Small to moderate	Low
Stock offering	Large	Large	Large

Figure 4-2. Financing Characteristics Comparison

likely to offer no advice whatsoever as long as you make payments of principal and interest on time and are not in violation of any other terms of your loan. You can learn more about the characteristics of each of these financing sources in Chapter 2.

Second, consider the amount of money you are likely to need. Any amount less than several million dollars is too small to be considered for a standard initial public offering of stock, for example. Venture capital investors are most likely to invest amounts of $2 million and up. Only the richest angel investor will be able to provide more than a few hundred thousand dollars, if that. See Figure 4–2 for comparisons.

Almost any source of funds, from a bank to a factor, has some guidelines about the size of financing it prefers. Anticipating the size of your needs now will guide you in preparing your plan.

The third consideration is cost. This can be measured in terms of interest rates and shares of ownership as well as in time, paperwork, and plain old hassle. At the top of the list are public offerings of stock, which may cost several hundred thousand dollars in legal and accounting fees to put together and require a great deal of your own time and attention.

Planning

Your business plan can be used for several things, from monitoring your company's progress toward goals to enticing key employees to join your firm. Deciding how you intend to use yours is an important part of preparing to write it.

BUZZWORD

Working capital *is the amount of money a business has in cash, accounts receivable, inventory, and other current assets. (Current assets are assets likely to be turned into cash within a year.)* Net working capital, *which is what this term usually refers to, is current assets minus current liabilities. (Current liabilities are things like accounts payable to suppliers and short-term loans due in less than a year.) The higher the amount of net working capital you require, the greater your financing needs are likely to be.*

59

▶ *Do you intend to use your plan to help you raise money?* In that case, you'll have to focus very carefully on the executive summary, management, and marketing and financial aspects. You'll need to have a clearly focused vision of how your company is going to make money. If you're looking for a bank loan, you'll need to stress your ability to generate sufficient cash flow to service loans. Equity investors, especially venture capitalists, must be shown how they can cash out of your company and generate a rate of return they'll find acceptable.

▶ *Do you intend to use your plan to attract talented employees?* Then you'll want to emphasize such things as stock options and other aspects of compensation as well as location, work environment, corporate culture, and

BU⚡WORD

Cash conversion cycle *is an arcane financial measure that is a powerful indicator of a business's health. It represents the time it takes to transform outlays into income. For a manufacturer, that means the number of days required to purchase raw material and turn it into inventory, then sales, and finally, collections. The shorter your cash conversion cycle, the better.*

When Is a Negative a Positive?

Cash is one of the major constraints on the growth of any business. It's the reason why even highly profitable, fast-growing companies frequently have to go hat in hand to borrowers, seeking money to allow them to fill their orders so they can turn sales into cash. There's one type of company, however, that doesn't have a problem with cash. It's one with a negative cash conversion cycle, and the best-known example in recent years has been Dell Computer Corporation.

The rapidly growing Austin, Texas, computer company actually has a cash conversion cycle of minus four days. That means the company collects from its customers, on average, four days before it has to pay its suppliers. Here's how it works:

First, Dell sells direct to customers. This cuts out the typical 90-day wait for payment experienced by manufacturers who sell through retailers. Dell bills individual customers' credit cards immediately upon shipping their computers. Its corporate customers are asked to pay within 30 days.

The second part is the way Dell manages outlays of cash. It gets 30-day terms from suppliers and also asks that they bill for components only when the parts actually leave the trucks and enter the factory. There, in as little as a few hours, components are assembled into computers and shipped, and individual customers' credit cards are charged or corporate buyers are invoiced.

The result is that Dell collects cash faster than its operations are spending it. That frees Dell from the delay, distraction, and cost of arranging and paying for loans or other external financing. It's one of the things that makes the company such a fearsome and successful competitor. It's estimated the company could grow at an annual rate of 500 percent using only internally generated cash.

opportunities for growth and advancement. If you're a high-tech start-up, top employees are likely to ask to see your plans for attracting venture capital and later selling out to a bigger firm or going public so they can realize the value of their stock options.

▶ *Do you anticipate showing your plan to suppliers to demonstrate that you are a worthy customer?* A solid business plan may convince a supplier of some precious commodity to favor you over your rivals. It may also help you to arrange supplier credit—one of the most useful forms of financing to a small business. You may want to stress your blue-ribbon customer list and spotless record of repaying trade debts in this plan.

▶ *Do you hope to convince big customers that you will be a dependable supplier?* Then you'll want to emphasize your staying power, innovation, and special capabilities. And in this plan, unlike the supplier-targeted one, you may want to play down relationships with other big customers, especially if they are foes of the one you're wooing.

▶ *Do you expect to use your plan only for internal purposes?* Then you'll want to build in many milestones, benchmarks, and other tools for measuring and comparing your future performance against the plan. Such things may be of little interest to a banker evaluating your loanworthiness but could make all the difference between a useful plan and one that's no good at all for monitoring corporate performance.

Plan of Action

Who you are has as much to do with how you prepare for writing your plan as what you hope to do with it. More than half the businesses started in the United States today are begun by women, a fact addressed in Minding Her Own Business *(Adams) by Jan Zobel, a book on business planning for women.*

These distinctions are not merely academic. A plan that's well suited for internal purposes would probably be completely wrong for taking to a potential *Fortune* 500 customer. Actually, the marketplace of business plan consumers is even more finely segmented than that. A plan for a bank, for instance, wouldn't accomplish much by including a strategy for selling the company to a large conglomerate several years down the road, whereas a venture capitalist would look for your exit strategy very early on.

Think about all this, and keep it in mind as you create your plan. Along the way, you'll have to make many decisions about what to include or leave out and what to stress or play down. Setting some direction now about how you intend to use your plan will make those later decisions faster and more accurate.

Hiring

One of the beauties of being an entrepreneur, as opposed to a solo practitioner or freelancer, is that you can leverage the activities and skills of all the people who are your employees. This is one of the secrets to building a personal fortune. And it's one you can use even if you didn't happen to be born with a silver spoon in your mouth or an oil well in your backyard.

To use a simple example of the profit power of people, say you start a public relations firm. You bill clients $60 an hour, plus mailing and other office expenses, for services provided by your account executives (AE). You pay your staff $30 an hour including benefits. Before expenses for rent and other overhead items, then, you clear $30 for every hour one of your AEs bills. If you can grow your AE staff very large (and generate enough business to keep them busy), it can leverage your earnings very rapidly indeed.

The flip side of all this is, to earn the $30 gross margin on each employee's billable hour, you have to manage the employee. You may also have to generate the sales, issue the invoices, make the collections, and otherwise run the company's functions. If you pay somebody else to do it, it costs you control plus more of that gross margin.

So one of the questions you need to ask yourself when assessing your goals and objectives is, "How many people do I plan to hire to work at my company?"

The decision of how many people you want to manage is entirely up to you. The decision of when to start thinking about it has been made for you. That time is now.

Assessing Your Company's Potential

For most of us, our desires about where we would like to go are not as important as our businesses' ability to take us there. Put another way, if you choose the wrong business, you're going nowhere.

Luckily, one of the most valuable uses of a business plan is to help you decide whether the venture you have your heart set on is really likely to fulfill your dreams. Many, many businesses never make it past the planning stage because their would-be founders, as part of a logical and coherent planning process, test their assumptions and find them wanting.

Test your idea against at least two variables. First, financial, to make sure this business makes economic sense. Second, lifestyle, because who wants a successful business that they hate? Figure 4–3 can help you focus on your financial and lifestyle goals.

Financial Potential

The main reason for businesses being abandoned is failure to live up to financial expectations. Part of your planning process is to see if you can reasonably expect to turn a profit with your business. You'll also want to know when that's going to happen and, crucially, how much of an investment it will take to get you to that point.

Assessing Your Company's Potential

Answer the following questions to help you outline your company's potential. There are no wrong answers. The objective is simply to help you decide how well your proposed venture is likely to match your goals and objectives.

Financial

1. What initial investment will the business require?

_____

_____

2. How much control are you willing to relinquish to investors?

_____

_____

3. When will the business turn a profit?

_____

_____

4. When can investors, including you, expect a return on their money?

_____

_____

5. What are the projected profits of the business over time?

_____

_____

6. Will you be able to devote yourself full-time to the business financially?

_____

_____

Figure 4-3. Assessing Your Company's Potential

7. What kind of salary or profit distribution can you expect to take home?

8. What are the chances the business will fail?

9. What will happen if it does?

Lifestyle

1. Where are you going to live?

2. What kind of work are you going to be doing?

3. How many hours will you be working?

4. Will you be able to take vacations?

5. What happens if you get sick?

6. Will you earn enough to maintain your lifestyle?

7. Does your family understand and agree with the sacrifices you envision?

Figure 4-3. Assessing Your Company's Potential, continued

Lifestyle Concerns

The decision to become an entrepreneur is as much a lifestyle choice as it is a business option. Entrepreneurs tend to work long hours, often for low pay in the beginning. As a natural consequence of their position as founders and owners, they bear a much greater burden of worry and pressure than other employees. The road to entrepreneurial success is frequently paved with 16-hour days and seven-day weeks. Now is the time to ask yourself if you really love what you plan to do that much, or if you'd be better off taking on a less demanding project.

You also may have to consider others' feelings about your proposed lifestyle changes. Entrepreneurship can be a great thing for a family because it provides flexibility and financial benefits that most employees can only dream about. Or it can represent considerable strain. Many entrepreneurs rarely take vacations, especially during the first years of getting their venture off the ground. Another issue has to do with how the business will accommodate the normal ups and downs of life. What happens if you get sick? Are you going to be able to take a few days off every now and then?

Lifestyle concerns are complex. They involve everything from where you are going to live to the kind and amount of work you'll be doing. Unlike the financial analysis of your company's potential, there are few hard-and-fast answers to lifestyle concerns and almost none that can be termed wrong or right. You simply have to think the matter over and decide whether you'll be happy with your venture.

> **BUZZWORD**
>
> *A lifestyle entrepreneur is one who starts a business not to dominate an industry or even to get rich but because he or she thinks it will be more enjoyable to own a company than to work for one. Lifestyle entrepreneurs may want to live in a certain place, to work flexible hours, or to simply be able to make their own decisions.*

✶ EXPERT ADVICE ✶

Let's take a look at Madeline Fisher, a would-be newsletter publisher who's drafting a plan to see whether her dream business is going to fly. She envisions making a decent living (or maybe better) moonlighting part-time producing a newsletter on a topic she knows and loves—marketing coffee bars. She's done some research and made some assumptions about the market, how she'll reach it, and the business's publishing operations. During the course of preparing her plan, she finds out whether a business built around those assumptions is going to work.

Her market research tells her there are 10,000 people in the United States whose work largely or entirely involves marketing coffee bars. She guesses, based on rates she's paid for other professional newsletters, that they'd be willing to pay $200 for 12 issues annually of a 16-page newsletter packed with tips and tricks for getting people to come in and buy coffee and accessories. Reading up on newsletters, she learns that a well-designed, direct-mail solicitation will generate subscriptions from 1 percent of recipients.

Checking with a local printer and mailing service, she learns that it will cost her around $1 to send a sales letter to each person on a rented mailing list. The same sources inform her that printing and mailing each copy of the 16-page newsletter will run her about $2. Because she works full-time in a retail marketing job, she'll have to hire a freelance or part-time editor to write and edit the contents, at around $100 a page, or $1,600 per issue.

The future publisher of "Coffee Bar Marketing News" has done a good research job. Now it's time to pull all this together to test its financial potential. She decides it would be reasonable to go for having 200 subscribers at the end of the first year. Then she'd like to double that annually until she has 1,600 subscribers. That represents 16 percent of the market today. But it's not ridiculous considering that she hasn't seen any competition and that the number of coffee bars and, presumably, coffee bar marketers, is growing at a healthy clip.

Punching a few numbers into her calculator, Madeline comes up with a figure for gross annual sales with 1,600 subscribers each paying $200 annually. Wow! $320,000. Even after paying $28,800 to print and mail the issues, $19,200 for writing and editing, and an estimated $4,200 in office costs, that still leaves:

Projected subscribers	1,600
Revenues ($200 x 1,600)	$320,000
Costs (printing, labor, and overhead)	$61,800
Gross profit	$258,200

Double wow! This is more than decent. Madeline dives into the rest of her calculations, dizzy with excitement. She quickly regains her balance. The problem, she finds, is twofold.

First, there's the cost of getting those subscribers. Getting 200 subscribers will require mailing 20,000 pieces, based on her hoped-for 1 percent return rate. At approximately $1 per direct-mail piece, plus labor, printing, postage, and overhead, she loses money on each new subscriber the first year.

Gross profit	$258,200
Annual revenue per subscriber	200
Marketing costs per subscriber ($1 mailing with 1 percent return)	100
Printing and mailing for one copy of 12 Issues	24
Fixed costs (labor and overhead/200)	117
Subtotal costs per subscriber	241
First year net loss per subscriber	−$41

Madeline figures, correctly, that the key is to get some more subscribers and to convince them to resubscribe year after year. She does some more research and learns that a 50 percent resubscription rate is doable. Then she does some more figuring. The results of her financial analysis show that she'll reach 1,600 subscribers, and a healthy profit, after four years.

First Year

Starting number of subscribers	0
Resubscribers (50 percent of starting number)	0
New subscribers (to give 100 percent annual increase)	200
Total subscribers	200
Annual subscription revenues	$40,000
Marketing costs (new subs x $100)	20,000
Printing and mailing costs (subs x $24)	4,800
Labor and overhead	23,400
Total costs	48,200
Pretax net profit or loss	($8,200)

Second Year

Starting number of subscribers	200
Resubscribers (50 percent of starting number)	100
New subscribers (to give 100 percent annual increase)	300
Total subscribers	400
Annual subscription revenues	$80,000
Marketing costs (new subs x $100)	30,000
Printing and mailing costs (subs x $24)	9,600
Labor and overhead	23,400
Total costs	63,000
Pretax net profit or loss	$17,000

Third Year

Starting number of subscribers	400
Resubscribers (50 percent of starting number)	200

Plan Pointer

Every type of business has one or more key indicators that hint at its long-term viability. For newsletters, for example, it's the number of people who resubscribe. For mail order sellers, it's the response rate to direct-mail marketing efforts. Find your business's key indicators, describe them in your plan, and monitor them carefully.

New subscribers (to give 100 percent annual increase)	600
Total subscribers	800
Annual subscription revenues	$160,000
Marketing costs (new subs x $100)	60,000
Printing and mailing costs (subs x $24)	19,200
Labor and overhead	23,400
Total costs	102,600
Pretax net profit or loss	$57,400

Fourth Year

Starting number of subscribers	800
Resubscribers (50 percent of starting number)	400
New subscribers (to give 100 percent annual increase)	1,200
Total subscribers	1,600
Annual subscription revenues	$320,000
Marketing costs (new subs x $100)	120,000
Printing and mailing costs (subs x $24)	38,400
Labor and overhead	23,400
Total costs	181,800
Pretax net profit or loss	$138,200

Madeline's analysis shows her newsletter venture has definite financial potential, even if it's not quite as rosy as this quick forecast suggests. She should, for instance, apply an inflation factor—4 percent a year is a good figure—to expenses such as overhead. She has a more serious problem with her marketing plan, however. Is it really reasonable to mail 120,000 pieces of mail a year to a marketplace of just 10,000 people? Probably not, but Madeline left out positives as well. For instance, there are a number of other marketing tools, such as publicity, that she hasn't considered in her plan. And with a good product, she should be able to beat the 50 percent renewal rate, saving her a bundle on marketing.

Chapter 12 covers how to make detailed financial forecasts and Chapter 10 marketing plans. For now, Madeline's quick analysis shows that her venture does have the potential to be financially rewarding.

Chapter 5

One Plan Does Not Fit All

BUSINESS PLANS HAVE A LOT OF ELEMENTS IN COMMON, SUCH AS CASH flow projections and marketing plans. And many of them share certain objectives as well, such as raising money or persuading a partner to join the firm. But all business plans are not the same any more than all businesses are.

Depending on your business and what you intend to use your plan for, you may need a very different type of business plan from what another entrepreneur needs. Plans differ widely in their length, their appearance, the detail of their contents, and the varying emphases they place on different aspects of the business. "They come thick, they come thin, they come ugly, they come pretty," says Benjamin M. Rosen of venture capital firm Sevin Rosen Management Co. "Mostly, they just keep coming."

Differences Among Industries

One of the reasons for differences among plans is that industries are different. A retailer isn't much like a manufacturer, and a professional services firm isn't much like a fast-food restaurant. Each of them requires certain critical components for success—components that may be irrelevant or even completely absent in the operations of another type of firm.

For instance, inventory is a key concern of both retailers and manufacturers. Expert, innovative management of inventory is a very important part of the success of Wal-Mart, one of the great all-time success stories of retail. And Dell Computer, with its direct-sales model, is another enterprise skyrocketing to global prominence with savvy inventory management. Any business plan that purported to describe the important elements of these businesses would of necessity have to devote considerable space to telling how the managers planned to reduce inventory, increase inventory turnover, and so on.

Now look at a professional services firm, such as a management consultant. The consultant has no inventory whatsoever. Her offerings consist entirely of the management analysis and advice she and her staff can provide. She doesn't have to pay now for goods to be sold later or lay out cash to store products for eventual sale. The management consultant's business plan, therefore, wouldn't have any section on inventory or its management, control, and reduction.

Sometimes even companies in more closely related industries have significantly different business plans.

This is just one pretty obvious example of the differences among plans for different industries. Sometimes even companies in more closely related industries have significantly different business plans. For instance, a fine French restaurant's plan might need a section detailing how the management intended to attract and retain a distinguished chef. At another restaurant, one catering to the downtown lunchtime crowd, a great deal of plan space might be devoted to the critical concern of location and very little to staffing issues.

Presenting Yourself in the Best Light

You want your plan to present yourself and your business in the best, most accurate light. That's true no matter what you intend to use your plan for, whether it's destined for presentation at a venture capital conference or will never leave your own office or be seen outside internal strategy sessions.

When you select clothing for an important occasion, odds are you try to pick items that will play up your best features. Think about your plan the same way. You want to reveal any positives that your business may have and make sure they receive due consideration.

When you select your plan type, it's a lot like picking a dress or suit for a big interview or social outing. Flip through your closet carefully—this outfit may have an important bearing on how useful your plan eventually turns out to be.

70

Types of Plans

Business plans can be divided roughly into five separate types. There are very short plans, or miniplans. There are working plans, what-if plans, presentation plans, and even electronic plans. They require very different amounts of labor, and not always with proportionately different results. That is to say, a more elaborate plan is not guaranteed to be superior to an abbreviated one, depending on what you want to use it for.

The Miniplan

It's safe to say that almost every business idea starts out as a miniplan of some sort. It may be no more than a quick jotting down—even a mental scrawl—of some basic business formula or statement. A thought such as, "I'm sure I can make one of those for less than he's selling them for!" could be considered a sort of business plan. Ideally, even a miniplan will be more elaborate than that.

A miniplan may be up to ten pages long. It should pay at least cursory attention to such key matters as business concept, financing needs, marketing plan, and financial statements, especially cash flow, income projection, and balance sheet. It's a great way to quickly test a business concept or measure the interest of a potential partner or minor investor. It can also serve as a valuable prelude to a full-length plan later on.

Be careful about misusing a miniplan. It's not intended to substitute for a full-length plan. If you send a miniplan to an investor who's looking for a comprehensive one, you're only going to look foolish.

A miniplan is a great way to quickly test a business concept or measure the interest of a potential partner or minor investor.

The Working Plan

A working plan is a tool to be used to operate your business. It has to be long on detail but may be short on presentation. As with a miniplan, you probably can afford a somewhat higher degree of candor and informality when preparing a working plan. In a plan you intend to present to a bank loan committee, you might describe a rival as "competing primarily on a price basis." In a working plan, your comment about the same competitor might be, "When is Jones ever going to stop this insane price-cutting?"

A plan intended strictly for internal use may also omit some elements that would be important in one aimed at those outside the firm. You probably don't need to include an appendix with resumes of key executives, for example. Nor would a working plan especially benefit from product photos.

Internal policy considerations may guide the decision about whether to include or exclude certain information in a working plan. Many entrepreneurs are sensitive about employees knowing the precise salary the owner takes home from the business. To the extent such information can be left out of a working plan without compromising its utility, you can feel free to protect your privacy.

Fit and finish are likely to be quite different in a working plan. It's not essential that a working plan be printed on high-quality paper and enclosed in a fancy binder. An old three-ring with "plan" scrawled across it with a felt-tip marker will serve quite well. That doesn't mean you should skimp on additions such as graphs and charts, however. These do more than look nice. They can be useful tools for communicating concepts and trends to other managers as well as for reinforcing them in your own mind.

Internal consistency of facts and figures is just as crucial with a working plan as with one aimed at outsiders. You don't have to be as careful, however, about such things as typos in the text, perfectly conforming to business style, being consistent with date formats, etc. This document is like an old pair of khakis you wear to the office on Saturdays or that one ancient delivery truck that never seems to break down. It's there to be used, not admired.

Internal consistency of facts and figures is just as crucial with a working plan as with one aimed at outsiders.

What-If Plans

When you face unusual circumstances, you need a variant on the working plan. You might want to prepare a *contingency plan* when you are seeking bank financing. A contingency plan is a plan based on the worst case scenario that you can imagine your business surviving—loss of market share, heavy price competition, defection of a key member of your management team. A contingency plan can soothe a banker's fears by showing that you have indeed considered more than a rosy scenario.

Your business may be considering an acquisition, in which case a *pro forma business plan* (some call this a *what-if* plan) can help you understand what the acquisition is worth and how it might affect your core business. What if you raise prices, invest in staff training, reduce duplicative efforts? Such what-if planning doesn't have to be as formal as a presentation plan. Perhaps you want to mull over the chances of a major expansion. A what-if plan can help you spot the increased needs for space, equipment, personnel, and other variables so you can make good decisions.

What sets these kinds of plans apart from the working and presentation plans is that they aren't necessarily describing how you will run the business.

They are more aids to thinking than operational blueprints. If you decide to acquire that competitor or grow dramatically, you will want to incorporate some of the thinking already invested in these special purpose plans.

The Presentation Plan

If you take a working plan, with its low stress on cosmetics and impression, and twist the knob to boost the amount of attention paid to its looks, you'll wind up with a presentation plan. This plan is suitable for showing to bankers, investors, and others outside the company.

Almost all the information in a presentation plan is going to be the same as your working plan, although it may be styled somewhat differently. For instance, you should use standard business vocabulary and omit the informal jargon, slang, and shorthand that's so useful in the workplace and is appropriate in a working plan. Remember, these readers won't be familiar with your operation. Unlike the working plan, this plan isn't being used as a reminder but as an introduction.

You'll also have to include some added elements. Among investors' requirements for due diligence is information on all competitive threats and risks. Even if you consider some to be of only peripheral significance, you need to address these concerns by providing the information. In the end, raising and dealing with such issues will only make your plan appear stronger.

Almost all the information in a presentation plan is going to be the same as your working plan, although it may be styled somewhat differently.

Sliding By

For Tod Loofbourrow, the presentation of his plan was everything—literally. The president and founder of Foundation Technologies, a human resources software company, grew his company to 70 employees without ever having a conventional plan written down on paper.

But that doesn't mean Loufbourrow didn't plan or use his plan wisely. Instead, he confined his planning to creating impressive presentations, primarily in the form of slides created in Microsoft PowerPoint®, that conveyed the mission and promise of Foundation to investors. "We raised $8 million in venture capital with eight PowerPoint slides," he says.

"Our plan was really about presenting our story in the form of slides and oral discussion," explains Loofbourrow. The key task of a plan, he feels, is the ability to convey the company's story economically and convincingly rather than to amass a pile of detail.

One big difference between the presentation and working plans is in the details of appearance and polish. A working plan may be run off on the office printer and stapled together at one corner. A presentation plan may instead be produced by a high-quality printing company. It will be bound expertly into a booklet that is durable and easy to read and include graphics such as charts, graphs, tables, and illustrations.

It's crucial that you have your presentation plan proofread repeatedly, in addition to using spell-checking software. Typos, misspellings, and grammatical errors will detract from the overall impression of smooth perfection that you want to impart and may suggest to readers that you are not as thorough as you should be.

It's also essential that a presentation plan be accurate and internally consistent. A mistake here could be construed as a misrepresentation by an unsympathetic outsider. At best, it will make you look less than careful. If the plan's summary describes a need for $40,000 in financing, but the cash flow projection shows $50,000 in financing coming in during the first year, you might think, "Oops! Forgot to update that summary to show the new numbers." The investor you're asking to pony up the cash, however, is unlikely to be so charitable.

The Electronic Plan

The majority of business plans are composed on a computer of some kind, then printed out and presented in hard copy. But more and more business information that once was transferred between parties only on paper is now sent electronically. And you may find it appropriate to have an electronic version of your plan available. An electronic plan can be handy for presentations to a group using a computer-driven overhead projector, for example, or for satisfying the demands of a discriminating investor who wants to be able to delve deeply into the underpinnings of complex spreadsheets.

An electronic plan may consist of a file on a floppy disk or one sent by electronic mail via the internet. It may be a document in the format of a popular word processing program or a slideshow-type presentation.

One of the nice things about an electronic business plan is the speed with which you can transmit it. If you receive an expression of interest in your company from a financier or potential partner, you can electronically mail a plan to this person in minutes. Relying on express mail will require at least a day, and even a cross-town courier will take hours.

Another potential advantage of an electronic plan is that it lets a reader, by loading any spreadsheets it contains into his or her computer, see the underlying formulas you use for figuring important numbers. It's fairly easy to make spreadsheets with interlocking formulas that are so complicated it's hard to tell exactly what is going on behind the scenes. Being able to view your calculations may give some readers an added comfort level that you're not trying to pull the wool over their eyes with your financial projections. This won't be the case, by the way, if your plan's spreadsheets consist of only the data copied into a grid format.

It's worth noting that an electronic plan is cheaper than a printed one. You can spend a bundle having several dozen copies of a long plan color-printed and professionally bound. Making a new copy of an electronic plan, on the other hand, is limited to the cost of a floppy disk.

There are some problems with electronic plans. The fact that they're easier to copy and disseminate makes it harder to control who sees your plan. The person you're sending it to has to have access to an appropriate computer and software to see it at all. Many people are not willing to look at electronic plans, preferring the convenience and familiarity of a paper plan. So despite some significant advantages to electronic plans, you aren't likely to be able to completely replace the paper version.

Plan of Action

You can take a look at electronic plans others have created by going to Palo Alto Software's online samples of business plans created with its software. (See Chapter 15 for more on Palo Alto's programs.) All it takes is a trip to the World Wide Web at www.bplans.com.

Why You May Want More than One Plan

So you've looked over the different types of plans. Which one is for you? Odds are good that you'll need more than one variety, perhaps even all these and more besides. If you want to get maximum impact from your plan, you'll need to tailor it to address the particular needs of your audience of the moment.

Target Audiences

The potential readers of a business plan are a varied bunch, ranging from bankers and venture capitalists to employees. Although this is a diverse group, it is a finite one. And each type of reader does have certain typical interests. If you know these interests up front, you can be sure to take them into account when preparing a plan for that particular audience.

Active venture capitalists see hundreds of plans in the course of a year. Most plans probably receive no more than a glance from a given venture capitalist before being rejected; others get just a cursory inspection prior to being mailed back. Even if your plan excites initial interest, it may receive only a few minutes of attention to begin with. It's essential with these harried investors that you make the right impression fast. Emphasize a cogent, succinct summary and explanation of the basic business concept, and do not stint on the details about the impressive backgrounds of your management team.

Bankers tend to be more formal than venture capitalists and more concerned with financial strength than with exciting concepts and impressive resumes. For these readers, you'll want to give extra attention to balance sheets and cash flow statements. Make sure they're fully detailed and come with notes to explain any anomalies or possible points of confusion.

Angel investors may not insist on seeing a plan at all, but as we pointed out in Chapter 2, your responsibilities as a businessperson require you to show them one anyway. For such an informal investor, prepare a less formal plan. Rather than going for impressive bulk, seek brevity. An angel investor used to playing her hunches might be put off by an imposing plan rather than impressed with your thoroughness.

If you were thinking about becoming a partner in a firm, you'd no doubt be very concerned with the responsibilities you would have, the authority you would carry, and the ownership you would receive in the enterprise. Naturally, anyone who is considering partnering with you is going to have similar concerns. So make sure that any plan presented to a potential partner deals comprehensively with the ownership structure and clearly spells out matters of control and accountability.

Customers who are looking at your business plan are probably doing so because they contemplate building a long-term relationship with you. They are certainly going to be more concerned about your relationships with your other customers and, possibly, suppliers, than most plan readers. So deal with these sections of your plan in depth. If your customer has special requirements, such as the ability to make hourly deliveries to a plant without variations of more than a few minutes, you'll want to talk about your record on these matters, which would probably be of little or no interest to other readers. On the other hand, customers presumably will already be familiar with trends in your industry, so you can probably skip or abbreviate these sections.

Suppliers have a lot of the same concerns as customers, except they're in the other direction on the supply chain. They'll want, above all, to make sure you can pay your bills, so be sure to include adequate cash flow forecasts and other financial reports. Suppliers, who naturally would like their customers to order more and more, are likely to be quite interested in your growth prospects. In fact, if you can show you're probably going to be growing a lot, you may be in a better position to negotiate terms with your suppliers.

Strategic allies usually come to you for something specific—technology, distribution, complementary customer sets, etc. So naturally, any plan you show to a potential ally will stress this aspect of your operation. Sometimes potential allies may also be potential competitors, of course. So you may want to present your plan in stages, saving sensitive information such as financials and marketing strategies for later in the process when trust has been established.

Managers in your company are using the plan primarily to remind themselves of objectives, to keep strategies clear, and to monitor company performance and market conditions. You'll want to stress such things as corporate mission and vision statements and analyses of current industry and economic factors. The most important part of a plan intended for management consumption is probably in the financials. You'll want to take special care to make it easy for managers to compare sales revenue, profitability, and other key financial measures against planned performance.

Employees in companies that use open-book management styles should receive a version of your plan edited for their understanding and needs as well as your own comfort level. It's good to be frank and open, but if you're uncomfortable with employees knowing exactly what all the managers earn, leave this information out. As is the case with managers, an employee's plan should make it easy to compare actual production levels, costs, and other measures against prior projections. You may also include some data, such as rates of workplace accidents or absenteeism, that would be of only peripheral interest to investors.

There's one caution to the plan-customization exercise. Limit your alterations from one plan to another to modifying the emphasis of the information you present. Don't show one set of numbers to a banker you're trying to borrow from and another to a partner you're trying to lure on board. It's one thing to stress one aspect of your operation over another for presentation purposes and entirely another to distort the truth.

Plan Pointer THIS WAY

Instead of writing a whole new plan for each audience, construct a modular plan with interchangeable sections. Pull out the resume section for internal use, for example, and plug it back in for presentation to an investor. A modular, mix-and-match plan saves time and effort while preserving flexibility.

⋆ Expert Advice ⋆

Help When You Are Ready to Create Your Business Plan

"Keep the plan as short as possible and very simple to read," says Scott Simpson of Battery Associates. "Remember that the plan is a road map and a catalyst for the business. Don't get bogged down on details that don't matter. It isn't going to be helpful to have 30 pages of analysis discussing why revenues five years out will be $100 million vs. $110 million."

Simpson says that companies need to concentrate on the important stuff, like why your business will provide a compelling solution to a big problem, and why your company and not the others will be successful. "There's no need to spend tons of money on the plan. Videos, CDs, color pages, and other gimmicks are cool but at the end of the day, the content must stand on its own," he says.

"Also, don't create your plan in a vacuum. Read analyst reports, attend trade shows, understand your competition, and, most importantly, talk to potential customers. A plan written without knowledge of what problem you're solving for your customer represents a business that will most likely fail. Finally, know your audience. If the business plan is intended to help secure financing for your company, make sure that it covers the most vital information on which investors will focus."

Jim Caruso of Telecom Alley Inc. offers this advice:

Clearly determine the audience for your plan and write the plan for that audience and its interests phrased in its own words. Understand and closely follow any guidelines provided by your venture's backers, such as VCs. Differences may include expected length of executive summary, number of years of financial projections, projected funding sources, and investment horizon and exit strategy. Each audience has its own leaning. Investors' interest often shifts with changes in market conditions, so stay on top of their considerations. . . .

Be careful not to propose ice cubes to Eskimos. Events in public stock markets can kill your opportunity if your idea falls from favor, and this is critical in attaining funding. An example of the recent shifts in favor are those from business-to-consumer, to business-to-business, to peer-to-peer forms of electronic commerce. Each gained ,then lost the favor of investors, so timing can be critical.

If you seek outside investors, understand valuation methods that determine what your venture is worth. Understand dilution of share-holding and how that affects your control of your own fate. Recognize that investors want the opportunity to cash out or exit. Most realistically, a successful exit comes from acquisition, not an IPO. Consider which companies are potential acquirers and figure these exit possibilities into your plan. This is actually a part of speaking directly to the interests of your audience, the investor.

Stay flexible and silent about what you believe the venture is worth until you are in serious negotiation. It is best to have a VC firm's term sheet without ever stating what you believe the value to be. This avoids leaving money and shares on the table that could be yours. Expect the business plan to be a living document that improves with every tough question asked by a potential investor, business partner, or customer.

Section Two

Writing Your Business Plan

Chapter 6

Executive Summaries Sell Ideas

THE FIRST PART OF YOUR PLAN THAT ANYBODY WILL SEE, AFTER THE title page and table of contents, is the summary. Sometimes called the executive summary, it could be considered an expanded table of contents because it's more than an introduction to the rest of the plan. It's supposed to be a brief look at the key elements of the whole plan—and it's critical.

The actual executive summary should be only a page or two. In it you may include your mission and vision statements, a brief of your plans and goals, a quick look at your company and its organization, an outline of your strategy, and highlights of your financial status and needs. If you've ever read a Cliffs Notes version of a classic novel, you get the idea. Your executive summary is the Cliffs Notes to your business plan.

Labor over your summary. Polish it. Refine it. Ask friends and colleagues to take a look at it, and then take their suggestions to heart. If your plan isn't getting the response you want when you put it to work, suspect a flaw in the summary. If you get a chance to look at another plan that was used to raise a pile of cash, give special scrutiny to the executive summary.

The summary is the most important part of your whole plan. Even if a plan is only 15 or 20 pages, it's difficult for most people to keep that much

Super Summary

Jimmy Treybig, the founder of Tandem Computers and now a venture capitalist in Austin, Texas, says that the executive summary is the most important part of the plans he reviews. "What I want is 20 sentences that tell me why someone who gives them money is going to get rich," says the veteran businessman.

Treybig's 20 sentences should contain information on how the business will address the market, the product idea, the competitive advantage, the amount of money that is needed, who is on the team, and how it will all come together. Most important of all, he says, the executive summary should convey urgency. Treybig wants to be told, "It's going to explode, and I'd better invest now or I'm going to miss out."

Fact or Fiction?

Because the executive summary comes first in your plan, you may think you should write it first as well. Actually, however, you should write it last, after you've spent considerable time mulling over every other part of your plan. Only then will you truly be able to produce a summary of all that is there.

information in their minds at once. It's much easier to get your arms around the amount of information—just one or two pages—in an executive summary. Your plan is going to be judged on what you include in the summary and on how well you present it.

A good rule of thumb for writing an effective and efficient business plan is to avoid repeating information. Brief is better and clearer, and needless repetition may annoy some readers and confuse others. Take extra care when writing your summary. You'll be glad you did.

Purposes of the Executive Summary

The executive summary has to perform a host of jobs. First and foremost, it should grab the reader's attention. It has to briefly hit the high points of your plan. It should point readers with questions requiring detailed responses to the full-length sections of your plan where they can get answers. It should ease the task of anybody whose job it is to read it, and it should make that task enjoyable by presenting an interesting and compelling account of your company.

The first question any investor has is, "How much?" followed closely by, "When will I recoup my investment?" Perceived risk and exit strategies are supportive information, and these in turn are supported by the quality of the management team and the proposed strategies.

It doesn't much matter whether you are presenting the plan to a family member, friend, banker, or sophisticated investors such as investment

Points to Include in an Executive Summary

A suggested format for an executive summary:

1. How much financing are you seeking?
2. What will the return be to the investor? Over what length of time?
3. What is the perceived risk level?
4. What is the exit strategy?
5. What is the management team?
6. What are the product and competitive strategies?

bankers or venture capitalists. They all need the same information. Concealing the amount and terms will only lessen your chances of a successful financing.

How Much Cash

If you are using your plan as a financing proposal, and you probably are, put this information right up front. Are you seeking a loan, convertible debt, or equity investment? What terms, both in interest and length of loan, are you requesting? If equity, what is the probable exit strategy—and when will the exit strategy be executed?

Some readers will stop right here. That's fine. Other readers will appreciate your frankness. Being coy about amounts and terms will only harm your venture.

Using the Cash

Provide a short explanation of how you'll use the proceeds of any financing you seek. Tell the investor why you need the money. It's not necessary to get into much detail here. You don't have to justify every penny and wind up feeling obligated to ask for a loan of $23,558.36 because that's the exact price of everything you need. It's perfectly acceptable to state that the proceeds will be used for equipment and working capital. The details will appear in the business plan.

You should let the reader know how the investment will help the company grow and/or increase its profits. Why else would you be seeking funding? The best use of somebody else's money is to buy or build something that will make more money, both for you and for that person.

Plan Pointer THIS WAY

Five minutes. This is how long an average reader will spend with your plan. If you can't convey the basics of your business in that time, your plan is in trouble. So make sure your summary, at least, can be read in that time and that it's as comprehensive as possible within that constraint.

85

The Goals of Financiers

In your executive summary, consider the following:

▶ Friends and family want to get their money back someday but are not very interested in timing and returns.

▶ Bankers look for free cash flow to pay back the principal and interest of their loan. They also look closely at management experience and marketing. They may ask for collateral. By law they have to be conservative, i.e. risk averse, so they are not great candidates for risky financing.

▶ Angel investors look for moderate rates of return, usually above the prime rate, plus some capital appreciation. They sometimes want to be involved at a hands-on level.

▶ Venture capitalists seek annual compound rates of return in the area of 35 to 50 percent per annum. They seldom want to go longer than three to five years to cash out. They always want to know what the exit strategy is.

It's a rare company that doesn't have any investment from the entrepreneur or entrepreneurs who started it.

You may have special considerations to address in any given plan, depending on its target. For instance, you may know or suspect that one of the conditions of getting a loan from your parents is that you employ your black-sheep sister. Be sure your summary of management has a slot—Director of Ephemera might work—for that unworthy individual.

Don't forget yourself: It's a rare company that doesn't have any investment from the entrepreneur or entrepreneurs who started it.

Who Will Own What

When a business starts generating profits and plowing them back into the firm, value can build rapidly. Even if you aren't in an industry likely to purchase buildings or patent valuable technology, the business derives value from the fact that it can generate profits into the future.

Because your business is valuable, spell out who owns what. If you have many equity investors coupled with a pile of creditors, this can get pretty complicated.

For the summary section of your plan, a basic description such as "Ownership of the company will be divided so that each of the four original partners owns 25 percent" will suffice. If you have to negotiate details of exactly what any equity investors will get, there's time to do that later. For now, you just want to give people an idea of how the ownership is divided.

Putting Your Best Fool Forward

Slant your executive summary to the intended audience. The special concerns of particular audiences were covered in the last chapter. For instance, if you're addressing a banker, stress cash flow, management experience, and balance-sheet strength. For a partner, highlight organizational flexibility and prospects for growth. A venture capitalist will want very high growth rates plus some hint that you'll be ready to go public or sell out in a few years.

If you tell a story in the summary, give it a happy ending. Although it's your duty to fully disclose to investors any significant risk factors, you can save that for later. The summary is the place to put your best foot forward, to talk up the upside and downplay the downside.

As always, accentuating the positive doesn't mean exaggeration or falsehood. If there is a really important, unusual risk factor in your plan—such as that one certain big customer has to make a huge order or the whole thing's kaput—then you will want to mention that in your summary. But

Plan Pointer

Assessing your own strengths and weaknesses is a lot harder than assessing others' good and bad points, right? So when it comes time to select your best features, it's also time to solicit feedback from others. Ask people whose opinions you trust—colleagues, associates, and peers—whether your assessment of your idea is off-base or on target.

Raising the Fund-Raising Roof

Raising money for a business is ordinarily considered a pretty staid line of work. But not when Howard Getson gets involved. The president and co-founder of IntellAgent Control Corporation is famous for his brash but effective requests for money to grow his sales automation software manufacturing company.

How brash? In 1996, Getson sent a letter to prospective investors with outrageous lines like, "Return this letter now! You may already have invested $10 million!" and "This is the most undervalued financing we've ever agreed to accept."

How effective? Getson raised $6.8 million from 70 investors over two years with similar pitches.

Why does it work? Getson melds his in-your-face style with solid financial acumen. "Really," he explains, "it is the perfect blend of direct-mail schlock and true business sense."

run-of-the-mill risks like unexpected competition or simply customer reluctance can be ignored here.

Paint a convincing portrait of an opportunity so compelling that only a dullard would not recognize it and desire to take part in it.

Company Description

If your company is complex, you'll need a separate section inside the plan with a heading like "Company Description" to describe its many product lines, locations, services, or whatever else it is that makes it a little too complicated to deal with quickly. In any event, you provide a brief description, no longer than a few sentences, of your company in the executive summary. And for many firms, this is an adequate basic description of their company. Here are some one- or two-sentence company descriptions:

▶ John's Handball Hut is the Hamish Valley's leading purveyor of handball equipment and clothing.

▶ Boxes Boxes Boxes Inc. will provide the people of the metropolitan area with a comprehensive source for packing materials, containers, and other supplies for the do-it-yourself move.

▶ Johnny AppleCD buys, sells, and trades used compact disc musical recordings through locations on the north and south side of town.

Optional Information

The following items are not a necessity in your business plan: mission statement and corporate vision. If you have honed either down to a clear and concise sentence, by all means, use it in your plan.

Mission Statement

Many mission statements communicate what your business is about and should include a description of what makes you different from everybody else in your field. Mission statements have a place in a plan: They help investors and other interested parties get a grip on what makes your company special.

A mission statement should be a clearly written sentence or two that tells what you sell and to whom and why they buy from you. It may also summarize your goals and objectives. Here are some examples:

- ▶ River City Roadsters buys, restores, and resells classic American cars from the 1950s and 1960s to antique-auto buffs throughout Central Missouri.

- ▶ Captain Curio is the Jersey Shore's leading antique store, catering to high-quality interior decorators and collectors across the tri-state area.

- ▶ August Appleton, Esq., provides low-cost legal services to personal-injury, workers' compensation, and age-discrimination plaintiffs in Houston's Fifth Ward.

Corporate Vision

A mission statement describes the goals and objectives you could "reasonably" expect to accomplish. A small software company whose mission statement included the goal of "putting Microsoft out of business" would be looked upon as foolishly naive.

In a vision statement, however, just those sorts of grandiose, galactic-scale images are perfectly appropriate. When you "vision"—to borrow the management consultant's trick of turning nouns into verbs—you imagine the loftiest heights you could scale, not the next step or several steps on the ladder.

Does a vision statement even have a place in a business plan? You could argue that it doesn't, especially because many include personal components such as "to love every minute of my work and always feel I'm doing my best." But many investors deeply respect visionary entrepreneurs. So if you feel you have a compelling vision, there's no reason not to share it in your plan.

Extract the Essence

The key to the executive summary is to pick out the best aspects of every part of your plan. In other words, you want to extract the essence. Instead of describing everyone in your company, tell only about your key managers. Instead of talking about all your products, mention only the major ones or discuss only product lines instead of individual products.

And when you talk about your company's purpose and mission, stick to the highlights. You have pages to come where you can get into the minutiae. The executive summary is the first thing people read, so make sure it's interesting and to the point.

Plan Pointer THIS WAY

Make your mission statement do double duty as a marketing slogan and employee motivator. Famous ones include Ford's (Quality Is Job One) and Avis (When You're Number Two, You Try Harder). Hint: Slogans are shorter—no more than six words—and more specific than most mission statements.

Fact or Fiction?

Must you have a mission statement? Not necessarily. Many entrepreneurs find it difficult to summarize their mission in a sentence. But people do pay attention to mission statements. Write one that steers them wrong, and they'll go wrong. So if you can't accurately describe your mission in a statement, do without.

✴ EXPERT ADVICE ✴

Adapted from www.entrepreneur.com/article/0,4621,270366,00.html.

Article Tools

Within the overall outline of the business plan, the executive summary will follow the title page. The summary should tell the reader what you want. All too often, what the business owner desires is buried on page eight. Clearly state what you are asking for in the summary.

The statement should be kept short and businesslike, ideally no more than half a page. It could be longer, depending on how complicated the use of funds may be, but the summary of a business plan, like the summary of a loan application, is generally no more than one page. Within that space you'll need to provide a synopsis of the entire business plan. Key elements that should be included are:

1. *Financial requirements.* Clearly states the capital needed to start or expand the business. Detail how the capital will be used, and the equity, if any, that will be provided for funding. If the loan for initial capital will be based on security instead of equity within the company, you should also specify the source of collateral.

2. *Business concept.* Describes the business, its product, and the market it will serve. It should point out just exactly what will be sold, to whom, and why the business will hold a competitive advantage.

3. *Financial features.* Highlights the important financial points of the business including sales, profits, cash flows, and return on investment.

4. *Current business position.* Furnishes relevant information about the company, its legal form of operation, when it was formed, the principal owners, and key personnel.

5. *Major achievements.* Details any developments within the company that are essential to the success of the business. Major achievements include items like patents, prototypes, location of a facility, any crucial contracts that need to be in place for product development, or results from any test marketing that has been conducted.

When writing your statement of purpose, don't waste words. If the executive summary is eight pages, nobody's going to read it because it will be very clear that the business, no matter what its merits, won't be a good investment because the principals are indecisive and don't really know what they want. Make it easy for the reader to realize at first glance both your needs and capabilities.

Chapter 7

Management Makes Money

I N THE MANAGEMENT SECTION OF YOUR PLAN YOU DESCRIBE WHO WILL RUN the company. This may be no more than a simple paragraph noting that you'll be the only executive and describing your background. Or it may be a major section in the plan, consisting of an organizational chart describing interrelationships between every department and manager in the company, plus bios of all key executives.

Capitalizing on Experience

For entrepreneur Bill Dunnam, his management experience really was the company. The basic idea behind Hanks Root Beer Co., the company he co-founded four years ago, was to compete in a soft drink industry dominated by Coke and Pepsi—not too promising. But Dunnam's 11 years' experience working for Coca-Cola had the power to convince everybody—well, everybody except former Coke colleagues. "They were like, 'You're nuts, Bill,'" he recalls. Investors didn't agree, and they helped him get Hanks off the ground and up to $2 million in sales the second year.

Time and again, financiers utter some variation of the following statement: "I don't invest in ideas; I invest in people." Although there's some question as to whether this is the whole story—investors certainly prefer capable people with good ideas to inept people with good ideas—there's no doubt that the people who run your company will receive considerable scrutiny from financiers as well as from customers, suppliers, and anyone else with an interest in your plan. People are, after all, a company's most important asset. To not adequately address this issue in a plan is a serious failing. Luckily, it's one of the easiest parts.

Your Managers

Identifying your managers is, however, more than giving their names. Plan readers want to know their qualifications to run your business. You can provide this by describing them in terms of the following characteristics.

Prior work experience in a related field is something many investors look for.

▶ *Education.* Impressive educational credentials among company managers provide strong reasons for an investor or other plan reader to feel good about your company. Use your judgment in deciding what educational background to include and how to emphasize it. If you're starting a fine restaurant and your chef graduated at the top of her class from the Culinary Institute of America, play that front and center. If you're starting a courier service and your partner has an anthropology degree from a little-known school, mention it but don't make a big deal out of it.

▶ *Employment.* You can be proud to be an entrepreneur without being ashamed of having worked for somebody else. In fact, prior work experience in a related field is something many investors look for. If you've spent ten years in management in the retail men's apparel business before opening a tuxedo outlet, an investor can feel confident that you know what you're doing. So describe any relevant jobs you've had in terms of job title, years of experience, names of employers, etc. But remember, this isn't a resume. You can feel free to skim over or omit any irrelevant experience, and you don't have to provide exact dates of employment.

▶ *Skills.* A title is one thing; what you learn while holding it is another. In addition to pointing out that you were a district sales manager for a stereo equipment wholesaler, you should describe your responsibilities and the skills you honed while fulfilling them. For instance, you'll note

Beading the Competition

Jerry Free had no experience as an inventor or manager of a product company when he came up with a better way to put up sheetrock walls. What he did have was vast expertise and understanding of the issues involved in putting up sheetrock developed through years of doing just that kind of work.

So when he went to a large company, U.S. Gypsum, asking for help marketing Speed Bead, an invention that makes corners easier to build in drywall construction jobs, it listened. Impressed by Free's grasp of drywall installation issues and Speed Beads well-thought-out design, U.S. Gypsum agreed to fund the patenting as well as marketing and distribution of the idea, in exchange for licensing rights.

"My idea was so simple, I couldn't believe it hadn't been done," Free says. "And if it hadn't, then why not?" The simple answer is, nobody else had the idea and the practical experience to make it workable. It also took several thousand dollars in advisors' fees and five years of waiting. But now Free's Speed Bead expertise is starting to pay off—he's still installing drywall, but he's doing it from a new truck bought with licensing royalties.

BUZZWORD

Functional organization *is a term describing a company or other entity with a structure that divides authority and reporting along functions such as marketing, or finance. These functions cross product lines and other boundaries.*

that you were responsible for hiring salespeople, planning and budgeting, working with key accounts, reporting to senior management, and so on. Each time you mention skills that you or a member of your management team has spent years acquiring at another company, it will be another reason for an investor to believe you can do it at your own company.

▶ *Accomplishments.* Dust off your plaques and trot out your calculator for this one. If one of your team members has been awarded patents, achieved record sales gains, or once opened an unbelievable number of new stores in the space of a year, now's the time to tell about it.

Don't brag; just be factual and remember to quantify. Say that you have 12 patents, your sales manager had five years of 30 percent annual sales gains, and you personally oversaw the grand openings of 42 stores in 11 months. Investors are looking to back impressive winners, and quantifiable results speak strongly to businesspeople of all stripes.

▶ *Personal.* Who cares about personal stuff? Isn't this business? Sure, but investors want to know with whom they're dealing in terms of the personal side, too. Personal information on each member of your

Whom Do You Describe in Your Plan?

If you're the only manager, this question is an easy one. But what if you have a pretty well-established organization already? Should you describe everyone down to shop foremen or stop with the people who are on your executive committee? The answer is, probably neither. Instead think about your managers in terms of the important functions of your business.

In deciding the scope of the management section of your plan, consider the following business functions and make sure you've explained who will handle those that are important to your enterprise:

- Accounting
- Advertising
- Distribution
- Finance
- Human Resources
- Legal

- Marketing
- Operations
- Production
- Purchasing
- Sales
- Training

Many businesses contain unique functions. For example, only product companies such as software publishers have product-testing departments. List functions that are unique to your company under the "Other" category.

management team may include age, city of residence, notable charitable or community activities, any relevant health conditions, and, last but far from least, personal motivation for joining the company. Investors like to see vigorous, committed, involved people in the companies they back. Describing the relevant personal details of your key managers will help investors feel they know what they're getting into.

What Does Each Do?

There's more to a job than a title. A director in one organization is a high and mighty individual, whereas in another company a person bearing the same title is practically nobody. And many industries have unique job titles, such as managing editor, creative director, and junior accountant level II, that have no counterparts in other industries.

So when you give your management team's background and describe their titles, don't stop there. Go on, and tell the reader exactly what each member of the management team will be expected to do in the company. This may be especially important in a start-up, in which not every position is filled from the start. If your marketing work is going to be handled by the CFO until you get a little further down the road, let readers know this up front. You certainly can't expect them to figure that out on their own.

Expanding Your Team

If you do have significant holes in your management team, you'll want to describe your plans for filling them. You may say, for example, "Marketing duties are being handled on a temporary basis by the vice president for finance. Once sales have reached the $500,000 per month level, approximately six months after start-up, a dedicated vice president of marketing will be retained to fulfill that function."

In some cases, particularly if you're in a really shaky start-up and you need solid talent, you may have to describe in some detail your plans for luring a hotshot industry expert to your fledgling enterprise.

Hiring Projections

Work, they say, expands to fill the time allotted. Nobody knows that like a small-business owner. A job such as balancing the books or unpacking a new shipment of goods that should have taken an hour expands to fill a day. When quitting time comes, there's still a whole day's work to be done and only you to do it. This is one of the reasons small-business owners tend to have a slightly harried look all the time.

You can't increase the number of hours in the day, but you can add hands to do it. The question often becomes: How many hands do you need? After you ponder this one for a while, you'll find yourself wondering: When do I need them? How long do I need them for? Whom, exactly, do I need? And many other questions. Making staffing projections is a tricky yet essential part of business planning.

Let's say, for example, you wish to add a second shift at your small factory manufacturing storage cases for CD-ROMs. Your day shift employs ten factory floor workers plus a supervisor. Can you just hire 11 people and start running the swing shift? Not necessarily. It may be that two of those workers only work part-time on the production line, spending much of their day helping the shipping department process incoming materials and outgoing orders. Two more may devote several hours to routine maintenance procedures that won't have be done twice a day even when a second shift is added. So your real needs may be for seven production workers and

Strategic Hiring Worksheet

To help you in your strategic staffing projections, consider these factors:

1. What are your key business objectives?

    _____

    _____

    (Hint: These may be things such as increasing sales or reducing costs. The idea is to make sure that your hiring decisions fit your strategy. If geographically expanding your retail store chain is a primary objective, for example, a staffing plan will have to include trained managers for each new location.)

2. What skills do your workers currently possess?

    _____

    _____

3. What new skills will they need to possess?

    _____

    _____

    (Hint: You may find you are better off with fewer workers who are more highly trained or have different skill sets.)

4. Which of these skills are central to your business—your core competencies?

    _____

    _____

    (*Hint*: You may want to outsource peripheral functions. Accounting, legal matters, and human resources are frequently outsourced by companies whose main business is elsewhere and who find it doesn't make sense to spend the effort to attract and retain skilled employees in these areas.)

5. List the jobs and job descriptions of the people it will take to provide these skills.

    _____

    _____

    (Hint: The idea here is to identify the workers whose job titles may mask their true function in the organization so you can figure out how many and what type of people you really need to staff a job.)

Now you should be able to make an accurate projection of not only how many but what kind of people you need to achieve your long-term objectives.

Figure 7-1. Strategic Hiring Worksheet

a supervisor—a savings of 20 percent in your projected staffing increase. It's decisions like this that easily can make the difference between a highly profitable operation and one barely scraping by. Figure 7.1 can help here.

Adding and Retaining Key Employees

When the first edition of this book was being written, the U.S. economy was at a near-historical level of prosperity, including the lowest unemployment levels seen in decades. That's great for workers who find themselves in a sellers' market of rare power. It's not so great for employers.

Finding and retaining employees of any kind in this type of job market is a serious difficulty for almost all businesses. Did it last? No, it never lasts forever. The balance of power shifted back to employers. When the number of help-wanted ads shrinks relative to the number of people reading them, it's easier to hire and keep employees.

Except for one kind of employee: Key employees, people who are smart and hardworking and unafraid to take risks, are always in great demand. They can always write their own tickets, and a lot of employers are happy to go along because these employees are gold. Bill Gates has said that Microsoft, which employs 22,000, would become an unimportant company if it lost its 20 best people. And the importance of key employees is no secret. That's why you need to address the issue of how you will attract and retain key employees in any enterprise in which they are likely to be important.

Plan Pointer

An organizational chart graphically sorts your company into its major functional departments—finance, administration, marketing, production, etc. It's the quickest, clearest way to say who is in charge of what and who reports to whom.

Are you starting a software company? You'll need an ace programmer or two. A gourmet restaurant? Then your executive chef becomes your key employee. An art gallery? Maybe you can pick great art, but a sales manager who knows how to close a deal will be essential. No matter what business you are in, unless you are one of the truly rare individuals who really can do it all, you are likely to find that one or more central tasks are really better farmed out to a key employee.

The things that make employees want to come to work for you and stay vary. At bottom, choosing an employer is a highly personal decision. That's why it's crucial to understand the individual needs of your key employees so that you can give them exactly what they want. If you only offer a higher salary to an employee whose most important concern is that she work at a job offering flexible hours so she can care for an elderly parent, then you probably won't retain that employee.

Here are some common concerns that drive employment decisions:

▶ *Benefits.* Paid holidays and sick leave, health insurance, and retirement plans such as 401(k)s are among the benefits most often listed as desirable by employees.

▶ *Compensation.* Salary, bonuses, stock options, profit sharing, and auto mileage allowances are among the most important compensation issues to employees.

▶ *Miscellaneous.* On-site child care, flexible work hours, paid memberships to business groups, and a personal day off on birthdays are hot buttons as well.

Your business plan should consider the above issues and describe the inducements you will offer key employees to encourage them to stay. Especially in a small company, an investor is likely to be very leery of a plan that appears to be based on the capabilities of a handful of employees unless the business owner has clearly given a lot of thought to keeping these important workers on board.

The above list is by no means comprehensive, however. Employee needs are as complex as humanity is. One worker may stay because she likes the view out her window on a high floor; somebody in an identical office may leave because heights make her nervous. One of the most important needs, especially for highly motivated employees, is maintaining a constant atmosphere of learning, challenge, and advancement. If you can find a way to let your employees grow as your company does, they're likely to do just that.

Plan of Action

Attracting and Rewarding Outstanding Employees *(Entrepreneur Press), by David Rye, quickly, economically, and precisely advises you on finding, hiring, and keeping the best employees.*

Board of Directors or Advisors

A board of directors gives you access to expertise, provided you choose them wisely, but at the cost of giving up control of the business to them. Technically, the officers of a corporation report to the board of directors, who bear the ultimate responsibility for the proper management of the company. Most boards will have financial, marketing, and organizational experts. Such a board lends great credibility to a company. Board members can provide more than oversight and sounding board skills; they provide a wealth of contacts and referrals.

A board of advisors is a less formal entity. You can have the same kind of people on an advisory board but you don't report to them. Beware of creating a rubber-stamp board. You need the variety and breadth of experience

Seek Consistent Outside Advice

Jim Caruso of Telecom Alley Inc. suggests a board of advisors. "You may create a board of advisors for your venture, offering each advisor a nominal shareholding in exchange for a couple of hours of good advice each month. The first advice would be reading and commenting on the business plan. These advisors should come from current or expected customers, business partners, or others that are CEOs or industry experts that approached and won a similar prospective customer."

and skills a board (of directors or advisors) brings to the table. Running a business is hard enough without adding an echo chamber. Your board should be able to challenge your thinking, help you solve knotty problems, and even change management if necessary.

Outside Professionals

Some of the most important people who'll do work for you won't work for you. Your attorney, your accountant, and your insurance broker are all crucial members of your team. A good professional in one of these slots can go a long way toward helping you succeed. The same may be true, to a lesser extent, for real estate brokers, management consultants, benefits consultants, computer consultants, and trainers.

Your business plan should reassure readers that you have your bases covered in these important professional positions.

Your business plan should reassure readers that you have your bases covered in these important professional positions. Readers don't necessarily want to see an attorney on staff. It's fine that you merely state that you retain the services of an attorney in private practice on an as-needed basis.

You don't even need to name the firm you're retaining, although a prestigious name here may generate some reflected respect for you. For instance, if your firm is audited by a Big Four firm instead of a local one-man accounting shop, then by all means play it up. Few things are more comforting to an investor than the knowledge that this investment's disbursement will be monitored regularly and carefully by an expert.

Investors invest in companies for profit. They don't just give money to people they like or admire. But it's also true that if they don't like, admire, or at least respect the people running your company, they're likely to look elsewhere. The management section of your plan is where you tell them

Checking It Twice

Here are some common licenses and certifications you may need. Check this list to see if there's anything you may have forgotten:

- Business license
- DBA (doing business as) or fictitious name statement
- Federal Employer ID Number
- Local tax forms
- Sales tax permit or seller's permit
- Health inspection certificate
- Fire inspection certificate
- Patent filing
- Trademark registration
- Zoning variance

Many of these forms and certificates will take days, weeks, months, or longer to arrive after you request them from the appropriate parties. So don't wait until the last minute to do so. Nothing is more frustrating than sitting in a ready-to-open store, with employees on the clock and interest charges on inventory and fixtures ticking away as well, but unable to serve customers because you don't have your sales tax permit

about the human side of the equation. You can't control your readers' responses to that, but you owe it to them and to yourself to provide the information.

Licenses and Certifications

Every business must file tax returns, and most businesses have to have certain licenses and certifications to do business.

Some paperwork is just paperwork, and some paperwork is essential. Every business must file tax returns, and most businesses have to have certain licenses and certifications to do business. Your plan should take notice, however briefly, of the fact that you have received or applied for any necessary licenses and certificates. If you don't mention the subject, some plan readers will assume all is hunky-dory. Others, however, may suspect the omission means you haven't thought about it or are having trouble getting the paperwork in order. Addressing those concerns now is a worthwhile idea.

Aside from the usual business licenses and tax forms, there are any number of certificates and notices you may require, depending on circumstances. Owners of buildings must have their elevators inspected regularly and, in some cities, post the safety inspection record in public. Plumbers must be licensed in many states. Even New York City hot dog vendors must be licensed by the city before they can unfurl their carts' colorful umbrellas.

For some businesses, their certification or occupational license is essentially what they sell. Think of a CPA. A lot of people sell accounting services. When you go to a CPA, you're paying for the probity and skill represented by the CPA designation, not just another accountant. You're basically buying those initials.

⋆ **EXPERT ADVICE** ⋆

Alex W. Thomson, Esquire, is the director of the Technology and Entrepreneurial Services Section at the Pittsburgh law firm, Houston Harbaugh. He offers this advice concerning other legal issues when putting together your business plan:

As you begin to create a business plan for your company, sound legal advice is important. Attorneys are an integral part of strategic business planning because they offer the guidance necessary to ensure short- and long-term stability. Proper planning and organization in the beginning will lessen the likelihood of problems arising as your business develops.

Prior to creating a business plan, four issues should be reviewed with your attorney:

1. What type of entity will the business be conducted in?

2. How will you raise money to fund the business endeavors?

3. How will you staff the business, and what compensation and benefits will you provide to your employees?

4. Does the business have important intellectual property or proprietary information, and if so, how will it be protected?

Attention to detail in each of these areas is imperative in creating a successful strategic business plan.

In establishing your company's legal entity, consider the advantages and disadvantages of each type—sole proprietorship, partnership, C corporation, S corporation, and limited liability company (LLC). Choosing the right business entity is imperative in a successful business venture because there are many tax and nontax implications. A good lawyer can help you determine which entity would be best for your particular company and situation.

BUZZWORD

Outsourcing *was a 1990s trend among big firms, but entrepreneurs have known about it for years. If you've ever fired your book-keeper and started sending payroll to a service, you've outsourced. Basically, you are using a service instead of your own employee(s) to do a specific task. Outsourcing can save time and money for support staff jobs and add flexibility in production staffing.*

Financing a business plan requires knowledge of the laws governing the ways in which companies may raise money. For instance, when taking on investors, whether they are family and friends, angel investors, or venture capital investors, there are securities laws issues that may inhibit the way in which money may be accepted.

An important question to ask is, "How do I raise money and not violate the law?" Legal professionals can guide you in your planning process to ensure that your company will not violate the laws regarding financing.

Determining staffing needs is yet another necessary component of a strong business plan. The first consideration is whether employees will be at will or contracted. A lawyer can develop contracts and other detailed documents important in the hiring process. Salary issues need to be determined, too—for example, will your employees be paid hourly or will they be salaried? Other considerations include incentive plans and employee benefits such as health insurance, retirement plans, and stock options. An employee handbook can also be a useful tool to set up a foundation for employee policies and procedures. All issues regarding employees may require lawyer presence to avoid the specific liabilities that your company may face.

Intellectual property and proprietary information can provide a company with a needed competitive advantage. Therefore, because of the potential importance of intellectual property and proprietary information, an attorney should be consulted to ensure that it is properly protected. Ensuring all employees sign proprietary information and invention agreements is one step in protecting your company's intellectual property and proprietary information. Obtaining patents or federal registration of the company's trademarks is also critical to proper protection.

Another aspect of the business plan should include how relationships with customers and suppliers will be established and what the terms of the legal relationship will be with them. The necessary question to ask and answer is whether standard terms and conditions will apply or whether each relationship will be contracted individually. In addition is the need to decide whether any of the Uniform Commercial Code (UCC) provisions will be overridden. Certain UCC provisions, such as implied warranties, will govern unless specifically disclaimed.

To find a competent attorney for your company, seek referrals from other business managers. It's important to meet with more than one firm to determine which one is best for your particular company. Look for experience in your industry as well as chemistry between you and the firm.

Don't be afraid to talk about fees. It is important to know what you're paying for to determine if you're getting your money's worth.

Successful businesses deal with a variety of laws and regulations on a daily basis, so it is important to hire an attorney who specializes in your business and can help facilitate growth of your company. Consulting an attorney before drafting your business plan will result in a more well thought out and better drafted business plan. This will lessen the likelihood of problems as the company grows, saving both time and money. Through knowledge and experience, a good lawyer can efficiently aid in the creation of a successful business plan.

(Alex W. Thomson, Esquire, is the director of the Technology and Entrepreneurial Services Section at the Pittsburgh law firm Houston Harbaugh. He can be reached at (412) 288-2227 or via e-mail at athomson @hh-law.com.)

Chapter 8

What You Are Really Selling

EVERY BUSINESS HAS SOMETHING TO SELL, AND THE PRODUCT SECTION is where you tell readers what it is you're selling. (For simplicity's sake, the term *product* is used to refer to both products and services unless otherwise indicated.) This is clearly a very important section of your plan. No matter how expert a team of managers you've assembled is, or how strong your financial underpinnings are, unless you have something to sell or at least plans to develop it, you don't really have a business at all.

They Sold the Bottle Before the Drink

When Dan DaDalt went after investors to back his idea for a new red-colored rum liquor, he and his partner didn't bother with mixing up any booze. They spent $1,000 on a Lucite mockup of the dramatic red bottle and showed that. Investors liked the flavor—to the tune of $800,000 for the two entrepreneurs. Now they're after $2 million, and even though the start-up, called Redrum, now has a real beverage, the main tool, says DaDalt, will be "an even cooler-looking bottle."

Although many businesses are founded to develop new, never-before-seen products, they're still built around a product, even though it may not exist at the moment. And even for these development-stage enterprises, it's just as important to describe the planned-for product.

What Is Your Product or Service?

It's easy to talk eloquently about a product you believe in. Some highly marketing-oriented businesses, in fact, are built as much on the ability to wax rhapsodic about a product as they are on the ability to buy or source compelling products to begin with. Think of J. Peterman, a catalog operation that became famous—and highly successful—by selling prosaic products with the help of romantic, overblown advertising copy.

Some highly marketing-oriented businesses, in fact, are built as much on the ability to wax rhapsodic about a product as they are on the ability to buy or source compelling products to begin with.

It's important in your plan to be able to build a convincing case for the product or service upon which your business will be built. The product description section is where you do that. In this section, describe your product in terms of several characteristics, including cost, features, distribution, target market, competition, and production concerns. Figure 8–1 can help you define your product.

Here are a few sample product descriptions:

▶ Street Beat is a new type of portable electronic rhythm machine used to create musical backgrounds for street dances, fairs, concerts, picnics, sporting events, and other outdoor productions. The product is less costly than a live rhythm section and offers better sound quality than competing systems. Its combination of features will appeal to sports promoters, fair organizers, and charitable and youth organizations.

▶ *Troubleshooting Times* is the only monthly magazine for the nation's 6,000 owners of electronics repair shops. It provides timely news of industry trends, service product reviews, and consumer product service tips written in a language service shop owners can understand.

▶ HOBO, the Home Business Organization, provides business consulting services to entrepreneurs who work out of their homes. The group connects home business owners with experts who have extensive experience counseling home business owners in management, finance, marketing, and lifestyle issues. Unlike entrepreneurial peer groups, which charge members for attending sessions whether or not they receive useful advice, HOBO will guarantee its services, asking home business owners to pay only if they derive solid benefit from the service.

Product Description Worksheet

Features describe the make, shape, form or appearance of a product, the characteristics that you use to describe products. These features convey benefits to the customer. Benefits (perceived benefits) are the emotional or other end results that your product or service provides that customer, the satisfaction or fulfillment of needs that a customer receives from your products or services. In the famous phrase "My factories make cosmetics, we sell hope," cosmetics are the products, hope is the benefit.

Product Description	Features	Benefit Conveyed	Importance for my Product
Physical characteristics:	Shape		
	Color		
	Size		
	Weight		
	Fresh		
Specified characteristics:	Made by…		
	Quality		
	Price		
	New! Improved!		
	Location		
	Delivery		
	Follow-up service		
	Availability		
	Durability		
	Reliability		
	Service		
	Ease of use		
	Used by		

Figure 8-1. Product Description Worksheet

A business plan product description has to be less image-conscious than an advertising brochure but more appealing than a simple spec sheet. You don't want to give the appearance of trying to snow readers with a glitzy product sales pitch. On the other hand, you want to give them a sampling of how you are going to position and promote the product.

A business plan product description is not only concerned with consumer appeal. Issues of manufacturability are of paramount concern to plan readers, who may have seen any number of plans describing exciting products that, in the end, proved impossible to design and build economically.

If your product or service has special features that will make it easy to build and distribute, say so. For instance, the portable rhythm machine maker should point out in the business plan that the devices will be constructed using new special-purpose integrated circuits derived from military applications, which will vastly increase durability and quality while reducing costs. Figure 8–2 shows potential unique selling propositions that any

Nothing If Not New

Gary Hoover is a guy to watch. He almost single-handedly invented and proved the concept of the warehouse-sized bookstore by opening the first Bookstop in Austin, Texas, in 1982.

His product (or, in this case, service)? A business that would do for books what Toys "R" Us did for toys and Home Depot did for hardware—create a category-killer superstore that stocked everything, had low prices, and offered great service.

Hoover was more than a visionary with an idea. He had worked as a retail stock analyst for Citibank, a buyer for Federated Department Stores, and vice president of marketing and planning for the shopping center arm of May Department Stores Co. So he could plan as well as dream.

His planning ability showed when he used his business plan to raise $350,000 from private investors to open the first Bookstop. Book superstores have since proved one of the great retailing innovations, with hundreds of Barnes & Noble and Borders superstores sprouting up nationwide.

Hoover, in fact, sold Bookstop to Barnes & Noble for $41.5 million in cash in 1989. Then he started an online information publisher, Hoover's Inc., and now he's moved on to a new idea—the travel superstore. There are just two TravelFest Superstores now, both in Austin, Texas. But if Gary Hoover's track record indicates anything, his product will spawn imitators—if not acquirers—soon.

Unique Selling Proposition Worksheet

When you've explained the selling propositions associated with your product in each of these categories, give each one a score from 1 to 10 based on your evaluation of how convincing a case you can make for that being a unique selling proposition. The one or two strengths with the highest scores will be your candidates for inclusion in business plan product description.

Features:

Price:

Service:

Financing:

Delivery:

Reputation:

Training:

Knowledge:

Experience:

Customers:

Other:

BUZZWORD

Unique selling proposition *is a term for whatever it is that makes you different from and better than the competition in the eyes of your customers. It's why they buy from you instead of someone else.*

Figure 8-2. Unique Selling Proposition Worksheet

product or service may be able to provide. Look at the list and ask yourself what your product has to offer buyers in each category.

What Makes It Worthwhile?

A product description is more than a mere listing of product features. You have to highlight your product's most compelling characteristics, such as low cost or uniquely high quality, that will make it stand out in the marketplace and attract buyers willing to pay your price. Even the simplest product has a number of unique potential selling strengths.

Many of the common unique selling strengths are seemingly contradictory. How can both mass popularity and exclusive distribution be strengths? The explanation is that it depends on your market and what its buyers want.

Plan Pitfall

Don't count on getting your product into a major retailer on its own merits. The glut of tens of thousands of new products introduced annually, combined with the existing plethora of more than 30,000 products stocked by a typical supermarket, puts retailers in the driver's seat. They demand—and get from almost all new product makers—slotting fees, which are simply payments for the right to be on store shelves.

- ▶ *Features.* If your product is faster, bigger or smaller, or comes in more colors, sizes, and configurations than others on the market, you have a powerful selling strength. In fact, if you can't offer some combination of features that set you apart, you'll have difficulty writing a convincing plan.

- ▶ *Price.* Everybody wants to pay less for a product. If you can position yourself as the low-cost provider (and make money at these rock-bottom prices), you have a powerful selling advantage. Conversely, high-priced products may appeal to many markets for their sheer snob value. One Amsterdam designer came out with a perfume that came in a sealed bottle that could not be opened. This "virtual perfume" was priced the same as Chanel No. 5 and found ready buyers.

- ▶ *Availability.* Ford Motor Company's F-series pickups and sedans such as the Taurus have been perennial bestsellers in the U.S. auto marketplace at least partly because there is a Ford dealership in every town in America. Similarly, if you can get your product into a major retailer such as Wal-Mart or Kmart, you create a powerful selling point by piggybacking on their redoubtable distribution powers.

- ▶ *Service.* Excellent service is perhaps the most important trait you can add to a plain-vanilla product to make it compelling. Many people look not for the best value or even the best product, but simply the one they can buy with the least hassle.

- ▶ *Financing.* Whether you "tote the note" and guarantee credit to anyone, offer innovative leasing, do buybacks, or have other financing alternatives, you'll find that giving people different, more convenient ways to pay can lend your product a convincing strength.

▸ *Delivery.* Nobody wants to wait for anything anymore. If you can offer overnight shipping, on-site service, or 24-hour availability, it can turn an otherwise unremarkable product or service into a very attractive one.

▸ *Reputation.* Why do people pay $10,000 for a Rolex watch that keeps worse time than a $10 Timex? The Rolex reputation is the reason. At its most extreme, reputation can literally keep you in business, as is the case with many companies, such as IBM and Sears, whose well-developed reputations have tided them over in hard times.

▸ *Training.* Training is a component of service that is becoming increasingly important in an era of high-technology products and services. For many sophisticated software products and electronic devices, a seller who couldn't provide training to buyers would have no chance at all of landing any orders.

▸ *Knowledge.* In the Information Age, your knowledge and the means you have of imparting that to customers is an important part of your total offering. Retailers of auto parts, home improvement supplies, and all sorts of other goods have found that simply having knowledgeable salespeople who know how to replace the water pump in an '85 Chevy will lure customers in and encourage them to buy.

▸ *Experience.* "We've been there. We've done thousands of installations like yours, and there's no doubt we can make this one work as well." Nothing could be more soothing to a skeptical sales prospect than to learn that the seller has vast experience at what he's doing. If you have ample experience, make it part of your selling proposition.

▸ *Customers.* There's a reason Tiger Woods makes $90 million a year from endorsements for Nike, Buick, and many more—and it's not because golf fans really think they'll play like Tiger if they buy Tiger-endorsed products. They just want to share the Tiger aura, if only obliquely.

▸ *Other factors.* There are many wild cards unique to particular products, or perhaps simply little used in particular industries, with which you can make your product stand out. For instance, consider a guarantee. When consumers know they can return a faulty product for a refund or repair, they're often more likely to buy it over otherwise superior competitors offering less powerful warranties.

Plan Pointer

THIS WAY

It's easy and essential for internet retailers to make information part of what they plan to give out. When pioneer online book retailer Amazon opened its music CD site, it included more than 750,000 pages of reviews, interviews, and articles to encourage data-hungry web surfers to visit and, more important, to buy.

113

High Flier

Today you can be a frequent shopper, frequent diner, and frequent just-about-anything-else in addition to being the consumer that started it all, the frequent flier. The innovation that revolutionized airline marketing and marketing of many other types of products and services is credited to Robert Crandall, former CEO of American Airlines.

In the early 1980s, Crandall faced a difficult situation. He and other airlines flew the same passengers on the same planes over the same routes and, because they were subject to the same economics, at about the same price. How to make travelers choose American over United, Delta, and other rivals?

Crandall's solution was the now-ubiquitous frequent flier club. Passengers who chose American would accumulate points for each trip. When they had enough, they could redeem the points for free or discounted travel and, later, other awards.

The idea neatly solved the problem of how to differentiate nearly identical transportation services and also encouraged American passengers to become fiercely loyal to the airline.

Fact or Fiction?

Don't assume too much when you're looking at a new product or service idea. For instance, you might think that horseshoers are an endangered breed in the automobile era. But actually the leisure and sport horse industry is thriving, and there are more farriers active today than when horses were the main mode of transport. Just because something seems out of fashion doesn't mean you're out of luck.

The business world is always looking for a new idea that will influence buying behavior, especially if it adds value without costing a lot. Real estate companies offer a month's free rent to new tenants who sign two-year leases, auto dealers give a year's free car washes to the purchaser of a $30,000 vehicle, and entertainment restaurants catering to kids let parents eat free. Put your imagination and knowledge of a market and your own business's workings to the problem, and you may be able to come up with an innovative world-beater, too.

Liability Concerns

To a typical consumer who's purchased her share of shoddy products from uncooperative manufacturers, it's cheering to hear of a multimillion-dollar settlement of a consumer's claim against some manufacturer. It provides proof that the high and mighty can be humbled and that some poor schmuck can be struck by lightning and receive a big fat check.

To manufacturers and distributors of products, however, the picture looks entirely different. Liability lawsuits have changed the landscape of a number of industries, from toy manufacturers to children's furniture retailers. If you visit public swimming pools these days, for instance, you don't see the diving boards that used to grace the deep ends of almost all such recreational facilities. The reason is that fear of lawsuits from injured divers, along with the allied increase in liability insurance premiums, have made these boards no longer financially feasible.

If you're going to come out with a diving board or offer diving board maintenance services, you need to be prepared for this legal issue. Dealing with it may be as simple as merely including a statement to the effect that you foresee no significant liability issues arising from your sale of this product or service. If there is a liability issue, real or apparent, acknowledge it and describe how you will deal with it in your plan. For instance, you may want to take note of the fact that, like all marketers of children's bedroom furniture, you attach warning labels and disclaimers to all your products and also carry a liability insurance policy.

If there is a liability issue, real or apparent, acknowledge it and describe how you will deal with it in your plan.

You must have an attorney's advice on this one. A layman's opinion on whether a product is more or less likely to generate lawsuits is not worth including in a plan.

On the subject of liability, here is a good place to deal with the question of whether you are already being sued for a product's perceived failings and, if so, how you plan to deal with it. If you can't find an answer, you may wind up like private aircraft manufacturers, many of which were forced out of the business by increases in lawsuits following crashes.

It's often difficult to get an attorney to commit himself on paper about the prospects for winning or losing a lawsuit. Many times plans handle this with a sentence saying something along the lines of, "Our legal counsel advises us the plaintiff's claims are without merit."

⋆ EXPERT ADVICE ⋆

The following are some key points about products.

▶ *Product knowledge is important but not critical.* Sure, you have to know the products and services you sell. You have to know a great deal about them. But product knowledge alone is useless, and that is where many marketing plans run afoul of the first law of marketing: Put the Customer First. Customers don't buy products or services. They buy solutions to problems, relief from an itch, satisfaction of a felt need. In short, they buy *benefits*.

▶ *Benefits are not features.* Features are characteristics of products or services that are independent of the buyer's perceptions. A tractor lawn mower may have a 3 hp gas motor, be green with a natty yellow design, have a warranty good for 2 years and cost $1,695, payable in 12 easy monthly installments. Those are all features.

The benefits to the buyer include confidence (3 hp is plenty powerful for a suburban lawn and will carry its owner in comfort up and down gentle slopes), prestige (John Deere knows how to make its buyers feel good), convenience and economy (price and terms). Benefits perceived differ from one customer to the next—another buyer might buy the same lawn mower because his son-in-law is the dealer, or because his neighbor says it's a great machine, or just because it caught his eye.

The key point is that benefits are dependent on the perceptions of the market, whereas features are dependent on the product or service.

▶ *The perceptions of the market are only determined by research.* Armchair research does not count. If you know your markets, and if you know what they perceive to be value, then and only then can you safely match your products or services to their demands. You get to know what your markets want by asking them, by knowing them, by researching their buying behaviors. Some of this is almost subliminal— but what sets the big winners apart is that they take the extra time to do this research.

▶ *Purchasing decisions are ultimately irrational.* Features and perceived benefits are great, but the buying decision is triggered by something more visceral than cold calculation. Even a price-driven purchase is, ultimately, a way to assuage an itch: habit, seeking approval, demonstrating compliance with early training. If decisions were rational, making the right products with the most effective blend of features and benefits would be easy.

Chapter 9

Riding Industry Trends

"It doesn't matter how hard you row.
What matters is what boat you're in."
—Peter Worrell, Investment Banker

PETER'S POINT IS THAT IT ISN'T ENOUGH TO JUST WORK HARD OR WORK harder. If you are in the wrong industry at the wrong time, making your business grow is going to be difficult. Not impossible. Just difficult. The investment community tends to believe that any business can be buoyed by an industry on the rise and that the opposite is true in an industry whose tide is ebbing. This means it's important for you to include an industry analysis in your business plan.

Readers of your business plan may want to see an industry on a fast-growth track with few established competitors and great potential. Or they may be more interested in a big if somewhat slower-growing market with competitors who have lost touch with the market, leaving the door open for rivals.

Whatever the facts are, you'll need to support them with a snapshot analysis of the state of your industry and any trends taking place. This can't be mere off-the-cuff thinking. You need to buttress your opinions

Local Is Profitable

Over 90 percent of all businesses are local. Unless your business is set up to market to regional or larger markets, focus on customers in your immediate geographic location. You can use your knowledge of the conditions and trends in the local economy to advantage. You can identify and study direct and indirect competitors in the local market far more thoroughly than in a wider area. The better you know your market area, the better you will be able to serve it—and make a profit.

with market research that identifies specific competitors and outlines their weaknesses and strengths and barriers to entry. Finally, and perhaps most important, you'll have to convincingly describe what makes you better and destined to succeed.

Convincing doesn't necessarily mean complex. Peter van Stolk, founder of Urban Juice & Soda, fulfills all desired functions of an industry description by merely pointing visitors to his bookcases full of the hundreds of new beverages he's been asked to distribute in his 12 years in business. Most are long gone, proving his main point: "The beverage industry is competitive, but there aren't a lot of smarts."

One of the things you will try to do with your plan is present a case for your industry being, if not the next big thing, at least an excellent opportunity.

The State of Your Industry

In the early 1980s, all an entrepreneur needed was the word "energy" in the title of his company to draw the attention of financial backers. At other times, fields such as biotechnology, computer software, or internet commerce have been seen as veins of gold waiting to be mined by gleeful investors. One of the things you will try to do with your plan is present a case for your industry being, if not the next big thing, at least an excellent opportunity. The section of your plan dealing with the state of your industry is the place to present this information.

When preparing the state of the industry section, you'll need to lift your eyes from your own company and your own issues and focus them on the outside world. Instead of looking at your business as a self-contained system, you'll describe the whole industry you operate in and point to your position in that universe.

This part of your plan may take a little more legwork than other sections because you'll be drawing together information from a number of outside

118

sources. You may also be reporting on or even conducting your own original research into industry affairs. See Figure 9–1.

Industry Analysis Worksheet

To start preparing your industry analysis and outlook, dig up the following facts about your field:

1. What is your total industrywide sales volume? In dollars? In units?

   _____

   _____

2. What are the trends in industry sales volume?

   _____

   _____

3. Who are the major competitors? What are they like?

   _____

   _____

4. What does it take to compete? What are the barriers to entry?

   _____

   _____

5. What technological trends affect your industry?

   _____

   _____

6. What are the main modes of marketing?

   _____

   _____

7. How does government regulation affect the industry?

   _____

   _____

8. In what ways are changing consumer tastes affecting your industry?

   _____

   _____

BUZZWORD

Psychographics *is the attempt to accurately measure lifestyle by classifying customers according to their activities, interests, and opinions. Although not perfect, a psychographic analysis of your marketplace can yield important marketing insights.*

Figure 9-1. Industry Analysis Worksheet

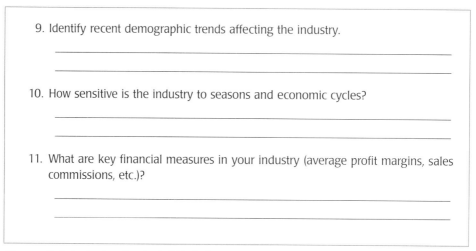

9. Identify recent demographic trends affecting the industry.

10. How sensitive is the industry to seasons and economic cycles?

11. What are key financial measures in your industry (average profit margins, sales commissions, etc.)?

Figure 9-1. Industry Analysis Worksheet, continued

Market Research

Successful entrepreneurs are famed for seemingly being able to feel a market's pulse intuitively, to project trends before anyone else detects them, and to identify needs that even customers are hardly yet aware of. After you are famous, perhaps you can claim a similar psychic connection to the market. But for now, you'll need to buttress your claims to market insight by presenting solid research in your plan.

Market research aims to understand the reasons consumers will buy your product.

Market research aims to understand the reasons consumers will buy your product. It studies such things as consumer behavior, including how cultural, societal, and personal factors influence that behavior. For instance, market research aiming to understand consumers who buy in-line skates might study the cultural importance of having a fit physique, the societal acceptability of marketing directed toward children, and the effect of personal influences such as age, occupation, and lifestyle in directing a skate purchase.

Market research is further split into two varieties: primary and secondary. Primary research studies customers directly, whereas secondary research studies information that others have gathered about customers. Primary research might be telephone interviews with randomly selected members of the target group, whereas secondary research might come from membership lists of clubs catering to the group's magazine subscription records and the like. For your plan, you can use either type. See Figure 9–2 for some basic market research questions.

Market Research Questions

About your buyers

Age _____

Annual income _____

Gender _____

Ethnicity _____

Occupation _____

Homeowner _____

Preferred media _____

About your competition

Market share _____

Advertising plans _____

Distribution _____

Product features _____

Length in business _____

About your products

Why purchased _____

Price _____

Service _____

Packaging _____

How used _____

How frequently purchased _____

What to improve _____

Plan Pointer THIS WAY

You can tell investors where you are in your industry with a good descriptive company name. Experts say to avoid the vague and generic in favor of the explicit and unique. So General Duplication is bad, while Xerox—a unique word that echoes "xerography," which is the technical name for the process of plain-paper copying—is perfect.

Figure 9-2. Market Research Questions

The basic questions you'll try to answer with your market research include:

▶ *Who are your customers?* Describe them in terms of age, occupation, income, lifestyle, educational attainment, etc.

▶ *What do they buy now?* Describe their buying habits relating to your product or service, including how much they buy, their favored suppliers, the most popular features, and the predominant price points.

▶ *Why do they buy?* This is the tricky one, attempting as it does to delve into consumers' heads. Answers will depend on the product and its uses. Cookware buyers may buy the products that offer the most effective non-stick surfaces, or those that give the most pans in a package for a given amount of money, or those that come in the most decorative colors.

Although some of these questions may seem very difficult, you'd be surprised at the detailed information about markets, sales figures, and consumer buying motivations that is available. Tapping these information sources to provide the answers to as many questions as you can will make your plan more convincing and your odds of success higher.

The industry of selling market research is a big one, and booming today. You can find companies that will sell you everything from industry studies

To Market, To Market

Following are some of the leading market research firms and their specialties:

- ACNielsen Corporation, 770 Broadway, New York, NY 10003–9595, (646) 654-5000, www.acnielsen.com. Specialties: TV-viewing habits, retail product sales.
- Arbitron Co., 142 W. 57th St., New York, NY 10019–3300, (212) 887-1300. Specialty: Local broadcast audience measurement.
- Burke Marketing Research Inc., 805 Central Ave, Cincinnati, OH 45202–5747, (513) 241-5663. Specialties: Various syndicated and custom research services.
- Gallup Organization Inc., 502 Carnegie Center, #300, Princeton, NJ 08542–3709, (609) 924-9600. Specialty: Public opinion polls.
- Yankelovich Partners, 20 Glover Ave., Norwalk, CT 06851–6206, (203) 846-0100. Specialty: Social attitudes research.

to credit reports on individual companies. Market research is not cheap. It requires significant amounts of expertise, manpower, and technology to develop solid research. Large companies routinely spend tens of thousands of dollars researching things they ultimately decide they're not interested in. Smaller firms can't afford to do that too often.

However, for existing companies the best market research can't be bought from any provider. It's the research you do on your own. In-house market research might take the form of original telephone interviews with consumers, customized crunching of numbers from published sources, or perhaps competitive intelligence you've gathered on your rivals.

But the most likely source of in-house market research is information you already have. This information will come from analyzing sales records, gathering warranty cards containing the addresses and other information about purchasers, studying product return rates and customer complaint cards, and the like.

You can get in-house market research data from your own files, so it's cheaper than buying it. It's also likely to be a lot fresher than third-party market research, which may have been moldering in some computer for years. Because it comes from your own operations, it will almost certainly be more precisely targeted than a packaged study and probably better even than a custom survey you hire someone else to do.

One limitation of in-house market information is that it may not include exactly what you're looking for. For instance, if you'd like to consider offering consumers financing for their purchases, it's hard to tell how they'd like it since you don't already offer it. You can get around this limitation by conducting original research—interviewing customers who enter your store, for example, or counting cars that pass the intersection where you plan to open a new location—and combining it with existing data. Follow these steps to spending your market research dollars wisely:

1. Determine what you need to know about your market. The more focused the research, the more valuable it will be.

2. Prioritize the results of the first step. You can't research everything, so concentrate on the information that will give you the best (or quickest) payback.

3. Review less expensive research alternatives. Small Business Development Centers can help you develop customer surveys. Your trade association will have good secondary research. Be creative.

BU⚡WORD

Positioning *is one of the most effective tools for marketing and for explaining your marketing approach in your business plan. Consider these slogans: "You Try Harder When You're Number Two." "The Uncola." "The Nonaspirin Pain Reliever." These famous phrases from Avis, 7UP, and Tylenol stress their positioning against bigger rivals Hertz, Coca-Cola, and Bayer.*

4. Estimate the cost of performing the research yourself. (It'll take more time than you expect.) You may find that hiring a consultant will be the most cost effective research method.

Trends

Plan Pointer

One of the most powerful trend-spotting tools available is the Statistical Abstract of the United States, *published by the U.S. Census Bureau. It contains comparative data on everything from national average household food expenditures to what Anchorage, Alaska, residents pay in rent. And it's available on CD-ROM. For more information, call the Census Bureau at (301) 763-4100.*

Timing, in business as in other areas of life, is everything. Marc Andreessen, founder of Netscape Communications, had the good fortune to develop software for browsing the World Wide Web just as the internet, which had been around for 20 years, was coming to widespread popular attention. The timing of his move made him hundreds of millions of dollars, but most of those who came later fell by the wayside.

The best time to address a trend is before it is even beginning and certainly before it is widely recognized. If you can prepare a business that satisfies a soon-to-be popular need, you can generate growth that is practically off the scale. (This is, by the way, the combination that venture capitalists favor most.) The problem, of course, is spotting the trends first.

There are a couple of different techniques you can use to identify trends and to present your identifications in your plan. A trend is basically a series

Soaking the Rich

Sometimes you don't need fancy market research to spot a customer need. Lonnie Johnson, an engineer at NASA's Jet Propulsion Laboratory, was tinkering with a heat-pump design when he attached a nozzle to a piece of tubing and stuck it on his bathroom faucet. It made a lousy heat pump, he noticed, but a great water pistol.

Johnson made a portable prototype for his daughter, who promptly soaked every kid in the neighborhood. Faced with mounting demands for defensive armament, Johnson took his prototype to the offices of a toy maker called Larami Corporation. When he squirted a jet of water across the meeting room, the executives were hooked.

Johnson's informal market research—and his dramatic presentation of his invention—led Larami to offer him a licensing agreement for the now-ubiquitous Super Soaker line of water pistols. The deal produces millions annually in licensing fees for Johnson, who has since started his own product-development company (www.johnsonrd.com). There's no word on how he does his market research nowadays.

of occurrences that indicates a pattern. So trend analysts look at past events (usually trends themselves) and project them forward. For example, a trend analyst would look at the aging U.S. population and project that in not too many more years, there will be far more old people than young. The problem with trend analysis is that it assumes the past is like the future. Often it's not; for instance, the aging population trend would get upset if a lot of young immigrants arrived and reared large families, throwing off the age curve.

Another good way to forecast trends is by test marketing. You try to sell something in a single store and see how it does before you roll it out in your whole chain. Key to this technique is trying it in a well-selected test market, one that closely resembles the market you'll try to sell to later on.

Focus groups and surveys try to catch hold of trends by asking people what's hot. You can ask open-ended questions: What type of portable computer would you like to see? Or show them product samples and see how they react. This is also tricky because you are dealing with a small group of, you hope, representative people and extrapolating to a larger group. If your group isn't representative, your results may be misleading.

Some other ways you can try to nail a trend in advance: talk to salespeople who are in touch with customer needs, quiz executives whose jobs are watching the big picture, read a wide variety of periodicals and try to spot connections, hire think tanks of experts to brainstorm over what the future might hold.

In most of these trend-forecasting techniques, statistics play a big role. Mathematicians assign numerical values to variables such as loyalty to existing brands, then build a model that can indicate trends that are invisible to intuitive analysis. Providing some statistics in the trends section of your plan can make it more convincing.

Barriers to Entry

If you want to become a semiconductor manufacturer, you'll need a billion-dollar factory or two. If you want to have a TV network, you'll need programming and affiliate stations in at least the major markets. Want to sell personal computer operating systems? There's a little problem of 60 million customers who run Windows, and Windows only.

These problems are called barriers to entry, and they exist to some extent in all industries. The barriers may be monetary, technological, or distribution- or

Plan Pointer *THIS WAY*

Forecast Pro is software that runs on your Windows PC and lets nonstatisticians produce sophisticated business forecasts. Engineered for lay users, it automatically selects the best forecasting technique for the job you're doing. For more information on Forecast Pro, contact Business Forecast Systems at 68 Leonard St., Belmont, MA 02748, (617) 484-5050.

125

market-related, or they may simply be a matter of ownership of prime real estate. (This last is frequently cited as the real competitive advantage of McDonald's, Big Macs notwithstanding. "Whenever you see a good site, you find out McDonald's already owns it," groused one fast-food competitor.)

An important part of analyzing your market is determining what the barriers to entry are and how high they stretch. If the barriers are high, as is the case with automobile manufacturing, you can be assured new competitors are likely to be slow in springing up. If they're low, as is the case with, say, screenwriting, where anybody with a typewriter can play, you know there will be an endless supply of competition lured by the low investment and chance of easy bucks.

Be alert for innovative competitors when writing the section of your plan in which you analyze barriers to entry. It may save you from a disastrous error and will certainly demonstrate to investors that you've thought your plan through and are not jumping to conclusions.

Identifing Competitors

You're not alone, even if you have a one-person homebased company. You also have your competition to worry about. And your backers will worry about competition, too. Even if you truly are in the rare position of addressing a brand-new market where no competition exists, most experienced people reading your plan will have questions about companies they suspect may be competitors. For these reasons, you should devote a special section of your plan to identifying competitors.

If you had to name two competitors in the athletic shoe market, you'd quickly come up with Nike and Reebok. But these by far aren't the only competitors in the sneaker business. They're just the main ones, and depending on the business you're in, the other ones may be more important. If you sell soccer shoes, for instance, Adidas is a bigger player than either of the two American firms. And smaller firms such as Etonic, New Balance, and Saucony also have niches where they are comparatively powerful.

You can develop a list of competitors by talking to customers and suppliers, checking with industry groups, and reading trade journals. But it's not enough to simply name your competitors. You need to know their manner of operation, how they compete.

Does a competitor stress a selective, low-volume, high-margin business, or does she emphasize sales growth at any cost, taking every job that comes

Fact or Fiction? ?❓?

Nobody beats Microsoft, right? Not quite. Intuit's Quicken rules personal-finance software, despite Microsoft's heavily promoted Money program. And an operating system for palm-top computers from tiny Palm Computing runs on nearly two million machines, ten times as many as Microsoft's rival Windows CE. The conclusion? Pick the right niche, and you can beat anybody.

along, whether or not it fits any coherent scheme or offers an attractive profit? Knowing this kind of information about competitors can help you identify their weaknesses as well as their names.

What Makes You Better?

This is one of the most important sections of your plan. You need to convince anybody thinking of joining with your company, as an investor or in another way, that you offer something obviously different and better than what is already available. Sometimes this is called your distinctive competence or competitive advantage, but it's not an overstatement to call it your company's reason for being.

Your distinctive competence may lie in any of the product features discussed in the last chapter, including cost, features, service, quality, distribution, and so forth. Or it could be something totally different. The success of a retail convenience store located on an interstate highway, for instance, might depend almost entirely on how close it is to an exit ramp.

Where the Elite Meet to Eat

The Elite Café in Waco, Texas, serves as a good case study of distinctive competence. The Elite has been near the campus of Baylor University, serving homestyle cooking for decades under the same ownership. Why do people stop there to eat instead of at one of the dozens of other restaurants along Interstate 35, many of them national chains with instantly recognizable names?

- *Convenience.* The Elite Café is near an exit ramp from both directions, and getting back onto the highway is easy.
- *Visibility.* The Elite has a big sign that is easy to spot in plenty of time to get off the highway.
- *Customer base.* After decades in the same spot, the Elite is a familiar dining place for thousands of Central Texas residents and travelers.
- *Geography.* The main reason, however, is probably related to the fact that the Elite is located very near the midpoint of the drive between Dallas and Austin, the state capital. Anybody making that drive is likely to decide to stop halfway through to ease the job, and when they do, there will be the Elite Café.

Plan Pitfall

Think twice before deciding barriers to entry are high for all potential competitors. For instance, you need billions of dollars to start a semiconductor company—but not if you contract out fabrication of the silicon chips to a manufacturer. Many semiconductor start-ups of the past few years do exactly that, providing serious competition for rivals who assumed the barrier was too high to allow many new entries.

Plan Pitfall

To prepare convincing industry studies, name all competitors, not just the biggies. Start with the primary ones. Then keep going to the secondary ones, trying to identify virtually every company that's a significant player in your field. Only when you have a comprehensive list of competitors can you truly understand what you're up against.

To figure out your competitive advantage, start by asking yourself:

1. *Why do people buy from me instead of my competitors?* Think about this question in terms of product characteristics. Ask your customers why they buy from you. Ask noncustomers why they don't. Ask suppliers, colleagues, and anybody you can find.

2. *What makes me different and, I hope, better?* The answers, carefully analyzed, should spell out your distinctive competence.

Distinctive competence is not quite as important if your company operates in the beginning stages of a new industry. When interest and sales in a new field are growing fast, you can survive and prosper even if you aren't clearly better than the rest. If, however, you plan to take market share away from established competitors in a mature industry, then distinctive competence is all-important. Without a convincing case for being very different and much better than the rest, your business plan will have a hard time swaying anybody.

✳ EXPERT ADVICE ✳

Centurion Consulting Group develops all types of plans for new and ongoing national and international companies, including strategic, business, marketing, growth, financial, feasibility, and operations plans. Barbara Lewis, a consultant with the company, also believes that a business plan is critical to the success of a company. "Just like you wouldn't build a house without a blueprint, you shouldn't build a business without a plan," she says. "The company's 'big picture' is the strategic portion of the plan, which includes the mission, vision, strengths, weaknesses, opportunities, and threats. Other essential elements of the plan include the marketing analysis and strategy and the operations and financial analysis and strategy."

One of the basic problems that she sees in plans is the market analysis. "Most plans don't define the market size, identify market characteristics, or have a realistic assessment of competitors," she says. "Yet the company's marketplace is one of the most important issues. Understanding the market goes a long way toward developing a cogent strategy and comprehensive tactical plan."

Chapter 10

Marketing: The Plan Within Your Plan

WHAT ARE YOU SELLING? HOW ARE YOU SELLING IT? WHY would anybody want to buy from you? These are the kinds of questions that run through the minds of people reading business plans. The marketing section of your plan is where you answer them.

Let there be no misunderstanding: Your marketing strategy is a very important part of your plan. Lack of sales is a primary reason for business failure. The marketing section is the place where you tell how you are going to avoid that fate. Nobody knows that better than Fred Gratzon. After founding Telegroup in 1989, Gratzon couldn't afford to hire salespeople or do much marketing. In fact, he was literally begging friends and neighbors to try the discount long-distance telephone service—mostly with no success. "I was humiliated," admits Gratzon. "But I needed to support my family." It was only after he came up with the idea of using independent salespeople that Telegroup connected. He never raised a dime of capital, but thanks to the marketing solution, Telegroup grew to pull in an estimated $280 million a year in less than eight years.

For the marketing section of your plan, start by describing your strategy in terms of the traditional four Ps of marketing: product, price, place, and promotion.

Defining Your Product

Product, the first of the four Ps, refers to the features and benefits of what you have to sell (as usual, we're using the term as shorthand for products and services). Many modern marketers have a problem with this "P" because it doesn't refer to customer service, which is an important part of the bundle of features and benefits you offer to customers. However, it's pretty easy to update *product* by simply redefining it to include whatever ancillary services are bundled into your offering.

There are a number of issues you need to address in your product section. You need to first break out the core product from the actual product. What does this mean? The core product is the nominal product. Say you're selling snow cones. A snow cone is your core product. But your actual product includes napkins, an air-conditioned seating area, parking spaces for customers, and so forth. Similarly, a computer store nominally sells computers, but it also provides expert advice from salespeople, a service department for customers, opportunities to comparison shop, software, and so on.

It's important to understand that the core product isn't the end of the story. Sometimes the things added to it are more valuable than the core product itself. That's not necessarily bad, but failing to understand this is likely to lead to trouble.

Defining Your Customer

The world's not going to beat a path to the door of the inventor of a passenger pigeon trap because there are no passenger pigeons anymore. Even the best product must meet a need in the market or it's a curio, not a foundation for a business plan. So make sure your plan identifies your markets and potential customers and tells why they're going to buy your product.

The first thing to do is identify the market you're going after. Talk about your market in terms of its characteristics, its needs, and, if possible, its numbers.

A new Italian restaurant might say it's going for families eating out on a budget who live within a five-mile radius of its location. It might quote

Tech It to the Limit

Sometimes merely applying technology to a product or service you're already offering can provide compelling marketing advantages. Timothy McCarthy founded Sales Building Systems in 1988 to help retail and restaurant chains boost individual store sales. But his business languished because he couldn't effectively teach or motivate store managers to do what he recommended.

In fact, the reverse happened. "Because I was creating additional work for them, the managers hated me," says McCarthy. The workbooks he wrote for them went unused, his advice went ignored, and his sales kept him barely scraping by.

Then a customer suggested he computerize his course material and, with the help of automation, ease the task of marketing for store managers instead of making it harder. "That's what I did," says McCarthy. The switch rapidly raised revenues, after nearly a decade of slow growth, to $4 million annually.

Census Bureau figures showing there are 12,385 such families in its service area. Even better, it would cite National Restaurant Association statistics about how many families it takes to support a new Italian restaurant.

A bicycle seat manufacturer might have identified as its market casual middle-aged cyclists who find traditional bike seats uncomfortable. It may cite American College of Sports Medicine surveys, saying that sore buttocks due to uncomfortable seats is the chief complaint of recreational bicyclists.

It is important to quantify your market's size if possible. If you can point out that there are more than six million insulin-dependent diabetics in the United States, it will bolster your case for a new easy-to-use injection syringe your company has developed.

In addition to fully defining your product, you need to address other issues in your marketing plan.

In addition to fully defining your product, you need to address other issues in your marketing plan. For instance, you may have to describe the process you're using for product development. Tell how you come up with ideas, screen them, test them, produce prototypes, and so on.

You may need to discuss the life cycle of the product you're selling. This may be crucial in the case of quickly consumed products such as corn chips and in long-lived items like household appliances. You can market steadily to corn-chip buyers in the hopes they'll purchase from you frequently, but it makes less sense to bombard people with offers on refrigerators when they need one only every 10 or 20 years. Understanding the product's life cycle has a powerful effect on your marketing plan.

Other aspects of the product section may include a branding strategy, a plan for follow-up products, or line extensions. Keeping these various angles on products in mind while writing this section will help you describe your product fully and persuasively.

Setting Prices

Plan Pointer

THIS WAY

Product beauty may be only skin deep. Packaging, far from merely containing goods, is an important part of your product. Attractive packaging lures looks. Sturdy packaging ensures goods arrive intact. Environmental consciousness means recycled or organic packaging may be more important than the product inside. So attend to outer as well as inner product beauty.

One of the most important decisions you have to make in a business plan is what price to charge for what you're selling. Pricing determines many things, from your profit margin per unit to your overall sales volume. It influences decisions in other areas, such as what level of service you will provide and how much you will spend on marketing. Pricing has to be a process you conduct concurrently with other jobs, including estimating sales volume, determining market trends, and calculating costs. There are two basic methods you can use for selecting a price.

One way is to figure out what it costs you altogether to produce or obtain your product or service, then add in a suitable profit margin. This markup method is easy and straightforward, and assuming you can sell sufficient units at the suggested price, it guarantees a profitable operation. It's widely used by retailers. To use it effectively, you'll need to know your costs as well as standard markups applied by others in your industry.

The other way, competitive pricing, is more concerned with the competition and the customer than with your own internal processes. The competitive pricing approach looks at what your rivals in the marketplace charge plus what customers are likely to be willing to pay and sets prices accordingly. The second step of this process is tougher—now you have to adjust your own costs to yield a profit. Competitive pricing is effective at maintaining your market appeal and ensuring your enterprise's long life, assuming you can sell your goods at a profit. See Figure 10–1 to determine your pricing objectives.

Pricing is inherently strategic. You can use prices to attack competitors, position your business, test a new market, defend a niche. The only hard and fast rule to follow in setting prices is: Set prices carefully, deliberately, knowledgeably, and with long-range goals in mind. All the rest are footnotes. See Figure 10–2 for help in determining your pricing strategy.

Further Pricing Thoughts

Why is setting prices so tough? Perhaps because nobody really understands it. Pricing is as much art as science. Price too low and lose money; price too high and lose customers; price in the middle and lose position. It seems like

Setting Pricing Objectives

Before you can select a pricing approach, you need to know your pricing objectives. Following are questions to ask yourself about your pricing goals:

1. Which is more important: higher sales or higher profits?

   _____

   _____

2. Am I more interested in short-term results or long-term performance?

   _____

   _____

3. Am I trying to stabilize market prices or discourage price-cutting?

   _____

   _____

4. Do I want to discourage new competitors or encourage existing ones to get out of the market?

   _____

   _____

5. Am I trying to quickly establish a market position, or am I willing to build slowly?

   _____

   _____

6. Do I have other concerns, such as boosting cash flow or recovering product development costs?

   _____

   _____

7. What will the impact of my price decision be on my image in the market? How does that fit the image I want?

   _____

   _____

Answer these questions first, then prioritize them to decide how each objective will weigh in setting your pricing strategy. That way, when you present your price objectives in your business plan, it will make sense and be supported by reasonable arguments integrated with your overall business goals.

Plan of Action

Price Wars *(Prima Publishing), by Thomas J. Winninger is a 275-page manual for avoiding or, if necessary, competing in and winning low-price competitions. The author provides many illuminating anecdotes of the dangers of price-cutting as well as practical steps to follow.*

Figure 10-1. Setting Pricing Objectives

Price Range Worksheet

Pricing is always considered in a competitive context. Part of your pricing strategy involves providing answers to the questions implicit in this worksheet.

Item: Price range: $ _____ (low) to $ _____ (high).

Establish a price floor

Mark-on (gross margin) is _____% of retail price.

Manufacturer's suggested price is $ _____.

Fixed costs are $ _____.

Variable costs are $ _____.

Break-even point is $ _____.

Special considerations for this product or service price:

Level of service: _____

Status: _____

Comparative quality: _____

Loss leader: _____

Demand: _____

Product life: _____

Overhead: _____

Market penetration costs: _____

Turnover rate is _____ times per year.

Industry average is $_____.

Going rate is $_____.

I estimate that _____ units will be sold.

Top price (what the market will bear) based on the customers' perceptions of value: $_____.

Figure 10-2. Price Range Worksheet

a no-win situation for most small business owners. There is no mechanical way to grind out the right price. There is no shortcut.

Small businesses simply cannot afford to compete on price. Low-balling drives small businesses out of business, cheapens their image, and costs them the opportunity to upgrade their customer base. It just does not work.

Small businesses simply cannot afford to compete on price.

There's always someone willing to sell a price or service on price alone. Sometimes the price competition comes from a giant like Wal-Mart, which buys in such huge quantities that suppliers cave in and pare their margins to the bone. (Wal-Mart has revolutionized inventory management and distribution, which allows them to make vast profits on thin margins. They aren't just competing on price.) Sometimes the competitor is a newcomer who thinks—erroneously—that the best way to enter a market is to buy market share with loss leader pricing.

The two main ways to deal with price competition are to meet the price (cave in and watch your margins evaporate) or to reposition yourself so the price competition is indirect (repositioning).

Filling in the Price/Quality grid in Figure 10–3 for your products is a useful exercise. Fill in the grid with autos or computers or whatever it is you are

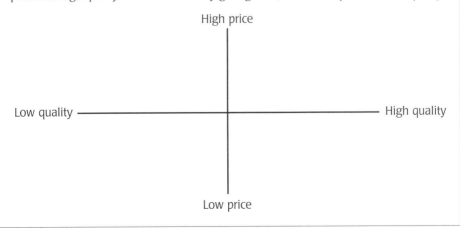

Price/Quality Grids

Use this grid to locate market gaps, areas where there may be an opportunity for your business to grow. Suppose there is no direct competitor in the high price/high quality sector, while the other areas are overserved. (Usually the low price range is jammed. Check it out.) That may open a market for you to fill. It's always interesting to note that high price and high quality do not necessarily go together, nor do low price and low quality.

Figure 10-3. Price/Quality Grid

135

selling. Knowing where your business operates best makes a big difference in your promotional plans.

Other useful grids are price/service, price/convenience, and so on. You can also use these grids to spot a market gap.

Place

Place refers to channels of distribution, or the means you will use to put your product where people can buy it. This can be very simple: retailers and many service businesses (restaurants, personal services, business services) rely pri-marily on location. For manufacturers, conventional distribution systems have three steps: producer, wholesaler, and retailer. You may occupy or sell to members of any one of these steps. Some companies with vertically inte-grated distribution, such as Dell Computer, occupy all the steps themselves. Others, like franchisors, are parts of systems that orchestrate the activities among all channels. Still others, such as independent retailers, operate in one channel only.

Location Considerations

For retailers, the big place question involves real estate. Location commonly determines success or failure for many retailers. That doesn't necessarily mean the same location will work for all retailers. A low-rent but high-traffic space near a housing project may be a poor choice for a retailer stocking those Armani suits but will work fine for a fast-food restaurant or conven-ience store. Your location decision needs to be tied to your market, your product, and your price.

Two of the most common tools for picking location are census data and traffic surveys. Retailers relying on walk-in traffic want to get a location that has a lot of people walking or driving past. You can usually get traffic data from local economic development agencies or by simply sitting down with a clipboard and pencil and counting people or cars yourself. Census data describing the number, income levels, and other information about households in the nearby neighborhoods can be obtained from the same sources. An ani-mal clinic, for example, wants to locate in an area with a lot of pet-owning households. This is the type of information you can get from census surveys.

Site Sensitivity

Manufacturers require certain basic conditions for their sites, but retailers and some service firms are exquisitely sensitive to a wide variety of location

136

factors. In some cases, a difference of a few feet can make the difference between a location that is viable and one that is not.

Site selection plans for retailers should include traffic data, demographics of nearby populations, estimated sales per square foot, rental rates, and other important economic indicators. Service firms such as restaurants will want many of the same things. Service firms such as travel agencies, pest control services, and bookkeeping businesses will want to provide information about local income levels, housing, and business activity.

Store design also must be addressed. Retailing can be as much about entertaining shoppers as it is about displaying goods. So store design becomes very important, especially for high-fashion retailers. Floor plans are probably not enough here. Retailers may want to include photos or illustrations of striking displays, in-store boutiques, and the like.

Distribution Concerns

There are three main issues in deciding on a placement strategy: coverage, control, and cost. Cost, it goes almost without saying, is an important part of any business decision, including distribution concerns. The other two issues, however, are unique to distribution and are trickier.

Coverage refers to the need to cover a large or a small market. If you're selling laundry soap, you may feel the need to offer it to virtually every household in America. This will steer you toward a conventional distribution scheme running from your soap factory to a group of wholesalers serving particular regions or industries, to retailers such as grocery stores, and finally to the consumer.

What if you are reaching out to only a small group, such as chief information officers of *Fortune* 500 companies? In this case, the conventional, rather lengthy distribution scheme is clearly inappropriate. You're likely to do better by selling directly to the CIOs through a company sales staff, sales reps, or perhaps an agreement with another company that already has sales access to the CIOs. In both these cases, coverage has a lot of say in the design of your distribution system.

Control is important for many products. Ever see any Armani suits at Target? The reason you haven't is that Armani works hard to control its distribution, keeping the costly apparel in high-end stores where its lofty prices can be sustained. Armani's need for control means that it deals only with distributors who sell to designer boutiques. Many manufacturers want similar control for reasons of pricing, after-sale service, image, and so forth. If you need control over your distribution, it will powerfully influence placement decisions.

If you need control over your distribution, it will powerfully influence placement decisions.

The distribution scheme is of critical importance to manufacturers. Say you make a mass-market consumer good such as a toy. Whether you plan effectively to get your product onto shelves in the major grocery, drug, and discount store chains may make all the difference between success and failure.

If you're selling an informational product to a narrow market, such as political consulting services to candidates for elected office, physical distribution is of less importance. However, for just about all companies, an effective placement strategy is a big determinant of success.

Promotion

Promotion is virtually everything you do to bring your company and your product in front of consumers. Promotional activities include picking your company name, going to trade shows, buying newspaper advertisements, making telemarketing calls, sending direct mail, using billboards, arranging co-op marketing, offering free giveaways, and more. Not all promotions are suitable for all products, of course, so your plan should select the ones that will work best for you, explain why they were chosen, and tell how you're going to use them. Figure 10–4 will help you see where your needs are.

Promotion aims to inform, persuade, and remind customers to buy your products. It uses a mix that includes four elements: advertising, personal selling, sales promotion, and publicity or public relations.

Advertising Concerns

Advertising is what most people think of when they think of promotion. About two-thirds of ads use newspapers, magazines, broadcast media, direct mail, and outdoor media or billboards to spread their message. The rest comes in the form of catalogs or specialty items such as pens, matchbooks, calendars, and the like.

One of the first things to decide about your ad campaign: what are we trying to do here? You may be advertising to raise your corporate profile, to improve a tarnished image, or simply to generate foot traffic. Whatever you're after, it's important to set specific goals in terms of such things as revenue increase, unit volume growth for new business, inquiries, and so forth. Without specific objectives, it's hard to tell what you can afford to do and whether the campaign is living up to expectations.

Fact or Fiction? ??

Ever feel you're going to have to cut prices to stay in business? Don't trust that feeling! Studies show 16 out of 17 businesses that lower prices to compete eventually go out of business.

BUZZWORD

Co-op promotions are arrangements between two businesses to cross-promote their enterprises. When a soft drink can carries a coupon good for a discount on the price of entry to an amusement park, that's a co-op. Countless variations exist.

138

Promotional Budget Worksheet

Select the advertising and promotional expenses you anticipate from the following list. Briefly describe the goal, such as "new leads" or "10 percent sales gain." Then estimate how frequently you'll insert an ad, run a spot, meet with a consultant, and so forth. Finally, determine how much this will cost. The bottom line is the starting figure for your marketing budget.

Medium	Purpose/Goal	How Often?	Annual Budget
Ad agencies			
Brochures			
Consultants			
Designers			
Direct mail			
Displays			
Internet			
Magazines			
Newspapers			
Trade journals			
Outdoor ads			
Public relations			
Radio			
Sales calls			
Samples			
Specialties			
Telemarketing			
Television			
Trade shows			
Yellow pages			
Total			

Plan of Action

You can get mounds of economic and demographic marketing information— much of it free— from the U.S. Census Bureau. To learn more, contact the following office: Economic and Demographic Statistics, Bureau of the Census, U.S. Department of Commerce, Data User Service Division, Customer Service, Washington, DC 20233, (301) 763-4100, www.census.gov.

Figure 10-4. Promotional Budget Worksheet

Other Kinds of Promotion

Personal selling is widely used in business-to-business models, in which sales cycles are long, products are complex, and the dollar amounts tend to be large. They are also used by Avon beauty consultants, car dealers, and barkers outside taverns on Bourbon Street in New Orleans. The key to effective personal selling is recruiting and training excellent salespeople.

The key to effective personal selling is recruiting and training excellent salespeople.

Sales promotion is kind of a grab bag of promotional activities that don't fit elsewhere. If you offer free hot dogs to the first 100 people who come to your store on Saturday morning, that's a sales promotion. This category also includes in-store displays, trade shows, off-site demonstrations, and just about anything else that could increase sales and isn't included in the other categories.

Publicity is the darling of small businesses because it lets them get major exposure at minimal cost. If you volunteer to write a gardening column for your local newspaper, it can generate significant public awareness of your plant nursery and position you as a leading expert in the field, all for the price of a few hours a week spent jotting down some thoughts on a subject you already know very well. To buy comparable exposure might cost thousands of dollars. Press releases announcing favorable news about

One Man's Pursuit of Excellence

In his book *In Praise of Excellence*, author and business expert Tom Peters wrote about an entrepreneur who was way ahead of his time when it came to putting together a publicity and marketing plan. Stew Leonard is an entrepreneur who owns a store in Norwalk, Connecticut, that he calls "the world's largest dairy." Leonard has combined the genius of Walt Disney and Dale Carnegie that delivers a message to his customers: "Have fun!" A few years ago, Leonard was grossing more than $150 million annually, making his store the most successful supermarket in the country. Customers will drive miles and miles out of their way to go there and enjoy the hoopla he has put together. He learned how to make the customers' shopping experience fun, and that is part of what keeps those customers coming back. Customer service is priority one with Stew Leonard. There is a three-ton granite boulder that sits at the entrance to his store, and it features the store's two cardinal rules. "Rule Number 1: The Customer is Always Right. Rule Number 2: If the Customer is ever wrong, go back and reread Rule Number 1."

your company are one tool of publicity; similar releases downplaying bad news are the flip side.

Public relations is a somewhat broader term that refers to the image you present to the public at large, government entities, shareholders, and employees. You may work at public relations through such tools as company newsletters, legislative lobbying efforts, your annual report, and the like.

Whatever you do, don't neglect public relations and publicity. There is no cheaper or more powerful tool for promotion.

Follow-Up Plan

Customers may ask, "What have you done for me lately?" Investors and others reading your business plan want to know, "What are you going to do for me tomorrow?" Any serious business plan has to take note of the fact that every product has a life cycle, that pricing pressures change over time, that promotions need to stay fresh, and that new distribution opportunities are opening up all the time. So the portion of your plan where you describe how you'll continue your success is a vital one.

The annals of business are full of companies that turned out to be one-trick ponies that introduced a product or service that zoomed to stardom but failed to follow it up with another winner. In the best cases, these companies survive but fade back into obscurity. In the worst, they fail to negotiate the switch from booming sales to declining sales and disappear completely.

Diversifying into more than one product is another good way to reduce the risk. It's a good idea to divert part of any boost in revenues to studying market trends and developing new products.

Investors looking at a plan, especially those contemplating long-term involvement, are alert to the risk of backing a one-trick entrepreneur. Showing competitive barriers you've erected and systems for developing new products is an important part of calming their fears.

There's one caveat when it comes to learning new tricks, however. Very simple concepts are the easiest to communicate, and extremely focused companies usually show the fastest growth—although not always over the long term. So you don't want to appear, in the process of reducing risk, that you've lost sight of the answers to the key questions: What are you selling? How are you selling it? And why would anybody want to buy from you?

Plan of Action

Not sure where to send a press release or to whom to address it? Bacon's Media Information Directories give names, addresses, and other contact information for virtually every newspaper, magazine, and radio and TV station in the United States and abroad. Directories come in various editions and cost $250 and up. For more details, contact Bacon's Information Inc. at 332 S. Michigan Ave., Suite 900, Chicago, IL 60604, (800) 621-0561, www.bacons.com.

One-Hit Wonder

Back in 1986, all any kid wanted for Christmas was a Teddy Ruxpin. Crazed demand for the $80 talking toy bear pushed its maker, a start-up called Worlds of Wonder Inc. (WOW), to sales of $327 million in just its second year in business. WOW went public and was valued at more than half a billion dollars.

What happened next was a lesson in the need to maintain a ceaseless stream of new ideas. First, competitors flooded the market with talking dolls that were often cheaper and of higher quality. Then overall demand declined as the fad faded.

WOW tried, to be sure. It came out with a game called Lazer Tag. Next was a gadget dubbed "the world's most intelligent doll." But they never found an understudy to Teddy. Within two years, the company was bankrupt, and soon it vanished from the scene.

It's hard to say that WOW would have done better if it had never had the Ruxpin doll. But there's little doubt that its failure to follow up meant that even its blazing initial success amounted to little.

⋆ EXPERT ADVICE ⋆

Clever Marketing

"I believe that generally the most important part of the plan is the marketing section," says Paul Hall, program director at the Mason Entrepreneurship Center in Virginia. "As a general observation, business plans are essential for financing, and desirable if the plan is only used to manage the business. We find that a start-up with a business plan is much more likely to succeed than one without. The larger and more complex the venture, the more important it is to have a plan written out."

"It is critical to know the market size and makeup (demographics and psychographics), the competition, the niche where you have a competitive advantage, and your projected market share. Next would be the economics of the business: gross and operating margins, profit potential, fixed and variable costs, break-even, months to profitable cash flow. As business philosopher Peter Drucker once said, 'The modern company has only two key elements, innovation and marketing. . . .'"

Marcia Yudkin, the author of *Internet Marketing for Less Than $500/Year* (Maximum Press), says her favorite, most effective marketing tool is not so much her web site but her weekly e-mail newsletter, "The Marketing Minute."

"People who spend a lot of time once at my web site aren't anywhere as likely to become fans and regular clients as subscribers who hear from me every week and may never have gone to my web site," she says. "They subscribed because they heard me speak or a friend forwarded them a copy. So my goal is to try to get as many casual web visitors as possible to sign up for my newsletter."

Marcia has written about how to start an e-mail newsletter and gives examples at www.clickz.com/article.php/831202.

Chapter 11

How Does Your Business Work?

T*HE MARKETING SECTION OF YOUR PLAN ADDRESSES A MAJOR PART OF* operations: how you identify and attract customers. Operations is concerned with how you buy, build, and prepare your product or service for sale. That covers a lot of ground, including sourcing raw materials, hiring labor, acquiring facilities and equipment, and shipping off the finished goods. And it's different ground depending on whether you're a manufacturer or a service firm.

Not surprisingly, investors and other plan readers pay careful attention to the part of your plan describing your operations. Most entrepreneurs are highly expert, interested in operations, and love to talk about it—in fact, one risk is that you'll go into too much detail here and wind up with what amounts to a technical treatise in which the essential marketing element seems lost. David Wheeler recognized that risk when seeking investors for his software start-up called InfoGlide Inc. So one of his first hires was someone to take on the job of CEO, to interface directly with investors and high-profile prospects, so Wheeler could get back to the operations he loved. "That's what I like," he says, "working with database code, not doing product demos."

The simplest way to treat operations is to think of it as a linear process that can be broken down into a sequence of tasks.

The basic rule for your operations section is to cover just the major areas—labor, materials, facilities, equipment, and processes—and provide the major details—things that are critical to operations or that give you competitive advantage. If you do that, you'll answer investors' questions about operations without overwhelming them.

The simplest way to treat operations is to think of it as a linear process that can be broken down into a sequence of tasks. Although several tasks may be performed simultaneously, leave the scheduling to a later part of the operations section. In Figure 11–1, each task is broken down into smaller elements, and as you run your business, you will naturally do so. For your business plan, make sure that the broad outlines of your operations are covered.

Once the initial task listing is complete, turn your attention to who is needed to do which tasks. Keep this very simple. You don't have to look at minor tasks (who opens the door? who fetches the mail?), but you do have to concentrate on major tasks such as producing a product or delivering a

What Has to Be Done: Task Listing

Task	Daily	Weekly	Monthly	Other (specify)
1.				
2.				
3.				
4.				
5.				
6.				
7.				
8.				
9.				
10.				

Figure 11-1. What Has to Be Done: Task Listing

Tasks Requiring More Than One Person

Name of task	
People needed	
Elements of the task	
Timing (when they do it)	
Time allotted	
Total time, including support	
Comments	

Figure 11-2. Tasks Requiring More Than One Person

service. Use your judgment. Then fill out the form in Figure 11–2 for each major task.

Operations for Retail and Service Firms

Service firms have different operations requirements from manufacturers. Companies that maintain or repair things, sell consulting, or provide health care or other services generally have higher labor content and lower investments in plants and equipment.

Another important difference is that service and retail firms tend to have much simpler operational plans than manufacturers. In the process of turning raw materials into finished goods, manufacturers may employ sophisticated techniques in a complex series of operations. By comparison, it's pretty simple for a retailer to buy something, ship it to his store, and sell it to a customer who walks in.

Companies that maintain or repair things, sell consulting, or provide health care or other services generally have higher labor content and lower investments in plants and equipment.

> ## Service Operations Checklist
> ❏ Staffing completed (or staffing plan completed)
> ❏ Organization chart completed
> ❏ Marketing implemented
> ❏ Sales policies
> ❏ Customer relations policies
> ❏ Service delivery policies
> ❏ Administering monitoring and control policies
> ❏ Follow-up procedures
>
> Note that staffing and organizational issues precede marketing, sales, and delivery of the service. Service operations are people-intensive and careful management goes a long way to making sure that your quality controls are effective.

That's not to say operations are any less important for retailers and service firms. But most people already understand the basics of processes such as buying and reselling merchandise or giving haircuts or preparing tax returns. So you don't have to do as much explaining as, say, someone who's manufacturing computer chips.

The Importance of People

For service and retail firms, people are the main engines of production. The cost of providing a service is largely driven by the cost of the labor it entails. And retail employees' skills and service attitudes drive their employers' productivity and market acceptance to a great degree.

A service firm plan, then, has to devote considerable attention to staffing. You should include figures on the local labor market for low-skilled employees such as counter clerks. Regional educational attainment data will help readers understand why you think you can hire sufficient semi- and high-skilled workers for a service or repair operation. You'll want to include background information and, if possible, describe employment contracts for key employees such as designers, marketing experts, buyers, and the like.

Buying

The ability to obtain reliable, timely, and reasonably priced supplies of easily salable merchandise is perhaps the prime skill of any retailer. Buying is

Retail Operations Checklist

- ❏ Marketing (include sales projections, location, promotional efforts)
- ❏ Staffing
- ❏ Training sales staff
- ❏ Buying procedures (include delivery times, freight-in, reorder points)
- ❏ Inventory control
- ❏ In-store sales tools
- ❏ Sales policies
- ❏ Customer service policies
- ❏ Service delivery policies
- ❏ Administering monitoring and control policies
- ❏ Follow-up procedures
- ❏ Back room operations staffed

Note the importance of training sales staff. Many retailers omit this to their economic loss. The major reason consumers give for not returning to a store is discourteous or unhelpful sales staff. Point out that you will train your sales staff so that they will act as a powerful resource for your company.

Fact or Fiction?

Is success a matter of buying low or selling high? Retailers say that, contrary to popular opinion, they really make their money when they buy, not sell, goods. The trick, mastered by successful retailers like Wal-Mart and Toys "R" Us, is to buy goods for a price low enough that you can sell them at a profit while still attracting customers and discouraging competitors.

both art and science. Knowing what the economical ordering quantities are for a given product is mechanical, but knowing which items to stock requires knowledge of customer desires and demand. Buying is based on your marketing plan. Without clear knowledge of the marketing environment, you cannot make wise purchasing decisions.

If you have what consumers want when few others do, you're almost guaranteed to have strong sales. If you run out of a hot item, on the other hand, disappointed consumers may leave your store, never to return.

Operations plans for retailers, therefore, devote considerable attention to sourcing desirable products. They may describe the background and accomplishments of key buyers. They may detail long-term supply agreements with manufacturers of in-demand branded merchandise. They may even discuss techniques for obtaining, on the gray market, desirable products from manufacturers who try to restrict the flow of goods to their stores.

As the owner, you have to juggle dozens of details and in the press of daily business, run the risk of not performing some essential step. Figure 11–3 can be used to plan your week before you get caught up in the chaos. Use it to focus your efforts on the most important items on your to-do list.

Weekly Time Plan

Name	Week Ending	
Problems/Objectives	**Schedule**	
	Monday	
	Tuesday	
	Wednesday	
	Thursday	
	Friday	
	Saturday	

Figure 11-3. Weekly Time Plan

Operations for Manufacturers

Product development, marketing, and distribution all play important roles, but it's the production process that sets manufacturers apart from all other enterprises.

Companies that make things have certain characteristics in common that set them apart from others, including retailers and service firms. They take raw materials and labor and transform them into sellable products. Although they may also distribute the products and sell direct to customers (thus involving the retail and service aspects of operations), most manufacturers concentrate on the production end and farm out the retail and service to other firms.

Process Points

The lead actor in manufacturing is the process of production. Product development, marketing, and distribution all play important roles, but it's the production process that sets manufacturers apart from all other enterprises. And the better your production process, the better a manufacturer you will be. It's the star that leads to your company's success.

Manufacturing Company Checklist

- ❏ Marketing plan completed
- ❏ Staffing completed (or staffing plan completed)
- ❏ Organization chart completed
- ❏ Product plan completed
- ❏ Basic manufacturing operations listed in sequence
- ❏ Raw materials purchased
- ❏ Equipment obtained
- ❏ Labor skills available and assigned
- ❏ Time lines and deadlines assigned
- ❏ Potential roadblocks identified
- ❏ Managerial controls in place
- ❏ Sales policies reviewed
- ❏ Customer relations policies outlined
- ❏ Service delivery policies developed
- ❏ Administering monitoring and control policies
- ❏ Follow-up procedures checked

Manufacturing is complex. Your checklist will most likely differ from the one given in this sidebar. A small contractor, for example, makes things but is less complex, so might have a checklist like this:

- ❏ Develop work schedule
- ❏ Hire labor
- ❏ Set up equipment
- ❏ Acquire necessary materials
- ❏ Monitor work schedule

The key point: Identify the major pieces or aspects of your operation in your business plan.

BUZZWORD

Kaizen, *a Japanese term for continuous improvement, swept the world of business operations in the 1980s and early 1990s. The idea is to constantly obtain small gains in productivity and quality over a long period.*

A manufacturing production process consists of several components. One step is usually fabrication, or the making of products from raw materials. There is also assembly of components, testing, and inspection of finished goods.

Manufacturing processes can become extremely detailed, down to calculating the number of seconds allowed for a sewing machine operator to complete the inseam on a pair of men's slacks. If you're an operations-minded entre-preneur, you may revel in these details. But control your enthusiasm for minutiae when it comes to writing a business plan. Stick to the important processes, those essential to your production or that give you a special competitive advantage.

Personnel and Materials

Manufacturers combine labor and materials to produce products. Problems with either one of these critical inputs spell trouble for your business and for its backers. So plan readers look for strong systems in place to make sure that personnel and materials are appropriately abundant.

You should show in your plan that you have adequate, reliable sources of supply for the materials you need to build your products. Estimate your needs for materials and describe the agreements with suppliers, including their length and terms, that you have arranged to fulfill those needs. You may also give the backgrounds of your major suppliers and show that you have backup sources available should problems develop.

It's an interesting spectacle, every now and then, to watch an industrial giant such as an auto maker or railroad paralyzed by a labor strike. It illustrates the importance of ensuring a reliable supply of adequately trained people to run your processes.

Plan Pointer

How much detail should you give about the technology you employ? Only a plan for internal use can tell all, so be careful not to let it reach the wrong hands. A plan for venture capitalists should contain fewer details. Venture investors are often expert in their fields but can't guarantee confidentiality. Bankers care less about details, so a basic outline should do.

The Making of a Baron

The person most famous for building an empire based on ownership of capital equipment is Andrew Carnegie. In the 19th century, this Scottish immigrant to America rose from beginnings as a textile-plant worker to become a baron of steel and oil.

Carnegie was always a hard worker—as a teenage delivery boy he was his family's primary source of income. But it was his savvy in acquiring capital equipment that made him a business legend.

At the age of 21, Carnegie borrowed to buy shares in a new railroad being built near his Pennsylvania home. A few years later, he acquired oil field assets in Titusville, Pennsylvania. In railroad car manufacturing, bridge building, and, finally, iron and steel mills, Carnegie followed the same strategy: control the means of production.

Shortly after 1900, Carnegie sold out to J.P. Morgan. Those holdings became U.S. Steel, today known as USX Corporation.

You'll first need to estimate the number and type of people you will require to run your plan. Start-ups can do this by looking at competitors' plants or by relying on the founders' prior experience at other companies. Existing firms can extrapolate what they'll need to expand from current operations. Then show that you can reasonably expect to be able to hire what you need. Look at local labor pools, unemployment rates, and wage levels using information from chambers of commerce or similar entities. If you plan to import sizable numbers of workers, check out housing availability and build an expense for moving costs into your budget.

Getting Equipped

Manufacturing a product naturally requires equipment. A manufacturer is likely to need all sorts of equipment such as cars, trucks, computers, telephone systems, and, of course, machinery of every description for bending metal, milling wood, forming plastic, or otherwise making a product out of raw materials.

Much of this equipment is very expensive and hard to move or sell once purchased. Naturally, investors are very interested in your plans for purchasing equipment. Many plans devote a separate section to describing the ovens, drill presses, forklifts, printing presses, and other equipment they'll require.

This part of your plan doesn't have to be long, but it does have to be complete. Make a list of every sizable piece of equipment you anticipate needing. Include a description of its features, its functions, and, of course, its cost.

Be ready to defend the need to own the more expensive items. Bankers and other investors are loath to plunk down money for capital equipment that can only be resold for far less than its purchase price.

The Facilities Section

Everybody has to be somewhere. Unless you're a homebased businessperson or a globe-trotting consultant whose office is his suitcase, your plan will need to describe the facilities in which your business will be housed.

Land and buildings are often the largest capital items on any company's balance sheet. So it makes sense to go into detail about what you have and what you need. Decide first how much space you require in square feet. Don't forget to include room for expansion if you anticipate growth. Now consider the location. You may need to be close to a labor

Plan Pitfall

Stay up on technology if you're in a so-called software industry—including books, movies, and music as well as computer programs. New tools for ripping off intellectual property—like copying recorded music with digital technology—make catching copycats tougher than ever. Increasingly, your secrets are only safe if you keep up with the high-tech highwaymen.

force and materials suppliers. Transportation needs such as proximity to rail, interstate highways, or airports can also be important. Next ask whether there is any specific layout that you need. Draw up a floor plan to see if your factory floor can fit into the space you have in mind.

To figure the cost of facilities, you'll first have to decide whether you will lease or buy space and what your rent or mortgage payments will be for the chosen option.

To figure the cost of facilities, you'll first have to decide whether you will lease or buy space and what your rent or mortgage payments will be for the chosen option. Don't forget to include brokerage fees, moving costs, and the cost of any leasehold improvements you'll need. Finally, take a look at operating costs. Utilities including phone, electric, gas, water, and trash pickup are concerns; also consider such things as maintenance and general upkeep. See Figure 11–4 to analyze your requirements.

These aren't the only operations concerns of manufacturers. You should also consider your need to acquire or protect such valuable operations assets as proprietary processes and patented technologies. For many businesses— Coca-Cola with its secret soft drink formula comes to mind—intellectual

Scaling Success by the Century

Would you like to create a company that will last 150 years? The solid foundation provided by a secure, broad-based patent could be just what you need. Take the case of Fairbanks Scales.

More than 150 years ago, a Vermont entrepreneur named Thaddeus Fairbanks grew dissatisfied with the scales available to weigh hemp processed by a company he'd started with his brother. Fairbanks had already invented a couple of modestly successful contraptions, including a stove and an iron plow, and he felt he could improve on the inaccurate and ponderous steelyard scales then in wide use.

After a spell in his invention shop, Thaddeus emerged with a new type of scale that used a system of levers and could be buried in the ground, allowing wagonloads of hemp and other materials to be easily, quickly, and accurately weighed. He obtained a patent on the invention and then, backed with $4,000, he and brothers Joseph and Erastus formed Fairbanks Platform Scale in 1830.

From that humble beginning, with the help of Thaddeus' patented scale technology, Fairbanks Scales would dominate the business of weighing everything from postal letters to canal barges for the next century. After a merger with its largest distributor in 1916, the company became known as Fairbanks Morse. In 1988, Fairbanks Scales was purchased back from Fairbanks Morse and is now the oldest continuing operating manufactuing company in America.

Facilities Worksheet

Use this worksheet to analyze your facilities requirements. Fill out the sections, then test available facilities against your requirements.

Space Requirements

Initial space _____

Expansion space _____

Total space _____

Location Requirements

Proximity to labor pool _____

Proximity to suppliers_____

Transportation availability _____

Layout Requirements: _____

_____

Cost Requirements (Dollar Amounts of Estimated Expenses)

Purchase/lease costs _____

Brokerage costs _____

Moving costs _____

Improvements costs _____

Operating costs _____

Total Cost _____

Figure 11-4. Facilities Worksheet

property is more valuable than their sizable accumulations of plants and equipment. Investors should be warned if they're going to have to pay to acquire intellectual property. If you already have it, they will be happy to learn they'll be purchasing an interest in a valuable technology.

Information Technology and Operations

No matter what business you are in, information technology probably looms larger all the time. Manufacturers link computers to speed orders directly from their customers' computers to their production control software. Retailers place their orders faster and more accurately using the same systems. Many service firms, such as travel agents, accountants, and web site designers, are also heavily dependent on technology.

If you use or anticipate using a promising new technology, whether it's a web site for online commerce or an interactive computer training course to improve customer service, include it in your description of operations. Investors are always looking for an operations edge, and if you have it, you should tell them about it in your business plan.

BUZZWORD

Logistics *is the science of moving objects from one location to another. For manufacturers and retailers, the logistics of supplies and products is crucial. For service firms, often the logistics of moving employees around is more important.*

✶ EXPERT ADVICE ✶

Many businesses succeed or fail on the basis of things that only people who work there ever notice. Wal-Mart didn't become the world's largest retailer because it snagged the best locations or hired the best ad agencies. It beat out Sears, Montgomery Ward, and the rest because of its extremely efficient systems for stocking and distributing the most profitable products in the most profitable manner. Its likely that your business is based in large part on some aspect of its operations—manufacturing, logistics, customer service—that plan readers will want to know about.

Chapter 12

Expressing Your Ideas in Financial Terms

FINANCIAL DATA IS ALWAYS AT THE BACK OF THE BUSINESS PLAN, BUT THAT doesn't mean it's any less important than up-front material such as the description of the business concept and the management team. Astute investors look carefully at the charts, tables, formulas, and spreadsheets in the financial section because they know that this information is like the pulse, respiration rate, and blood pressure in a human—it shows whether the patient is alive and what the odds are for continued survival.

Financial statements come in threes: income statement, balance sheet, and cash flow statement. Taken together they provide an accurate picture of a company's current value, plus its ability to pay its bills today and earn a profit going forward. This information is very important to business plan readers.

Income Statement

An income statement shows whether you are making any money. It adds up all your revenue from sales and other sources, subtracts all your costs, and comes up with the net income figure, also known as the bottom line.

Keep Spreadsheets Simple

Robert Crowley, vice president of Massachusetts Technology Development Corporation, a state-owned venture firm, once described it as "this horrible disease . . . called spreadsheet-itis. It's the most common ailment in business plans today." Crowley says electronic spreadsheet software allows business plan writers to easily crank out many pages and many varieties of financial documents. But this is a case of the more, the less merry. As a rule, stick with the big three: income, balance sheet, and cash flow statements.

These three statements are interlinked, with changes in one necessarily altering the others, but they measure quite different aspects of a company's financial health. It's hard to say that one of these is more important than another. But of the three, the income statement may be the best place to start.

Income statements are called various names—profit and loss statement (P&L) and earnings statement are two common alternatives. They can get pretty complicated in their attempt to capture sources of income such as interest and expenses such as depreciation. But the basic idea is pretty simple: if you subtract costs from income, what you have left is profit.

To figure your income statement, you need to gather a bunch of numbers, most of which are easily obtainable. They include your gross revenue, which is made up of sales and any income from interest or sales of assets; your sales, general, and administrative (SG&A) expenses; what you paid out in interest and dividends, if anything; and your corporate tax rate. If you have those, you're ready to go.

Sales and Revenue

Revenue is all the income you receive from selling your products or services as well as from other sources such as interest income and sales of assets.

Gross Sales

Your sales figure is the income you receive from selling your product or service. Gross sales equal total sales minus returns. It doesn't include interest or income from sales of assets.

Interest and Dividends

Most businesses have a little reserve fund they keep in an interest-bearing bank or money market account. Income from this fund, as well as from any other interest-paying or dividend-paying securities they own, shows up on the income statement just below the sales figure.

Other Income

If you finally decide that the branch office out on County Line Road isn't ever going to turn a decent profit, and you sell the land, building, and fixtures, the income from that sale will show up on your income statement as "other income." Other income may include sales of unused or obsolete equipment or any income-generating activity that's not part of your main line of business.

Costs

Costs come in all varieties—that's no secret. You'll record variable costs, such as the cost of goods sold, as well as fixed costs—rent, insurance, maintenance, and so forth. You'll also record costs that are a little trickier, the prime example being depreciation.

Cost of Goods Sold

Cost of goods sold, or COGS, includes expenses associated directly with generating the product or service you're selling. If you buy computer components and assemble them, your COGS will include the price of the chips, disk drives, and other parts, as well as the wages of the assembly workers. You'll also include supervisor salaries and utilities for your factory. If you're a solo professional service provider, on the other hand, your COGS may amount to little more than whatever salary you pay yourself.

Sales, General, and Administrative Costs

You have some expenses that aren't closely tied to sales volume, including salaries for office personnel, salespeople compensation, rent, insurance, and the like. These are split out from the sales-sensitive COGS figure and included on a separate line.

Depreciation

Depreciation is one of the most baffling pieces of accounting wizard work. It's a paper loss, a way of subtracting over time the cost of a piece of equipment or a building that lasts many years even though it may get paid for immediately.

Plan Pitfall

Profit and loss statements rightly get lots of attention. Without long-term profits, the future is questionable. But long-term profits aren't the whole answer. You need balance sheets to know your financial position and cash flow statements to see how that position has changed.

BUZZWORD

What sounds like Elmer Fudd is actually a common acronym used on many financial statements. EBIT stands for earnings before interest and taxes—an admirably descriptive accounting term that probably needs no further clarification.

159

Depreciation isn't an expense that involves cash coming out of your pocket. Yet it's a real expense in an accounting sense, and most income statements will have an entry for depreciation coming off the top of pretax earnings.

If you have capital items that you are depreciating, such as an office in your home or a large piece of machinery, your accountant will be able to set up a schedule for depreciation. Each year, you'll take a portion of the purchase price of that item off your earnings statement. Although it hurts profits, depreciation can, it should be noted, reduce future taxes.

In Figure 12–1, the income statement for NetKnowledge Internet Training Center, total receipts from tuition charged to students came to $23,568. The company got an extra $115 from interest on bank accounts.

Sample Income Statement

Sales Receipts	$23,568
Interest Income	115
COGS	12,615
Gross Margin	11,068
Expenses	4,835
Depreciation	1,125
Operating Earnings	5,108
Interest Expense	1,410
Pretax Earnings	3,698
Income Tax	1,109
Net Income	**$2,589**

Cost of goods sold amounted to $12,615. Subtracting COGS from sales gives the gross margin of $11,068. Subtracting expenses and depreciation from that returns a figure of $5,108 for operating earnings.

NetKnowledge racked up interest charges of $1,410. When this is removed from operating earnings, the resulting net income before taxes is $3,698. With income taxes calculated at $1,109, that leaves a net income of $2,589.

Figure 12-1. Sample Income Statement

Interest

Paying the interest on loans is another expense that gets a line all to itself and comes out of earnings just before taxes are subtracted. This line doesn't include payments against principal, it should be noted. Because these payments result in a reduction of liabilities—which we'll talk about in a few pages in connection with your balance sheet—they're not regarded as expenses on the income statement.

Taxes

The best thing about taxes is that they're figured last, on the profits that are left after every other thing has been taken out. Tax rates vary widely according to where your company is located, how and whether state and local taxes are figured, and your special tax situation.

The best way to figure taxes is to have your accountant do a projection of your tax rate based on past years' filings and this year's projected results. Then multiply that percentage times your earnings before tax. We've used an estimated effective tax rate of 30 percent, which is not usually too far off the mark, for this section. Whatever you use, you'll have your net income—the much talked-about bottom line—after you take out taxes.

Balance Sheet

If the income sheet shows what you're earning, the balance sheet shows what you're worth. A balance sheet can help an investor see that a company owns valuable assets that don't show up on the income statement or that it may be profitable but is heavily in debt. It adds up everything your business owns, subtracts everything the business owes, and shows the difference as the net worth of the business.

Actually, accountants put it differently and, of course, use different names. The things you own are called assets. The things you owe on are called liabilities. And net worth is referred to as equity.

The three elements are governed by a simple equation:

Liabilities + Equity = Total Assets

It can also be useful to look at it another way:

Assets – Liabilities = Net Worth

Both formulas mean the same thing.

Fact or Fiction?

You always want to maximize profits, right? Not always. Savvy entrepreneurs know that managing reported profits can save on taxes. Part of the trick is balancing salaries, dividends, and retained earnings. Tax regulations treat each differently, and you can't exactly do whatever you want. Get good advice, and be ready to sacrifice reported profits for real savings.

Plan Pitfall

Almost anything can lose value, but for accounting purposes, land doesn't. As a rule, you never depreciate land, although you may depreciate buildings as well as other long-lived purchases.

A balance sheet shows your condition on a given date, usually the end of your fiscal year. Sometimes balance sheets are compared. That is, next to the figures for the end of the most recent year, you place the entries for the end of the prior period. This gives you a snapshot of how and where your financial position has changed.

A balance sheet also places a value on the owner's equity in the business. When you subtract liabilities from assets, what's left is the value of the equity in the business owned by you and any partners. Tracking changes in this number will tell you whether you're getting richer or poorer.

Assets

An asset is basically anything you own of value. It gets a little more complicated in practice, but that's the working definition.

Assets come in two main varieties: current assets and fixed assets. Current assets are anything that is easily liquidated or turned into cash. They include cash, accounts receivables, inventory, marketable securities, and the like.

Fixed assets include stuff that is harder to turn into cash. Examples are land, buildings, improvements, equipment, furniture, and vehicles.

The fixed asset part of the balance sheet sometimes includes a negative value—that is, a number you subtract from the other fixed asset values. This number is depreciation, and it's an accountant's way of slowly deducting the cost of a long-lived asset such as a building or a piece of machinery from your fixed asset value.

Intangibles are another asset category. They include such things as patents, long-term contracts, and that ephemeral something called goodwill. Goodwill consists of such things as the value of your reputation, which is not really susceptible to valuation. Probably the best way to think of goodwill is like this: If you sell your company, the IRS says the part of the sales price that exceeds the value of the assets is goodwill. As a result of its slipperiness, some planners never include an entry for goodwill, although its value may in fact be substantial.

Patents, trademarks, copyrights, exclusive distributorships, protected franchise agreements, and the like do have somewhat more accessible value. They may never be turned into cash, but you can estimate their worth, or at least figure out what you paid for them and use that.

Liabilities

Liabilities are the debts your business owes. They come in two classes: short-term and long-term.

Plan Pointer THIS WAY

The two sides of a balance sheet—assets and liabilities—can be presented side by side or one on top of the other. The first is called columnar format; the second, report format. There's no rule about which is best. Do whatever looks or feels natural.

Sample Balance Sheet

December 31, 2005

ASSETS		LIABILITIES	
Cash	$4,387	Notes Payable	$11,388
Accounts Receivable	12,385	Accounts Payable	2,379
Inventory	1,254	Interest Payable	1,125
Prepaid Expenses	3,548	Taxes Payable	3,684
Other Current Assets	986	Other Current Liabilities	986
Total Current Assets	22,560	Total Current Liabilities	19,562
Fixed Assets	27,358	Long-term Debt	4,896
Intangibles	500	Other Noncurrent Liabilities	1,156
Other Noncurrent Assets	0	**Total Liabilities**	**$25,614**
		Net Worth	**24,804**
Total Assets	**$50,418**	**Total Liabilities & Net Worth**	**$50,418**

Figure 12-2. Sample Balance Sheet

Plan Pointer THIS WAY

Legendary investor Warren Buffett reads thousands of financial statements describing businesses every year. He says that in most cases, the first thing he goes to is the balance sheet to check a company's strength. So if you'd like to attract an investor of Buffett's stature, spend time on the balance sheet.

Short-term liabilities are also called current liabilities. Any debt that is going to be paid off within 12 months is considered current. That includes accounts payable you owe suppliers, short-term bank loans (shown as notes payable), and accrued liabilities you have built up for such things as wages, taxes, and interest.

Any debt that you won't pay off in a year is long-term. Mortgages and bank loans with more than a one-year term are considered in this class. Figure 12–2 shows a typical balance sheet.

Cash Flow Statement

The cash flow statement monitors the flow of cash over a period of time (a year, a quarter, a month) and shows you how much cash you have on hand at the moment.

The cash flow statement, also called the statement of changes in financial position, probes and analyzes changes that have occurred on the balance

Plan Pointer THIS WAY

One of the key characteristics of a balance sheet is that it balances. The bottom lines of both halves of the balance sheet, assets in one half and liabilities in the other, are always equal, or balanced.

Plan Pointer THIS WAY

Many people are uncomfortable with figuring any value at all for goodwill but don't want to ignore it completely. One common alternative is to just enter $1 for intangibles and leave it at that.

sheet. It's different from the income statement, which describes sales and profits but doesn't necessarily tell you where your cash came from or how it's being used.

A cash flow statement consists of two parts. One follows the flow of cash into and out of the company. The other shows how the funds were spent. The two parts are called, respectively, sources of funds and uses of funds. At the bottom is, naturally, the bottom line, called net changes in cash position. It shows whether and by how much you improved your cash on hand during the period.

Sources of Funds

Sources of funds usually has two main sections in it. The first shows cash from sales or other operations. In the cash flow statement, this figure represents all the money you collected from accounts during this period. It may include all the sales you booked during the period, plus some collections on sales that actually closed earlier.

The other category of sources of funds includes interest income, if any, plus the proceeds from any loans, line of credit drawdowns, or capital

BUZZWORD

Balance sheets help answer the question: What is the book value of the business? The book value of the business is the Net Worth (or Owner's Equity). Most valuation methods for small and midsized businesses use the Net Worth plus an adjusted earnings or free cash flow multiple to create a rough and ready valuation.

Penny's Lack of Pennies

When Penny McConnell's dreams came true, her cash flow fell short. The owner of an eight-person cookie bakery, McConnell had been making a living selling low volumes of fresh Penny's Pastries brand cookies to local stores. Then a buyer from Southwest Airlines called and said the airline wanted to serve her new cookies on all its flights. It would be a year's worth of sales—every month.

Inexperienced at planning for such volume, McConnell made crucial mistakes. She cut prices to meet Southwest's budget, which reduced profits. Then she borrowed heavily to buy equipment, order supplies, hire employees, and rent a new facility, increasing expenses sharply.

When costs rose after a technical problem cropped up, profits vanished completely. Then losses mounted. Within six months Penny's Pastries filed for bankruptcy. What happened? Too much spending, too much discounting, and too little planning doomed her from the start. Now in business with another venture, McConnell says a well-thought-out plan might have confirmed what her instincts suggested. "It was such a tremendous increase in volume," she says, "that I had a gut feeling from the beginning it wasn't going to work."

received from investors during the period. Again, these figures represent money actually received during the period. If you arranged for a $100,000 line of credit but only used $10,000 during this period, your sources of funds would show $10,000.

Uses of Funds

The sources of funds section often has only one or two entries, although some cash statements break out sources of funds by businesses and product lines. But even simple statements show several uses of funds. A cash flow statement will normally show uses such as cost of goods sold; sales, general, and administrative expense (SG&A); and any equipment purchases, interest payments, payments on principal amounts of loans, and dividends or draws taken by the owners.

Net Change in Cash

Few things feel better for a start-up businessperson than having plenty of cash in the bank. And few things tell better what's going on with cash on hand than the net change in cash line on your business plan. Net change in cash equals the difference between total funds in and total funds out. If you bring in $1 million and send out $900,000, your net change in cash is $100,000. Ideally, you want this number to be positive and, if possible, showing an upward trend.

Other Financial Information

If you're seeking investors for your company, you'll probably need to provide quite a bit more financial information than what is in the income statement, balance sheet, and cash flow statements. For instance, a personal finance statement may be needed if you're guaranteeing loans yourself. Applying business data to other ratios and formulas will yield important information on what your profit margin is and what level of sales it will take for you to reach profitability. Still other figures, such as the various ratios, will help predict whether you'll be able to pay your bills for long. These bits of information are helpful to you as well as to investors, it should be noted. Understanding and, if possible, mastering them, will help you run your business more smoothly.

Figure 12–3, Sample One-Month Cash Flow Statement for Net-Knowledge Internet Training Centers, reflects $23,568 in sales receipts. That includes sales booked and collected during the period and accounts receivable

Fact or Fiction?

Is it possible to have too much cash? In fact, it is. If your cash is simply sitting in a bank account, it may be drawing little or no interest. In a typical inflation environment, it will often lose purchasing power from one day to the next. If you have large amounts of cash and nothing to do with it, consider reinvesting in your company—or perhaps another.

Sample Cash Flow Statement

Sources of Cash

Sales	$23,568
Other Sources	0
Interest	115
Invested Capital	10,000
Total Cash In	**$33,683**

Uses of Cash

COGS	$12,615
SG&A	4,835
Interest	1,410
Taxes	1,109
Equipment Purchase	8,354
Debt Principal Payments	2,000
Dividends	0
Total Cash Out	**$30,323**
NET CHANGE IN CASH	**$3,360**
Beginning Cash on Hand	**$4,387**
Ending Cash on Hand	**$7,747**

COGS stands for cost of goods sold and includes primarily salaries paid to NetKnowledge's educators and staff. Sales, general, and administrative (SG&A), expenses include the base salary for NetKnowledge's single salesperson. The interest outlay is for interest on NetKnowledge's line of credit. The $8,354 entry is for a new computerized presentation projector. NetKnowledge paid its credit line down by $2,000 during the same period, and the owners took no draw out of the business.

The net result, equal to total cash in minus total cash out, comes to $3,360, and that is NetKnowledge's net cash flow for the month.

The bottom two entries sum up NetKnowledge's current cash position. You add the amount of cash on hand from the prior period's cash flow statement to the net cash flow figure on this statement.

Figure 12-3. Sample Cash Flow Statement

that were collected. The interest entry reflects interest received on NetKnowledge's cash reserves account at the bank. The $10,000 was an injection of capital by one of the firm's partners.

Personal Financial Statement

Investors and lenders like to see business plans with substantial investments by the entrepreneur or with an entrepreneur who is personally guaranteeing any loans and has the personal financial strength to back those guarantees. Your personal financial statement is where you show plan readers how you stack up financially as an individual.

The personal financial statement comes in two parts. One is similar to a company balance sheet and lists your liabilities and assets. A net worth figure at the bottom, like the net worth figure on a company balance sheet, equals total assets minus total liabilities.

A second statement covers your personal income. It is similar to a company profit and loss statement, listing all your personal expenses, such as rent or mortgage payments, utilities, food, clothing, and entertainment. It also shows your sources of income, including earnings from a job, income from another business you own, child support or alimony, interest and dividends, and the like.

The figure at the bottom is your net income; it equals total income minus total expenses. If you've ever had to fill out a personal financial statement to borrow money for a car loan or home mortgage, you've had experience with a personal financial statement. You should be able to simply update figures from a previous personal financial statement.

Financial Ratios

Everything in business is relative. The numbers for your profits, sales, and net worth need to be compared with other components of your business for them to make sense. For instance, a $1 million net profit sounds great. But what if it took sales of $1 billion to achieve those profits? That would be a modest performance indeed.

To help understand the relative significance of your financial numbers, analysts use financial ratios. These ratios compare various elements of your financial reports to see if the relationships between the numbers make sense based on prior experience in your industry.

Plan Pointer

Investors like to see entrepreneurs who are sharing the risk and living frugally, especially when the entrepreneur's living expenses are coming out of the investors' money. For that reason, many start-ups pay minimal salaries and allow little or no dividends or draws against profits to be paid to the owners until profits are steady.

Some of the common ratios and other calculations analysts perform include your company's break-even point, current ratio, debt-to-equity ratio, return on investment, and return on equity. You may not need to calculate all these. Depending on your industry, you may also find it useful to calculate various others, such as inventory turnover, a useful figure for many manufacturers and retailers. But ratios are highly useful tools for managing, and most are quick and easy to figure. Becoming familiar with them and presenting the relevant ones in your plan will help you manage your company better and convince investors you are on the right track.

Plan of Action

Wondering how good your credit is? You can get a copy of your credit report from any large credit rating agency, such as Experian, for a nominal sum. You can call them toll-free at (866) 200-6020 or visit their web site at www. experian.com.

Break-Even Point

One of the most important calculations you can make is figuring your break-even point. This is the point at which revenue equals costs. Another way to figure it is to say it's the level of sales you need to get to for gross margin or gross profit to cover all your fixed expenses. Knowing your break-even point is important because when your sales are over this point, they begin to produce profits. When your sales are under this point, you're still losing money. This information is handy for all kinds of things, from deciding how to price your product or service to figuring whether a new marketing campaign is worth the investment.

The process of figuring your break-even point is called break-even analysis. It may sound complicated, and if you were to watch an accountant figure your break-even point, it would seem like a lot of mumbo-jumbo. Accountants calculate figures with all sorts of arcane-sounding labels, such as variable cost percentage and semifixed expenses. These numbers may be strictly accurate, but given all the uncertainty there is with projecting your break-even point, there's some question as to whether extra accuracy is worth all that much.

There is, however, a quicker if somewhat dirtier method of figuring break-even. It is described in Figure 12–4. Although this approach may not be up to accounting-school standards, it is highly useful for entrepreneurs, and more important, it can be done quickly, easily, and frequently, as conditions change.

Once you get comfortable with working break-even figures in a simple fashion, you can get more complicated. You may want to figure break-even points for individual products and services. Or you may apply break-even analysis to help you decide whether an advertising campaign is likely to pay any dividends. Perform break-even analyses regularly and often, especially as circumstances change. Hiring more people, changing your product mix, or becoming more efficient all change your break-even point.

Break-Even Analysis Worksheet

To determine your break-even point, start by collecting these two pieces of information:

1. *Fixed costs.* These are inflexible expenses you'll have to make independently of sales volume. Add up your rent, insurance, administrative expenses, interest, office supply costs, maintenance fees, etc. to get this number. Put your fixed costs here: _____.

2. *Average gross profit margin.* This will be the average estimated gross profit margin, expressed as a percentage, you generate from sales of your products and services. Put your average gross profit margin here: _____.

   Now divide the costs by profit margin, and you have your break-even point. Here's the formula:

   $$\frac{\text{Fixed costs}}{\text{Profit margin}} = \text{Break-even point}$$

   If, for instance, your fixed costs were $10,000 a month and your average gross profit margin 60 percent, the formula would look like this:

   $$\frac{\$10,000}{0.6} = \$16,667$$

   So in this case, your break-even point is $16,667. When sales are running at $16,667 a month, your gross profits are covering expenses. Fill your own numbers into the following template to figure your break-even point:

   $$\frac{\$\rule{2cm}{0.4pt}}{\rule{2cm}{0.4pt}} = \$\rule{2cm}{0.4pt}$$

Figure 12-4. Break-Even Analysis Worksheet

Plan Pitfall

Financial reports should be prepared according to Generally Accepted Accounting Principles. GAAP— pronounced "gap"—isn't precise. For instance, you can often choose faster or slower methods of depreciating an asset. Stretching GAAP too far may lead to trouble, such as a shareholder lawsuit. Accountant audits are designed to ensure you don't fall into the gap between GAAP and trouble.

Current Ratio

The current ratio is an important measure of your company's short-term liquidity. It's probably the first ratio anyone looking at your business will compute because it shows the likelihood that you'll be able to make it through the next 12 months.

Figuring your current ratio is simple. You divide current assets by current liabilities. Current assets consist of cash, receivables, inventory, and other assets likely to be sold for cash in a year. Current liabilities consist of bills that will have to be paid before 12 months pass, including short-term

Accounting through the Ages

If you don't understand accounting as well as you should, you can't blame it on recent innovations. Double-entry accounting dates at least from 1340, and the first book on accounting, by a monk named Luca Pacioli, was published in 1494.

Surprisingly, a medieval accountant would feel quite comfortable with much of what goes on today in an accounting department. But accountants haven't been sitting back and relaxing during the intervening centuries. They've thought up all kinds of ways to measure the health and wealth of businesses (and businesspeople).

There are more ratios, analyses, and calculations than you can shake a green eye shade at. And wary investors are prone to using a wide variety of those tests to make sure they're not investing in something that went out of style around the time Columbus set sail. So although accounting may not be your favorite subject, it's a good idea to learn what you can. Otherwise, you're likely to be seen as not much more advanced than a 15th-century monk.

notes, trade accounts payable, and the portion of long-term debt due in a year or less. Here's the formula:

$$\frac{\text{Current assets}}{\text{Current liabilities}} = \text{Current ratio}$$

For example, say you have $50,000 in current assets and $20,000 in current liabilities. Your current ratio would be:

$$\frac{\$50,000}{\$20,000} = 2.5$$

The current ratio is expressed as a ratio; that is, the example in Figure 12–4 shows a current ratio of 2.5 to 1 or 2.5:1. That's an acceptable current ratio for many businesses. Anything less than 2:1 is likely to raise questions.

Quick Ratio

This ratio has the best name—it's also called the acid-test ratio. The quick ratio is a more conservative version of the current ratio. It works the same way but leaves out inventory and any other current assets that may be a little harder to turn into cash. You'll normally get a lower number with this one than with the current ratio—1:1 is acceptable in many industries.

Sales/Receivables Ratio

This ratio shows how long it takes you to get the money owed you. It's also called the average collection period and receivables cycle, among other names. Like most of these ratios, there are various ways of calculating your sales/receivables cycle, but the simplest is to divide your average accounts receivable by your annual sales figure and multiply it by 360, which is considered to be the number of days in the year for many business purposes. Like this:

$$\frac{\text{Receivables}}{\text{Sales}} \quad x \quad 360$$

If your one-person computer consulting business had an average of $10,000 in outstanding receivables and was doing about $120,000 a year in sales, here's how you'd calculate your receivables cycle:

$$\frac{\$10,000}{\$120,000} \quad = \quad 1/12$$

$$1/12 \times 360 = 30$$

If you divide 1 by 12 on a calculator, you'll get .08333, which gives you the same answer, accounting for rounding. Either way, your average collection period is 30 days. This will tell you how long, on average, you'll have to wait to get the check after sending out your invoice. Receivables will vary by customer, of course. You should also check the receivables cycle number against the terms under which you sell. If you sell on 30-day terms and your average collection period is 40 days, there may be a problem that you need to attend to, such as customer dissatisfaction, poor industry conditions, or simply lax collection efforts on your part.

Inventory Turnover

Retailers and manufacturers need to hold inventory, but they don't want to hold any more than they have to because interest, taxes, obsolescence, and other costs eat up profits relentlessly. To find out how good they are at turning inventory into sales, they look at inventory turnovers.

The inventory-turnover ratio takes cost of goods sold and divides it by inventory. The COGS figure is a total for a set period, usually a year. The inventory is also an average for the year; it represents what that inventory costs you to obtain, whether by building it or by buying it.

$$\frac{\text{Average COGS}}{\text{Average inventory}} = \text{Inventory turnover}$$

BU⚡WORD

Leverage *refers to the use of borrowed funds to increase your purchasing power. Used wisely, leverage can boost your profitability. Overused, however, borrowing costs can eradicate operating earnings and produce devastating net losses.*

171

An example:

$$\frac{\$500,000}{\$125,000} = 4$$

In this example, the company turns over inventory four times a year. You can divide that number into 360 to find out how many days it takes you to turn over inventory. In this case, it would be every 90 days.

It's hard to say what is a good inventory-turnover figure. A low figure suggests you may have too much money sitting around in the form of inventory. You may have slow-moving inventory that should be marked down and sold. A high number for inventory turnover is generally better.

Debt-to-Equity Ratio

This ratio is one that investors will scrutinize carefully. It shows how heavily in debt you are compared with your total assets. It's figured by dividing total debt, both long- and short-term liabilities, by total assets.

$$\frac{\text{Total debt}}{\text{Total assets}} = \text{Debt-to-equity ratio}$$

Here's a sample calculation:

$$\frac{\$50,000}{\$100,000} = 1:2$$

You want this number to be low to impress investors, especially lenders. A debt-to-equity ratio of 1:2 would be comforting for most lenders. One way to raise your debt-to-equity ratio is by investing more of your own cash in the venture.

Profit on Sales

This is your ground-level profitability indicator. Take your net profit before taxes figure and divide it by sales.

$$\frac{\text{Profit}}{\text{Sales}} = \text{Return on sales}$$

For example, if your restaurant earned $100,000 last year on sales of $750,000, this is how your POS calculation would look:

$$\frac{\$100,000}{\$750,000} = 0.133$$

Is 0.133 good? That depends. Like most of these ratios, a good number in one industry may be lousy in another. You need to compare POS figures for other restaurants to see how you did.

Return on Equity

Return on equity, often abbreviated as ROE, shows you how much you're getting out of the company as its owner. You figure it by dividing net profit from your income statement, by the owner's equity figure—the net worth figure if you're the only owner—from your balance sheet.

$$\frac{\text{Net profit}}{\text{Net worth}} = \text{Return on equity}$$

Take a look at the ROE for NetKnowledge, the company whose sample income statement and balance sheet was used earlier in the chapter.

$$\frac{\$2,589}{\$21,403} = 12\%$$

NetKnowledge's owners are getting a 12 percent return on their equity. To decide whether this is acceptable, compare it with what you could earn elsewhere, such as in a bank certificate of deposit, stock, mutual fund, or the like, as well as with other companies in your industry.

Return on Investment

Your investors are interested in the return on investment, or ROI, that your company generates. This number, figured by dividing net profit by total assets, shows how much profit the company is returning based on the total investment in it.

$$\frac{\text{Net profit}}{\text{Total assets}} = \text{Return on investment}$$

For NetKnowledge, this would be:

$$\frac{\$2,589}{\$47,017} = 5.5\%$$

Notice that the ROE, which reflects the return on the owners' equity alone, is a lot higher than the ROI. This is because NetKnowledge's leverage—the fact that it has borrowed against its assets—increases the ROE.

Plan of Action

Making sense of financial ratios requires knowing the normal ratios for your industry. Check two books, Industry Norms and Key Business Ratios (D&B) and Statement Studies (Robert Morris), to compare your apples with other people's apples. Both are available in many libraries.

EVA Sigh of Relief

EVA is an acronym standing for economic value added, and it's one of the most interesting financial management tools available to business owners. The aim of EVA is to find out whether you're doing better with the money you have than you could by, say, investing in U.S. Treasury bills.

EVA has been pioneered by consulting firm Stern Stewart, which has counseled hundreds of companies on how to apply EVA. And experts say that entrepreneurs in particular already understand EVA on a gut level. In any event, the basic concept is fairly simple—you measure EVA by taking net operating earnings before taxes and subtracting a reasonable cost of capital, say 12 percent.

In practice, however, it's complicated. Stern Stewart has identified more than 160 adjustments a company may potentially need to make to accounting procedures before EVA can be effectively implemented.

Forecasts

Business plans and financing proposals are based on projections. Past financial data can only support your projections; financial projections in your business plan express in common financial terms and formats how you expect the immediate future to play out the scenarios you created in the body of the plan. You can forecast financial statements such as balance sheets, income statements, and cash flow statements to project where you'll be at some point in the future.

Forecasts are necessities for start-ups, which have no past history to report on.

Forecasts are necessities for start-ups, which have no past history to report on. Existing businesses find them useful for planning purposes. Forecasts help firms foresee trouble, such as a cash flow shortfall, that is likely to occur several months down the road, as well as give them benchmarks to which they can compare actual performance.

Projected Income Statement

Business planning starts with sales projections. No sales, no business. It's that simple. Even if you're in a long-range development project that won't produce a marketable product for years, you have to be able to look ahead and figure out how much you'll be able to sell before you can do any planning that makes sense.

Now that the pressure's on, making a sales projection and the associated income projection may look a little tricky. So let's do it step by step.

First pick a period to project for. You should start with a projection for the first year. Then make projections for the next two years as well.

Next, come up with some baseline figures. If you're an existing business, what were last year's sales? The prior years'? What's the trend? You may be able to simply project out the 10 percent annual sales increase that you've averaged the past three years for the next three.

If you're a start-up and don't have any prior years' figures to look at, look at some other things. The most important question to ask is: What has been the experience of similar companies? If you know that car dealers across the nation have averaged 12 percent annual sales gains, that's a good starting point for figuring your dealership's projections.

Sometimes conditions are expected to change so much that past experience isn't helpful. Internet retailing has been around for nearly ten years, for instance, but that doesn't really mean much for where sales in this revolutionary new channel will be in several years. In these circumstances, you can look at constraints, such as your business's production capacity. Your restaurant is unlikely to sell more meals than its kitchen can cook, for example. Now you can take that high-end limit and adjust it to reflect economic conditions such as interest rate trends, the expected emergence of competitors, and any other important factors. Don't forget to include very specific future factors of which you may be aware, such as the well-publicized fact that the highway department is going to tear up the road in front of your restaurant for several months next year. When you add up all these past experiences, sales constraints, and modifiers, you should be able to come up with a forecast you can have some confidence in.

Forecasting expenses is your next step, and it's much easier. You can often take your prior year's cost of goods sold, adjust it either up or down based on trends in costs, and go with that. The same goes for rent, wages, and other expenses. Even start-ups can often find good numbers on which to forecast expenses because they can just go to the suppliers they plan to deal with and ask for current price quotes plus anticipated price increases. You'll hope, of course, to uncover good news with regard to expenses. You may find that unit costs go down thanks to economies of scale, for instance. And fixed costs, as the name suggests, are not likely to change significantly.

Plan Pointer

There are four kinds of financial ratios: liquidity ratios like the current ratio, asset management ratios like the sales/receivable cycle, debt management ratios like the debt-to-equity ratio, and profitability ratios like return on investment.

Projected Balance Sheet

Balance sheets can also be projected into the future, and the projections can serve as targets to aim for or benchmarks to compare against actual results. Balance sheets are affected by sales, too. If your accounts receivable or inventory go up, your balance sheet reflects this. And, of course, increases in cash show up on the balance sheet. So it's important to look ahead to see how your balance sheet will appear given your sales forecast.

When you sit down to prepare a projected balance sheet, it will be helpful to take a look at past years' balance sheets and figure out the relationship of certain assets and liabilities that vary according to sales. These include cash, receivables, inventory, payables, and tax liabilities.

If you have any operating history, you can calculate the average percentages of sales for each of these figures for the past few years and use that for your balance sheet projection. You can simply take last year's figures, if you don't think they'll change that much. Or you can adjust the percentage to fit some special knowledge you have about the coming year—you're changing your credit terms, for instance, so you expect receivables to shrink, or you're taking out a loan for an expensive new piece of equipment. Firms without operating history can look at one of the books describing industry norms referred to earlier to get guidance about what's typical for their type of company.

Figure 12–5, the Projected Income Statement for Small Bites, a catering service specializing in children's birthday parties, shows that the planner expects year 2005 revenues to follow the steady trend of 25 percent increases annually; it also shows the effect of opening a second operation in a nearby city.

The expenses section generally tracks expense trends as well, with many costs showing sharp jumps associated with opening the new location. The result is that depressed earnings are projected for the first year of the expanded operation, despite higher revenues.

Cash Flow Pro Forma

BUZZWORD

Cash flow forecasts are commonly called cash flow pro formas to distinguish them from the projected cash flow statement.

Businesses are very sensitive to cash. Even if your operation is profitable and you have plenty of capital assets, you can go broke if you run out of cash and can't pay your taxes, wages, rent, utilities, and other essentials. Similarly, a strong flow of cash covers up a multitude of other sins, including a short-term lack of profitability. A cash flow pro forma (or cash budget) is your attempt to spot future cash shortfalls in time to take action.

A cash budget differs from a cash flow statement in that it's generally broken down into periods of less than a year. This is especially true during start-up, when the company is especially sensitive to cash shortages, and management is still fine-tuning its controls. Start-ups, highly seasonal businesses, and others whose sales may fluctuate widely should do monthly cash

Sample Projected Income Statement

INCOME PROJECTION

	2005	2006	2007	2008 (projected)
INCOME				
Net Sales	$138,899	$173,624	$217,030	$271,287
Cost of sales	69,450	83,339	99,834	135,644
Gross profit	$69,449	$90,285	$117,196	$135,643
OPERATING EXPENSES				
General and Administrative Expenses				
Salaries and wages	$13,890	$17,362	$21,703	$27,129
Sales commissions	6,945	8,681	10,851	13,564
Rent	5,400	5,670	5,954	11,252
Maintenance	1,389	1,458	1,531	2,89
Equipment rental	2,452	2,575	2,703	5,109
Furniture and equipment purchase	3,232	3,394	3,563	6,735
Insurance	1,207	1,267	1,331	1,99
Interest expenses	3,008	3,158	3,316	6,268
Utilities	1,250	1,563	1,953	3,692
Office supplies	776	750	899	977
Marketing and advertising	6,256	6,805	7,150	9,204
Travel	550	750	1,000	1,000
Entertainment	323	301	426	555
Bad debt	139	174	217	323
Depreciation and amortization	1,800	2,700	4,050	6,075
TOTAL OPERATING EXPENSES	$48,617	$56,608	$66,647	$96,776
Net income before taxes	20,832	33,677	50,549	38,867
Provision for taxes on income	3,125	5,051	7,582	5,830
NET INCOME AFTER TAXES	$17,707	$28,626	$42,967	$33,037

Plan Pitfall

Pro forma and projected financial statements are based on the future and, as such, are imprecise. You need to make them as realistic and reasonable as possible but not believe in them too explicitly. Be extra-sure not to overstate revenue or understate expenses.

Figure 12-5. Sample Projected Income Statement

The Most Important Financial Statement

If you have only one financial statement to manage your business by—and to use in your business plan—let it be the cash flow pro forma. Only the cash flow pro forma can tell you how much capital you will need in a startup (add the startup costs, project the cash flow, then make the cash flow positive by providing capital in the indicated amount). Only the cash flow pro forma will tell you when you will need to borrow money—and how much you will need to borrow. Only the cash flow pro forma will tell you when it is time to pull the plug and bail out before you create negative value in your business.

Used as a budget, your cash flow pro forma will keep you from making spontaneous purchases, help evaluate the cost (in cash flow) of growth, hiring new people, adding facilities or equipment, or taking on more debt.

No business can prosper without a cash flow pro forma.

Plan Pointer

THIS WAY

When making forecasts, it's useful to change dollar amounts into percentages. So if you figure sales will rise 20 percent next year, you'll enter 120 percent on the top line of the projection. Using percentages helps highlight overly optimistic sales projections and suggest areas, especially in costs, for improvement.

flow projections for a year ahead, or even two. Any business would do well to project quarterly cash flow for three years ahead.

In Figure 12–6 balance sheet projects variable expenses and liabilities by taking each item's percentage of the previous year's sales and multiplying that by the estimated sales for the coming year. This generates numbers for all but long-term debt, which the owner knows will rise slightly, and other noncurrent debt, consisting of a note to the owner.

The added detail makes monthly cash flow forecasts somewhat more complicated than figuring annual cash flow because revenues and expenses should be recorded when cash actually changes hands. Sales and cost of goods sold should be allotted to the months in which they can be expected to actually occur. Other variable expenses can be allocated as percentages of sales for the month. Expenses paid other than monthly, such as insurance and estimated taxes, are recorded when they occur.

As with the balance sheet projection, one way to project cash flow is to figure out what percentage of sales historically occurs in each month. Then you can use your overall sales forecast for the year to generate monthly estimates. If you don't have prior history, you'll need to produce estimates of such things as profit margins, expenses, and financing activities, using your best guesses of how things will turn out.

The cash flow pro forma also takes into account sources of cash other than sales, such as proceeds from loans and investments by owners.

Sample Projected Balance Sheet

		2004	% Sales	2005 (projected)
	Sales	**$87,740**		**$110,000**
ASSETS				
Cash		$4,387	5.0%	$5,500
Accounts Receivable		12,385	14.1%	15,510
Inventory		1,254	1.4%	1,540
Other Current Assets		986	1.1%	1,210
Total Current Assets		$19,012	21.7%	$23,870
Fixed Assets		27,358	31.2%	34,320
Intangibles		500	0.6%	660
Other Noncurrent Assets		0	0.0%	0
Total Assets		**$46,870**		**$58,850**
LIABILITIES				
Notes Payable		$11,388	13.0%	$14,300
Accounts Payable		2,379	2.7%	2,970
Interest Payable		1,125	1.3%	1,430
Taxes Payable		3,684	4.2%	4,620
Other Current Liabilities		986	1.1%	1,210
Total Current Liabilities		$19,562		$24,530
Long-Term Debt		4,896		5,200
Other Noncurrent Liabilities		1,156		1,156
Total Liabilities		**$25,614**		**$30,866**
Net Worth		**$21,256**		**$27,984**
Total Liabilities & Net Worth		**$46,870**		**$58,850**

Figure 12-6. Sample Projected Balance Sheet

Sample Cash Flow Pro Forma: Monthly Sales Percentages

Month	% of Sales
Jan.	5.0%
Feb.	6.1%
Mar.	7.5%
Apr.	10.5%
May	11.9%
Jun.	13.8%
Jul.	12.2%
Aug.	9.0%
Sep.	7.6%
Oct.	5.5%
Nov.	4.8%
Dec.	6.2%

Figure 12-7. Sample Cash Flow Pro Forma: MonthlySales Percentages

Figure 12–7 is a cash flow pro forma for The Boardroom, a sailboard rental shop. The forecast begins by calculating what percentage of sales occurs in each month. Note that the percentages do not add up to exactly 100 because of rounding. This is still adequately accurate for your purposes. The sales by month portray a tolerably seasonal business, with close to half the annual sales occurring in the late spring and summer months. All the sales are for cash.

Translating these monthly percentages of sales to the cash flow projection provides you with beginning figures. The rest of the figures, for the most part, flow from these sales forecasts, as in Figure 12–8.

Notice that there are two nonsales sources of cash: $7,500 in proceeds from a bank loan and $10,000 in a loan from the owner. At the end of the year, after steady payments of interest on the bank loan, the principal is paid in a balloon payment. The loan proceeds are used at the beginning of the year to purchase a new mobile surfboard display stand. Additional personnel are trained during this period to be ready when the busy season starts up. Another equipment purchase occurs just as the busy season gets under way.

The forecast for The Boardroom shows a company that will wind the year up in a strong cash position. It will probably be able to not only pay its

Sample Cash Flow Forecast
Projected Cash Flow: 2005

	Jan.	Feb.	Mar.	Apr.	May	Jun.	Jul.	Aug.	Sep.	Oct.	Nov.	Dec.	TOTAL
CASH RECEIPTS													
Income from Sales													
Cash Sales	$6,550	$7,991	$9,825	$13,755	$15,589	$18,078	$15,982	$11,790	$9,956	$7,205	$6,288	$8,122	$131,131
Total Cash from Sales	6,550	7,991	9,825	13,755	15,589	18,078	15,982	11,790	9,956	7,205	6,288	8,122	$131,131
Income from Financing													
Loan Proceeds	5,000	0	0	2,500	0	0	0	0	0	0	0	0	$7,500
Other Cash Receipts	10,000	0	0	0	0	0	0	0	0	0	0	0	$10,000
Total Cash Receipts	21,550	7,991	9,825	16,255	15,589	18,078	15,982	11,790	9,956	7,205	6,288	8,122	148,631
CASH DISBURSEMENTS													
Expenses													
COGS	2,948	3,596	4,421	6,190	7,015	8,135	7,192	5,306	4,480	3,242	2,830	3,655	$59,010
SG&A	11,555	2,507	3,083	4,316	4,891	5,672	5,014	3,699	3,124	2,261	1,973	2,548	$50,643
Interest	0	80	80	80	80	80	80	80	80	80	80	80	$880
Taxes	0	0	0	1,500	0	1,500	0	0	1,500	0	0	0	$4,500
Equipment Purchase	5,000	0	0	5,000	0	0	0	0	0	0	0	0	$10,000
Debt Principal Payments	0	0	0	0	0	0	0	0	0	0	0	7,500	$7,500
Dividends	0	0	0	0	0	0	0	0	0	0	0	0	$0
Total Cash Disbursements	19,503	6,183	7,584	17,086	11,986	15,387	12,286	9,085	9,184	5,583	4,883	13,783	$132,533
Net Cash Flow	2,047	1,808	2,241	-831	3,603	2,691	3,696	2,705	772	1,622	1,405	-5,661	$16,098
Opening Cash Balance	0	2,047	3,855	6,096	5,265	8,868	11,559	15,255	17,960	18,732	20,354	21,759	$0
Cash Receipts	21,550	7,991	9,825	16,255	15,589	18,078	15,982	11,790	9,956	7,205	6,288	8,122	$148,631
Cash Disbursements	-19,503	-6,183	-7,584	-17,086	-11,986	-15,387	-12,286	-9,085	-9,184	-5,583	-4,883	-13,783	($132,533)
Ending Cash Balance	$2,047	$3,855	$6,096	$5,265	$8,868	$11,559	$15,255	$17,960	$18,732	$20,354	$21,759	$16,098	$16,098

Figure 12-8. Sample Cash Flow Forecast

181

The Unreal Thing

If you're having trouble envisioning how you could run out of cash while experiencing strong and profitable sales growth, take a peek at the iThink business-simulation software from High Performance Systems. It runs on your PC and uses just six variables to give you a new appreciation for the importance of cash.

You're a start-up business owner. You have $30,000 and access to lenders if you need it. You can set your selling prices, hire and lay off workers, and order raw materials. Competitors will affect the outcome of some decisions.

You have only two years of simulated time while making money and capturing significant market share. Easy? Sure, once you figure out the interlocking variables. For instance, you can lower prices to boost sales—until back orders pile up and poor service drives away business. Raise prices to slow sales, and competitors jump in.

High Performance's simulation isn't quite like being there. But it will give you a feel for the real thing. For more information, contact High Performance Systems Inc. at 46 Centerra Parkway, Suite 200, Lebanon, NH 03766, (603) 643-9636, www.hps-inc.com.

bills but also to finance further growth internally. The financial vital signs in the cash flow statement show a patient that is alive and well.

☆ EXPERT ADVICE ☆

Some key points about cash flow:

Positive cash flow = Survival

Cash flow buys time (if necessary), builds assets and profits, and keeps suppliers, bankers, creditors, and investors smiling. Without positive cash flow, survival becomes questionable. Negative or feebly positive cash flow is painful, and unless corrected will either kill a business or damage it so seriously that it never lives up to its potential. Although short periods of negative cash flow occur in almost every business, cash flows have to be positive at least on an annual basis. Some farmers do very well indeed with cash flows that are strongly negative for 11 months of the year. So do some manufacturers (especially in the garment trade). The key is that they know what their cash flow patterns are—and take steps to finance the negative periods, offsetting that cost against the occasional strong positive cash influx from operations.

Unfortunately, the smaller and more thinly capitalized the company, the less able it is to survive extended negative cash flows. This is one reason why so many start-ups fail. The business idea may be terrific, but sales always come much more slowly than expected while cash goes out twice as fast. And the initial investment is rarely enough to tide the business along until cash flow turns and stays positive.

How can a small business attain positive cash flow? Discipline. A cash flow budget is an unbeatable tool if followed carefully. If there is to be just one financial statement, make sure it's the cash flow pro forma. It acts at once as a cash flow budget and as a benchmark for sales.

Some people have trouble differentiating the cash flow pro forma from the projected P&L. The concept "profit" is so pervasive that it poses a barrier to understanding that positive cash flow does not equal profit (or vice versa). The example of a profitable growing company with negative cash flow succumbing to illiquidity and tumbling into Chapter 11 bankruptcy is commonly cited to disprove the identity. If the sales don't turn to cash soon enough, the company goes broke. Revenues are up, receivables are up, expenses are up, even profits are up. Yet the company runs out of cash, can't pay its bills, and becomes another cash flow victim.

Another conceptual problem is equating P&L losses with negative cash flow. A loss on the P&L can reflect a negative cash flow, but it doesn't have to. For example, publishing companies enjoy some accounting foibles such as deferred income (which suppresses sales by deferring revenues to a later period). The cash comes in December, but because the revenue is not earned until the following year, the company can show a nice loss for tax purposes, while enjoying strongly positive cash flow.

Some ways to understand cash flow (as distinct from P&L categories) include:

▶ *Students are adept at managing skinny cash flows.* They postpone bill paying, share space to lower costs, use secondhand books whenever possible (if they have to pay the bill, that is), minimize food costs, and so forth. Few of them think of this as cash flow management, but it is— and of a very high order. If they want a ticket to a concert or ball game, they find a way to scrape up the cash. Very few companies are as carefully managed.

▶ *Emphasize timing.* Timing is everything for cash flow. The transfers of cash, even the dates bills fall due or discounts can or cannot be taken. Although timing is always important in business, it is especially important in managing cash flow. A P&L can stand a bit of looseness—it doesn't matter whether a bill is received January 31 or February 10. That ten days can make a big difference in cash flow if the bill falls due before you have the cash in hand to pay it.

▶ *Compare cash flow to a checking account.* Cash is deposited (cash inflow). Checks are written (cash outflow). The aim is to always have some cash on hand (positive cash flow).

▶ *For the literate, recall Micawber's definition of happiness: "Income of £20.00.00, expenses of £19.19.19.* Result: happiness. Expenses of £20.00.01. Result: misery." Dickens was right; he understood cash flow. Cash flow deals with the ebb and flow of cash. If the flow is positive, good. If negative, do something to change it.

The cash flow pro forma is the most important single financial statement in the business plan. Every business needs an annotated cash flow pro forma (by month for the first year, by quarter thereafter) reflecting its business idea.

Section Three

Enhancing Your Business Plan

Chapter 13

Enlightening Extras:
Appendices

A BUSINESS PLAN IS A STORY, THE NARRATIVE OF YOUR ENTERPRISE, and you want to maintain a certain amount of flow as you lead readers from concept to management, through marketing, and on to financials. Some material that you'd probably like to fit into your plan somewhere just doesn't fit well into any of those sections. For instance, you may want to include resumes of some of your management team, product samples, product photos, advertising samples, press clippings, facility photos, or site plans.

For these and other items that the plan writer wants in the plan but that don't seem to belong anywhere, many plans include appendices and attachments. This is material that is optional and that many plan readers may not need to refer to. However, for those readers who want to delve deeper into the workings of the company, appendices provide additional answers.

Key Employee Resumes

The management section of your business plan will contain a listing and brief descriptions of the senior managers and other key employees on your

Make No Mistake

Here are five resume mistakes (and exceptions):

1. *Too long.* Most resumes should be one page. After ten years, go to two pages. Exception: Health care, academic, and scientific curricula vitae may run many pages and cover virtually every paper published or seminar attended by the subject.

2. *Too individualistic.* A resume is generally conservative in tone, appearance, and content. You don't want to use a wild typeface or an odd format, or include highly personal information such as the fact that you had no date to the senior prom. Exception: People in creative fields such as advertising or entertainment can let it all hang out.

3. *Too boring.* A resume should be more than a leaden list of job titles and dates of employment. You should stress what you learned while working at each position (or, in the case of serial entrepreneurs, each prior company you founded). Exception: If you organize your resume with a separate section where you detail all your skills and accomplishments, it's appropriate to briefly list jobs below.

4. *Inconsistent or error-filled.* If you say you have experience with software marketing but then fail to describe a prior position with that responsibility, it's going to look odd. The same holds true if you misspell a former employer's company name or make an obvious error in dates of employment. Exception: None.

5. *Too detailed.* Overly technical jargon, complicated descriptions of responsibilities in prior jobs, and irrelevant information such as the street address of a prior employer are only going to throw resume readers off the track you want them on. Limit the information to what's relevant, and don't try to impress anyone with your mastery of minutiae. Exception: If you're in a highly technical field, judicious use of insider expressions can help convince a skeptic that you are as knowledgeable as you claim to be.

team. However, many investors and lenders are going to want to know more about you and your important associates than you give them in this section. For that purpose, you can include full resumes in an appendix.

Product Samples

If your products are portable enough, you may be able to include samples in your appendix. Some examples of products that are suitable for inclusion in a plan are fabric swatches, stationery samples, printing samples, software screenshots, or even floppy disks.

It's important not to overdo it with product samples. Investors tend to regard many entrepreneurs as being somewhat more product-focused than operations or marketing minded. By all means, provide samples if it's feasible and helpful. But don't expect appealing samples to overcome deficiencies in the concept, management, marketing, operations, or financing schemes presented in your plan.

Product Photos

Appendices are good places to include photographs of products whose appearances are important or whose features are difficult to explain in words. It's normal and acceptable to include line drawings of products in the main sections of your plan. But again, most investors are more interested in such items as your balance sheet, management experience, and cash flow projections than they are in glossy product photos.

Advertising Samples

It may be advisable to include examples of the advertising you intend to use to market your products or services. For many companies, innovative and persuasive advertising approaches are essential to the success of the firm. Without actual examples of the ads, it may be difficult for readers to grasp the appeal and power of your marketing ideas.

Copies of newspaper and magazine ads, photos of billboards, still photos from TV spots, web site banner ads, and transcripts of radio spots are all acceptable. However, keep in mind that this information is optional. If you have an unimpressive advertising campaign, it won't help you to expose investors to the fact.

Press Clippings

Reviews and articles in influential publications and broadcast shows drive many product sales. If your new software program got rave reviews in a major computer magazine, by all means include it here. Readers knowledgeable about the industry will recognize the value that such intangible assets as favorable press notice can provide.

Plan Pointer THIS WAY

Don't draw the line at two dimensions when considering illustrations of products and other key features of your plan. Three-dimensional models, mock-ups, and prototypes let investors get a hands-on feel for what you're proposing. If you've prepared a 3-D sample or model, you can use it to give your plan a high degree of physical reality.

Generating favorable publicity is one of the more valuable things you can do for your business. To learn how to do it on your own, consult one of the many excellent manuals that have been written on the topic.

You may also want to include complimentary ratings, certifications, or other endorsements by entities such as travel guides, associations, and watchdog groups. If your hotel got an impressive number of stars from the Mobil or Michelin guides, you'll probably want to mention it more prominently in your plan, such as in your main marketing or concept sections. And it might not be a bad idea to include a copy of the actual certificate bearing the seal.

Other Appendix Contents

There is no one correct or comprehensive list of what you should include in your appendices. Your business, your intended use of the plan, your audience will all affect what you want to put in. Photos of a building or a sketch of a proposed development might appeal to a real estate investor. Investors in a software company won't be excited by a picture of a jewel box or a happy customer but may be interested in a flowchart. Keep your audience in mind. Ask yourself what additional information they might like you to include. Then provide it.

Facility Photos

Few real estate investors will buy a property without firsthand knowledge of its appearance, state of repair, and general impression. When an investor is being asked to put money into your company, perhaps in exchange for partial ownership of your plan or, often, for the specific purpose of purchasing a building, it's a good idea to calm any concerns about the facility's condition by providing a few photos.

Make sure any facility photos you provide are more informative than glitzy. Skip over the sculpture at the entrance in favor of an outside shot illustrating that the property is in overall good repair.

Site Plans

You may want to include basic factory layouts and store floor plans in the operations section of your plan. If your site plan is complex and you feel some readers would benefit from seeing some of the additional details, provide them here rather than cluttering up the main part of the plan with them.

Plan of Action

Jay Conrad Levinson's low-cost marketing manuals, beginning with Guerrilla Marketing *(Houghton Mifflin) in 1985, and continuing with books focusing on topics from online marketing to marketing homebased businesses, provide countless tips for generating and capitalizing on publicity.*

If you have a number of store locations with varying layouts, for instance, you could give an idea of how several of them look.

Credit Reports

Credit reports could be included in the financial statements section of your plan. However, because bankers are the main ones who will be interested in credit reports, you may want to place them in a separate appendix to make it easier to customize your plan.

Leases

The devil is in the details when it comes to leases. It's not appropriate to discuss every last clause of even an important lease in the main section of your plan. However, there's a chance that diligent readers will have questions about any especially significant leases that can only be answered by reading the actual documents. For these discriminating plan readers, you can include the actual leases, or at least the more important sections.

Customer Contracts

Few things are better to include in a plan than a long-term contract to supply an established customer. If you're lucky enough to have such a powerfully appealing deal in your pocket, you'll surely want to refer to it early on in your plan.

Like leases, however, the value of a contract may lie in its details. So it might be a good idea to include copies of relevant sections of any really significant contracts as appendices. If the deal is as good as you think (it had better be—otherwise, you wouldn't highlight it in your plan), then exposing potential investors to the beneficial details can only do you good.

There's no hard-and-fast rule about the overall length of a plan. Most new-venture plans should be under 20 pages. And though plans for complicated enterprises can legitimately run much longer, it's probably a good idea to exercise restraint when it comes to packing things into an appendix. Recall the idea of diminishing returns, and make sure that anything you put in your plan contributes significantly to presenting a clear, compelling picture of your business.

> **Plan Pointer**
>
> THIS WAY
>
> *If you don't have an eye-popping contract with a marquee client, but you have a lot of lesser arrangements with more or less impressive customers, use the laundry list approach. Many plans effectively devote a page or so to a dense roster of all existing clients, conveying a positive impression of having a robust customer base.*

⋆ EXPERT ADVICE ⋆

Sometimes the most interesting insights into a proposed investment come from the supporting documents. Most business plan writers know enough about the way bankers and investors read plans to provide marketing, management and financial information. A few go further and use the appendices to provide extra pieces of information that just don't fit into the main text.

Resumes are obviously important. Financial and credit information on the business and its principals, especially for a very small venture, can make a difference in the investment decision.

Here are a few suggestions:

▶ Quotes and estimates from suppliers of goods and services

▶ Letters of intent from qualified prospects

▶ Letters of support (or names and addresses) of references

▶ Census and other marketing information that is more general than the specifics included in the plan itself

▶ Economic data and predictions that might impact the business

▶ Leases and other legal documents relevant to the business

▶ Marketing materials such as brochures, advertisements, fliers, and so on

▶ Customer and prospect surveys

▶ Flow charts (work flow, distribution)

Ask yourself what other information your prospective investors might wish to see. The easier you make it for them the better. Their time is valuable. You can't do their due diligence for them, but they will appreciate your helping them by providing the sources of your information and the grounds of your assumptions.

Chapter 14

You Only Make a First Impression Once

I
T DOES NOT MATTER HOW COMPELLING YOUR STORY IS IF THE READER STARTS with a negative impression. A shopworn plan reeks of failure from the git-go. Make sure that the cosmetics are right: clean paper, crisp type, clear pictures and a professional (non-colloquial) presentation go a long way towards securing a fair reading or hearing of your business plan.

As always keep your audience in mind. Don't squander your money on leather bindings or professional printing without a compelling reason. Businesslike is almost always best as a fallback decision on how to make a good first impression.

Cover Letters

A cover letter is a brief missive introducing your plan to the person you have sent it to. In some cases it may never be read; in others it may be the only part of your plan that is read. But in any event, it serves several important functions.

First, the cover letter serves as an introduction to the plan. It should briefly explain why you've contacted this person—basically, to get him to

Plan Pointer

THIS WAY

Remove "To Whom It May Concern" from your vocabulary. Program your computer to explode if this phrase is typed into it. Never address a plan cover letter to something as vague as "Loan Department." Strive to get the name of an actual person whom you can identify as a "Mr." or "Ms." and use the proper honorific. If this person is not the right one, he or she will forward the plan to the right person. "To Whom It May Concern" is off-putting. Don't use it.

look at your plan. You should also explain generally what you're looking for—an investor, a loan, a long-term supplier relationship. Often this will be obvious from the circumstances. A banker, for instance, is going to recognize a business plan package immediately and guess why he's received it. But if there's any question, the cover letter is the place to resolve it.

The cover letter provides a valuable forum for you to explain why you're contacting this particular person. If you've received a personal referral, you'll want to say who gave you the referral very early on, probably in the first sentence following the salutation. Never underestimate the power of a personal referral from a friend, colleague, or acquaintance of the person you're writing to. It may not land you an investor, but it gets your foot in the door.

You may have some personal connection to the person other than a referral. For instance, perhaps you once met the person. Perhaps you even worked together at a company or organization. A shared interest, such as a hobby, is of less value, but it may be worth mentioning if your shared interest is unusual or marked by a close degree of identification among those who share it. For instance, it may not mean much to point out that you, like the reader, are a fan of professional basketball. However, if you both have competed as crew members on long-distance ocean racing sailboats, this might be worth mentioning. In any case, the cover letter, not the plan, is obviously the place to bring up this type of personal connection.

Finally, the cover letter may detail the terms under which you are presenting your plan. You may, for instance, say that you are not submitting the plan to any other investor. You may explicitly point out that you are currently seeking financing from a number of sources, including this one. If there is a deadline for responding to your plan, if you wish to stress that the plan is confidential and must be returned to you, or if you would like to ask the recipient to pass it on to someone else who may be interested, this is the place to do so.

The cover letter is also an opportunity to expand upon any concerns that you didn't include in your plan. Perhaps a late-breaking development, such as the hiring of a new key employee, occurred too late to be included in the finished plan. Or perhaps you have come across a brand-new market research report that validates some of the assumptions you made in your marketing section. The cover letter gives you a chance to provide updated, expanded, or other important information that isn't in your plan. See Figure 14–1.

Sample Cover Letter

Leonard Mineo
Mineo Capital
123 Bankston Blvd., Ste. 100
Tulsa, OK 74138

Dear Mr. Mineo:

Alf Walton suggested I write to you to alert you to the opportunity to invest in a new enterprise I am starting up.

The enclosed business plan details the strategy and concept behind Pairing Off, the new internet dating service I am beginning. Initial reception to the plan among focus group members, industry experts, and prospective suppliers has been excellent. We are now at the point when it is appropriate to seek additional equity investors.

Recently, I've become even more enthused about the prospects for Pairing Off. Some hot-off-the-press trend reports say that internet use is growing even faster than we projected in our plan. And personal recreation, including finding relationship partners, is one of the fastest-growing areas of use.

We've also had excellent recent success in attracting talented new members to our team. Among others, we've recently hired a dynamic programmer from one of the leading companies in the internet commerce field. Additionally, we have signed a long-term deal with Laura Manchaca, whose "Home by Midnight" syndicated column of dating advice for teenagers appears in more than 200 newspapers.

In closing, I'm very pleased to offer you the opportunity to come on board with Pairing Off. I can be reached at my office during most times. Please feel free to call me on my cell phone, (918) 555-5555, at any time. I look forward to hearing from you.

Sincerely,

Eduardo Aleman

Figure 14-1. Sample Cover Letter

Cover Sheets

The first thing anyone looking at your business plan will see is the cover page. After that, they may never look at it again. But the fact is your plan's cover page will contribute strongly to the first impression you make. Take care in how you present it, and make sure it fits with the overall image you want to portray.

A few cover-page components are essential. You should definitely have your company name, address, phone number, and other contact information. Another good item to include is the date, as well as perhaps a notice that this is, indeed, a business plan. Format this information in large, black, easily readable type, and place it toward the top of the page. You want, above all else, for a plan reader to know which business this plan is for and how to contact you.

If you have a striking, well-designed corporate logo, it's also a good idea to include that on the cover page. A corporate slogan, as long as it's not too long, is also a good identifying mark that does something to communicate your strategy as well.

Some plans include a confidentiality notice or nondisclosure request on the cover page. For your own tracking purposes, if your plan contains highly sensitive information, you may want to number the copies of your plans and include the number of this copy on the cover page.

It's tempting to put all kinds of stuff on the cover page, but you should probably resist it. Your business concept, the amount you're trying to raise, and other details can go on the inside. The cover page must identify the company. More than that is likely to be too much.

You wouldn't show up for a meeting with an investor wearing the clothes you normally wear for cleaning out the warehouse. Don't send your business plan out improperly clothed, either. You spend a lot of time and energy on your plan. It would be a shame to have it marred by spelling, typographical errors, and a poor general appearance.

Stationery, Printing, and Design

A three-ring binder is the ideal container for a business plan you're using only for internal management purposes. You'll find it easy to remove and replace pages with updated figures. And the plan will lie flat on a conference table for easy reference when you're discussing strategy, forecasts, and other issues with your team.

However, you'll want to use something different for sending out to bankers or other investors. The most common approach is to copy the plan onto good-quality white paper, using both sides of the paper, then bind pages together permanently into a booklet. Any copy shop or printer can do such a binding for you, or you may purchase a do it yourself binding kit at an office supply store. Cover your plan with a clear plastic binder so that the cover page shows, or print your cover page information on a heavy piece of paper to serve as a cover for the binder.

Permanent binding helps plan readers keep all the pages of your plan together and makes it easier to read. It's important to keep these reasons for permanent binding in mind—it's a decision that improves the functionality of the plan, not its looks. Spending a lot of money creating a beautiful, perfectly bound plan is not a wise investment. Plan readers are interested in information, not entertainment.

The same thing goes for choosing the paper and typeface you'll use in your plan. Pick white paper, or at most perhaps gray, cream, or some shade of off-white, but leave the colored paper to fliers from the pizza place down the street. To make a businesslike impression, use businesslike stationery.

Your general guide to selecting paper is the fact that investors tend to be conservative. Don't be less conservative than they are if you want to win a hearing.

Plan Pitfall

It's easy to go wild with fonts these days. Every computer comes with dozens of more-or-less standard fonts, and you can get on the Internet and download almost any number of crazy, unique software type-faces. But don't do it. Stick to a standard—Courier or Times Roman on a Windows PC, Palatino or another standard on a Macintosh.

Charts, Graphs, and Tables

Graphs and charts are invaluable tools for conveying certain types of information. Common visuals in business plans include organizational charts, product illustrations, sales trends, break-even points, market trends, competitor market shares, and the like. If you are including such information in your plan, consider using graphs or charts to help get the message across.

Many computer software programs, including general-purpose spreadsheet applications and word processors, can be used to construct serviceable charts. Be sure to use a good-quality printer to create the charts. Often small type is unreadable on a chart that has to be compressed to fit on a page and is then output from a low-quality printer. This type of chart isn't going to help your case.

Not all plan readers are comfortable with charts, just as not all are comfortable with endless columns of numbers. So use charts and graphs to supplement, not replace, information presented in text or report form. A visual is a way to emphasize and ease the communication of detailed material, but it can't replace the actual detail.

197

Multimedia Presentations

Some plans have to be more than paper. If your plan is going to be presented at a venture capital conference, before a company planning meeting, to a conclave of potential suppliers, at an industry conference, or in a similar group setting, you'll need slides instead of simple sheets of paper. Be prepared to talk attendees through the plan instead of relying on them to navigate it on their own.

You can use a variety of presentation programs to quickly generate slides or transparencies suitable for an overhead projector, sometimes with nothing more than the outline or text of your original plan. Remember to keep the amount of information presented on each page of a multimedia presentation brief and to give people time to read and absorb it before moving on to the next page of your presentation.

A word to the wise: If you plan on a multimedia presentation, rehearse, rehearse, and rehearse again—and have a seamless transference to a simpler presentation just in case your computer, slide projector, or other high-tech tool fails.

You'll also have to choose carefully what and when to present details culled from your full-length plan. One reason for the need for careful editing is the fact that a presentation plan is a lot shorter than a printed plan. People aren't going to sit while you read through 30 pages of text. Nor can they control the pace or direction of a presentation the way they can in a written plan they peruse on their own. You'll have to ask yourself such questions as: Will this group be more interested in the marketing or financial aspects of the plan? and present accordingly.

Fact or Fiction?

If a plan is used for internal purposes only, it doesn't matter what it looks like as long as it's functional, right? That's true to some extent, but it's also true that part of a plan's functionality is to convince and persuade. A plan that looks shabby and casually thrown together won't command as much respect among other managers and employees as one that's polished and professional looking.

✶ EXPERT ADVICE ✶

Some people have lots of success in presenting business plans, and some people have less. But nobody is always successful. Even a talented entrepreneur with a long track record of starting up winners will run up against an investor who doesn't want to play. Investors may not be interested in your particular industry, may not have any funds to invest at the moment, may need a larger or smaller amount to invest, or may have any of a hundred other reasons for turning you down.

As an example, your bank may be "loaned up" in your industry. If your proposal for a restaurant is turned down, it may be because your bank

Presenting—Your Business Plan!

Once you've prepared your plan for presentation, put it in front of the right people. There are five steps:

1. *Obtain leads and referrals.* Find names, addresses, and telephone numbers of investors of the type you wish to target. Ask people you know for referrals.
2. *Research your target.* Learn as much as possible about how much money people have to invest, industries they're interested in, and other requirements. Search venture capital directories, Who's Who, news articles, and similar sources.
3. *Make your pitch.* First, mail or messenger your plan to the target. Assuming you don't hear immediately, follow up with a letter or telephone call in a few weeks. If this doesn't produce a meeting, look elsewhere.
4. *Defuse objections.* Although you may think you've answered everything in your plan, you haven't. Prepare a list of possible objections—potential competitors, hard-to-buttress assumptions, etc.—that your investor may raise. Then prepare cogent answers.
5. *Get a commitment.* You won't get an investment unless you ask for it. When all objections have been answered, be ready to offer one last concession—"If I give your representative a board seat, can we do this today?"—and go for the close.

Plan Pointer

Use as many charts, tables, and other graphic elements as it takes to get your point across. But don't count on lavish visuals to sway a skeptical reader. Some readers actually are put off by plans that seem to be trying to wow them with presentation.

already has sufficient exposure in the hospitality sector. If so, ask your banker to refer you to another interested lender.

So the question is not: Will you get turned down? The question is: What do you do when it happens?

The first thing you should do is try to find out why, really, you got the thumbs-down. Is it truly because the person is out of the country, or is it something else?

Your purpose is not to uncover someone's evasion or white lie. An investor has the right to turn you down for any reason whatsoever (unless, of course, you're dealing with an institution such as a bank that must abide by equal opportunity lending guidelines). Instead of pointing fingers at the investors, you should really be interested in pointing fingers at your plan.

If there is a problem with your plan, you want to know about it. If the projected return to investors is so low that nobody is going to take you seriously, now's the time to find out, not after you've presented it unsuccessfully dozens of times.

So gently probe, asking questions that focus on your plan, to find out whether you've made a mistake or just hit an unreceptive audience. If you identify a failing, of course, fix it before submitting your plan to another party.

Plan of Action

The standard software for presentations these days is PowerPoint from Microsoft. It's included in most versions of the Microsoft Office suite and is available as a standalone package as well. For more information, visit Microsoft's web site at www. microsoft.com.

Get a Referral

Even a total refusal to consider your plan is helpful if the person suggests another place where you might be successful. You should always ask for a referral from anyone who turns your proposal down. It can't hurt—you've already been nixed. And a referral from a knowledgeable, respected investor can carry a lot of weight when you use it as an introduction (even if he or she is just trying to get rid of you.)

Venture investing is very much a network-driven business. Venture capitalists are always asking for referrals, and they're usually willing to give them as well.

Keep the Door Open

Leigh Steinberg, the well-known sports agent who has negotiated more than $2 billion worth of contracts for star athletes, says you should always keep in mind that one negotiation leads to the next. Keep that next negotiation in mind while working toward and planning for the one at hand. What that means in a business plan context is don't burn any bridges.

If an investor doesn't respond to your plan, brushes you off, or even rudely tells you to get lost, your response should still be unfailingly courteous and professional. If you let your frustration, disappointment, hurt feelings, and anger show, it could cost you plenty. That investor may be having a bad day and change her mind tomorrow. She may recall your name and the way you behaved so well under pressure and mention it to a more open-minded associate the next week. Or perhaps next year, when you're promoting a more exciting concept, she'll be willing to back the improved idea.

None of these scenarios is certain or even probable in any individual instance. But considering the aggregate potential to help or hurt you that all the people you'll present your plan to will possess, any of these scenarios is quite likely. And they're only possible if you keep the door open for the future.

Chapter 15

Information Creates Capital

MUCH OF THE BUSINESS-PLANNING PROCESS INVOLVES RESEARCH and communication—research about your product, its market, financial resources, your customers, and your competition along with communication with others in your line of work: industry experts, suppliers, and prospective customers. That's why the internet is an invaluable tool for small business owners. Whether you're writing a business plan for a new business or for one that's already established, the internet is a goldmine of information, as well as an indispensable link to future customers, investors, and market opportunities.

Market Research

Thanks to the internet, market research for business-planning purposes has become much easier and less time consuming. For example, by logging on to the U.S. Census Bureau web site (www.census.gov), you can learn everything you need about population trends in your market, which helps you determine market share—a key piece of information in any business plan. Using your web site or e-mail, you can set up an online focus group to get a handle on what prospective customers want from a product or service like yours, how they'd use it, where they'd like to buy it, and how often they'd purchase it. This kind of information will help you establish pricing, distribution, and promotional strategies.

You can garner a wealth of valuable information via the web on your competitors—and on businesses similar to yours operating in other markets. Visit these companies' web sites to see what their product/service lines are, what their "unique selling propositions" are, who their target markets are and what media are used to reach them, what their prices are, and where and how their product is distributed. If their web sites have a section called "News" or "Upcoming Events," you can learn about their plans for future marketing efforts and determine how they'll affect your business.

E-mail is a convenient and inexpensive way to stay connected to colleagues who own businesses like yours in other markets. You can build and maintain a network of other business owners, to whom you can field questions or from whom you can solicit advice.

You can garner a wealth of valuable information via the web on your competitors—and on businesses similar to yours operating in other markets.

Trade Associations: Key Source of Targeted Information

Trade associations are an excellent source of specific trade and industry information. Suppose you are an artisan specializing in concrete countertops and related items. Is there a trade association? Sure, see www.concretenetwork .com/newsletter.htm for specialized information.

Because there are over 30,000 trade associations in the United States, you will be hard-pressed not to find one that will include your business. Most have periodicals—magazines or newsletters—whose editor are eager to justify their positions by providing the membership with up-to-date information of all kinds. You can call the editor direct (they like to hear from members) or send him or her an e-mail with your particular questions.

Trade associations often sponsor trade shows, which can help you get information on suppliers, industry trends, consultants, and even seminars directly related to your business. The people you meet and the informal exchange of knowledge that results provide the greatest value: production tips, problem solutions, contacts, and ideas.

General Research

Use the internet to research your industry. Go to your favorite search engine and type in the words "trade association." You'll be amazed at how many are listed. Refine your search by inserting appropriate words like "manufacturing," "retail—clothing," "publishing," "advertising," or whatever is relevant to your business. Check out those trade associations that represent your business, and think seriously about joining one. Trade associations provide lots of information specific to their industries, in addition to publishing reports and newsletters or magazines, and many host trade shows—all boons to your marketing efforts.

By reading publications and reports available online, you can stay current with what's happening in your industry as well as plan for your business's future. *The Wall Street Journal, BusinessWeek, The New York Times, The Economist,* and countless others are only a click away. There you can learn about trends for new products, new manufacturing methods, new technology, and the economic outlook—all important considerations in the business planning process.

By reading publications and reports available online, you can stay current with what's happening in your industry as well as plan for your business's future.

Communication

If your business is already established and you have a web site, use it to solicit valuable feedback from your customers. Stay in touch with them to foster customer loyalty. After a sale is made, ask them whether they're satisfied or if more service is needed. Let them know about upcoming events and specials. Ask them what changes, if any, they'd like to see made in your product or service and how it's delivered.

Use the web and e-mail to get the information you need about vendors and suppliers. Get a list of customers you can e-mail or phone, so you can assess their business relationships before you make any commitments.

Financing

If your business plan will double as a financing proposal, visit the U.S. government's Small Business Administration (SBA) site at www.sba.gov to learn more about the many different types of financing programs available. In addition to financial assistance through guaranteed loans, the SBA also offers counseling services, help in getting government contracts, management assistance through programs like SCORE (Service Corps of Retired Executives), and lots of publications.

The SBA also sponsors the Angel Capital Electronic Network (ACE-Net), a nationwide internet-based listing service that allows angel investors to obtain information on small, growing businesses seeking $250,000 to $5 million in equity financing. You can access ACE-Net at www.sba.gov/services/acenet.html.

Other government organizations also offer financing to small businesses, including the U.S. Department of Agriculture (www.rurdev.usda.gov/rbs/busp), the U.S. Department of Commerce's Export Assistance Centers (www.ita.doc.gov/uscs/domfld/html), and the Department of Energy's Office of Industrial Technologies (www.oit.doe.gov), to name a few.

Computers are very handy when it comes to writing a plan.

To find nongovernment organizations that provide financing to small businesses in your area, visit the Association for Enterprise Opportunity (AEO) at www.microenterpriseworks.org, and ask which programs serve businesses in your area. Your banker and state economic development office can also help.

Software for Writing Business Plans

By the time you've read this book, completed the worksheets, and tried your hand at a few of the various components of a plan, you should be ready to go ahead and complete your own. However, there's always room for improvement, and there are a number of resources you can tap into for the purpose of increasing your expertise in plan writing.

It should be made clear: You don't have to have any particular software or even have access to a computer to write a plan. You can do all the calculations and draft all the text using nothing more than a calculator or even pencil and paper for the figuring and a typewriter for the writing. Until computers came into wide use 15 or 20 years ago, of course, that's the way all plans were done. Yours may look old-fashioned if it comes in with the telltale traits of manual typewriting, but if the information in it is compelling, that may not matter.

Be that as it may, computers are very handy when it comes to writing a plan. Numerous computer programs of various descriptions ease the creation of business plans. They range from word processing software such as WordPerfect to electronic spreadsheet programs such as Excel and even software for tapping into the internet for research and data-gathering jobs. If you plan to present your plan to a group of people, you may want to use a program such as Microsoft PowerPoint to create slides or an electronic version of your plan.

However, these are general-purpose software programs that are only incidentally of use for creating business plans. The Microsoft Excel spreadsheet program may be chock-full of useful formulas you can use for such otherwise tricky tasks as figuring the depreciation of an asset, but it won't help you with business plan-specific questions such as: How should I format the executive summary?

For these questions, you can go to software specially made for writing business plans. Numerous such products exist, and the category has been around for a while.

Business Plan Pro

The Business Plan Pro program from Palo Alto Software is one of the best business plan programs on the market. It's full-featured, helping you write a plan with complete text, financial tables for forecasts and analysis, and even charts for illustrating points graphically.

Business Plan Pro's split-screen interface is one of its most useful features. The two-screen setup splits your display in half, showing one thing, such as instructions, in one window while you see another, such as the material you're entering, in the second window. A click of the mouse takes you from one window to the other. This feature helps you simultaneously view and move easily between different sections of the program.

Business Plan Pro also has a complex set of menu commands to do such jobs as select a chart for display, go to the outline, and print the plan. A number of always-visible buttons helps you navigate between previous and next tasks or steps you've worked on.

Using Business Plan Pro requires you to work in three modes: Text Mode, Table Mode, and Chart Mode. Respectively, they roughly correspond to a word processing, a spreadsheet, and a chart program. However, they're specially set up for making business plans. For instance, the chart program has ready-made charts to show such things as cash flow projections and break-even analyses.

You use the Text Mode in Business Plan Pro to write the words. Before you start typing, however, take a look at the outline, always available by clicking the big Plan Outline button at the bottom of the screen. This is your command center for navigation throughout your plan, as well as for understanding the

Plan Pitfall

Thanks to plan-writing software's built-in financial formulas, you just have to plug in the data. Because you don't enter the formulas yourself, however, you won't have the same understanding of your financial statements as if you had to think about and manually enter them. So if you use plan-writing software, look under the hood and see what is going on inside all those spreadsheets.

BU✕✕WORD

Rich Text Format (RTF) *is a standard word processing format in which most plan-writing software lets you export your work. RTF will convert into almost any word processing program.*

organization of it. The outline, recognizing that not all businesses or business plans are the same, adjusts its topics to whatever type of business you're planning for. For instance, it will include an inventory section for a bicycle manufacturer but not for an architect.

Table Mode is preprogrammed for preformatted financial statements. The tables are linked to one another to help provide consistency in your business analysis. That's something you can do with any decent general-purpose electronic spreadsheet program, but it's nice that it's done for you. It makes it harder to be inconsistent, which is only too likely when you change a number in one table—say, the income projection—but neglect to do the same in another, like the cash flow plan.

Chart Mode plugs you into a set of business charts that are developed from the data entered in your financial statements. This makes it easy to include attractive and informative charts in your plan. And if you change the data, the charts are automatically updated.

Business Plan Pro formats and prints plans with page headings and numbers and various styles for topic headings, table titles, and chart titles. You can print text, tables, and charts individually or do the whole plan all at once. Individually printed tables and charts may be useful for appendices or special presentations.

Business Plan Pro comes with several sample plans, along with an outline that it will automatically customize to fit the needs of the type of business you specify. Business Plan Pro comes in versions for Windows and Macintosh. Visit Palo Alto Software's Web site at www.pasware.com or call (800) 229-7526 to order.

Plan Pointer

THIS WAY

Built-in spreadsheet templates in plan-writing software ease the task of computing financials considerably. They come with preprogrammed formulas and are often linked so you only have to enter information once to have it appear in several places—a real time-saver.

BizPlanBuilder

Jian Software's BizPlanBuilder is consistently one of the top-rated business planning software packages. Reviewers give it high marks for being easy to use and flexible. Two of its distinguishing characteristics are the question-and-answer process, which you use to enter information about your company, and an interactive document creator that leads you through the writing and organization of your plan. These are powerful aids if you are building a plan from scratch.

You don't have to start at square one, however. BizPlanBuilder comes with a robust selection of more than 90 typed pages of templates and sample text. One of the coolest features is that the data entry blanks in the templates are hot linked. That means, for example, you can type your company name into the correct spot on one of the templates and have it appear automatically in scores of other appropriate spots throughout your plan.

BizPlanBuilder comes with built-in word processing and spreadsheet software so you don't have to purchase these programs separately. However, if you already have favorite word processing or spreadsheet programs, BizPlanBuilder will let you use those instead of its integrated applications.

If you're trying to compare the results you can expect using several different scenarios, it can be a real pain to prepare complete projections for each of them. BizPlanBuilder has a much simpler approach. A tool called Sensitivity Analysis lets you compare best- and worst-case scenarios to your plan on a single page.

The program disc also has a number of supporting documents. There's an exhaustive description of various funding methods and contact information for resources such as the Small Business Administration and other government agencies. It also has ideas for presenting your plan and suggestions for cover sheets and nondisclosure agreements.

To sum up, BizPlanBuilder is a powerful and easy-to-use program with the sophistication and flexibility to help you with planning even complex businesses. It is available in versions for Windows and Macintosh systems. Contact Jian Software at 800-346-5426 or www.jian.com.

Books and How-To Manuals

Scores of books have been written on how to write a business plan. Most provide skimpy treatment of the issues while devoting many pages to sample plans. Sample plans are useful, but unless planners understand the principles of the planning process, they can't really create sophisticated, one-of-a-kind plans. The following books will help you with the details of various sections in your plan:

- *Dictionary of Business Terms* (Barron's). This compact, 650-page dictionary is a cure for jargon overexposure. It provides concise definitions of business terms from "abandonment" to "zoning ordinance." Appendices explain common business acronyms, provide tables of compounded interest rate factors, and more. It's the kind of book you'll turn to again and again.

- *Thomson/Polk Bank Directory* (Thomson Financial Publishing Inc.). A great resource for finding the right bank to fund your business.

Plan of Action

Small Business Development Centers are one-stop shops set up by the Small Business Administration to give entrepreneurs free to low-cost advice, training, and technical assistance. There are SBDCs in each state and territory. Learn more online at www.sba.gov or call (800) 8-ASK-SBA.

> ▶ *Guerrilla Marketing* (Houghton Mifflin), by Jay Conrad Levinson. The most recent release of this marketing classic provides updated marketing techniques for those with little cash but high hopes. Levinson's insistence on the central role of planning and his simple but effective explanations of how to do it will serve business planners well.

> ▶ *Guts & Borrowed Money* (Bard Publishing), by Tom Gillis. This practical guide is organized like an encyclopedia so you can quickly and easily look up detailed explanations of everything from arbitration to vision statements.

Web Sites

Plan Pointer

Lack time and budget to buy and learn a business plan software program? Try Adarus Business Plan. This shareware consists of Visual Basic wizards that use Microsoft Office applications to build a plan in Word. If you know Office, it saves time. At $40, it saves money, too.

The internet provides a virtually inexhaustible source of information for and about small business, including numerous sites with substantial databases of tips and ideas concerning business planning. Some of the best include the following:

> ▶ *Entrepreneur.com (www.entrepreneur.com).* This is the web site of *Entrepreneur* magazine, a monthly business magazine with the nation's largest readership, and the parent corporation of this book's publisher. The site contains a vast array of information resources, practical advice, interviews with experts, profiles of successful entrepreneurs, product and service reviews, and more.

> In addition to articles from past and present issues of the print magazine, the site offers resources for beginning businesses in Business Start-Ups, franchise information in the FranchiseZone, and Business Opportunity 400, where you can search a wide variety of businesses for sale. There are also resources for home businesses and e-businesses.

> The *Entrepreneur* web site also hosts *Entrepreneur* magazine's entre preneurpress.com, a source for books—including this one—that offer expert advice on starting, running, and growing a small business. These include business start-up guides, step-by-step start-up guides to specific businesses, and business management guides, which offer in-depth information on financing, marketing, and more.

> • *Small Business Administration (www.sba.gov).* The SBA's web site is a vast directory to services provided by the federal agency devoted to helping small businesses. These include special lending programs,

Homemade but Not Half-Baked

Lindsay Frucci created a fat-free brownie mix and built it into a homebased business success. No Pudge! Foods Inc. began in January 1995 with Frucci baking in her home kitchen in Elkins, New Hampshire. The start-up notched just $6,000 in first-year sales, reached $42,000 the second year, and exploded to $253,000 the third year.

Frucci's secret ingredient was a pair of SCORE (Service Corps of Retired Executives) counselors who told her to find outside manufacturing and get No Pudge! out of her kitchen. The flexibility and increased capacity allowed Frucci to handle large orders, package products with UPC codes, and devote her own energy to product development and marketing.

Frucci had faith in the SCORE counselors' advice because they'd already helped her draft a business plan when she needed more money to expand the homebased firm. They had faith in her, as they showed when they advised her to turn down a bank's offer of a loan because the bank required her husband to cosign. Insisting the business should be financed on its own merits, without personal guarantees, they went to a second bank, which saw the light.

Frucci says flexibility is her watchword, and it's reflected in the way she runs and plans her business. "Sometimes businesses fail because they have a business plan that says, 'This is the way I'm going,' and they don't consider changing midstream," she says. "Allow your business plan to change. It's not set in stone."

electronic databases of minority- and disadvantaged-owned businesses, directories of government contracting opportunities, and more.

There is also a generous selection of answers to frequently asked questions, tip sheets, and other advice. You can get a list of questions to ask yourself to see if you have the personality of an entrepreneur, find help with selecting a business, and browse an entire area devoted to help with your business plan.

Two things are of particular interest. First, is the vast collection of nearly 3,000 links to other small-business-related sites. Second, the online library to publications contained on the SBA site. The library provides online access to dozens of forms, legislation, regulations, reports, studies, FAQ (frequently asked questions) lists, and more. There are even hundreds of downloadable shareware and freeware computer programs for managing time, preparing invoices, tracking inventory, calculating loan payments, and many other business activities.

- *American Express Small Business Exchange (www.americanexpress. com/smallbusiness).* This site, sponsored by American Express, has a broad array of well-organized files providing advice and tips about all kinds of business problems, from buying or selling a business to issues related to working at home. There are a few come-ons for American Express services, such as equipment financing, financial planning, and, of course, applying for the well-known charge card. But the information is generally well-presented, factual, and unbiased.

Trade Groups and Associations

You're not in this alone. There are countless local and national organizations, both public and private, devoted to helping small businesses get up and running. They provide services ranging from low-rent facilities to financial assistance, from help in obtaining government contracts to help with basic business-planning issues. Many of these services are provided for free or at nominal cost.

▶ *SCORE.* The Service Corps of Retired Executives, known as SCORE, is a nonprofit group of mostly retired businesspeople who volunteer to provide counseling to small businesses at no charge. SCORE has been around since 1964 and has helped more than three million entrepreneurs and aspiring entrepreneurs. SCORE is a source for all kinds of business advice, from how to write a business plan to investigating marketing potential and managing cash flow.

SCORE counselors work out of nearly 400 local chapters throughout the United States. You can obtain a referral to a counselor in your local chapter by contacting the national office.

▶ *National Business Incubation Association.* The NBIA is the national organization for business incubators, which are organizations specially set up to nurture young firms and help them survive and grow. Incubators provide leased office facilities on flexible terms, shared business services, management assistance, help in obtaining financing, and technical support.

NBIA says there are nearly 600 incubators in North America. Its services include providing a directory to local incubators and their services.

▶ *Chambers of commerce.* The many chambers of commerce throughout the United States are organizations devoted to providing networking,

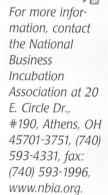

Plan of Action

For more information, write to SCORE Association at 409 Third St. SW, 6th Fl., Washington, DC 20024, or contact at (800) 634-0245, www.score.org.

Plan of Action

For more information, contact the National Business Incubation Association at 20 E. Circle Dr., #190, Athens, OH 45701-3751, (740) 593-4331, fax: (740) 593-1996, www.nbia.org.

lobbying, training, and more. If you think chambers are all about having lunch with a bunch of community boosters, think again. Among the services the U.S. Chamber of Commerce offers is a Web-based business solutions program that provides online help with specific small-business needs, including planning, marketing, and other tasks such as creating a press release, collecting a bad debt, recruiting employees, and creating a retirement plan.

The U.S. Chamber of Commerce is the umbrella organization for local chambers, of which there are more than 1,000 in the United States. If you're planning on doing business overseas, don't forget to check for an American chamber of commerce in the countries where you hope to have a presence. They are set up to provide information and assistance to U.S. firms seeking to do business there. Many, but not all, countries have American chambers.

Plan of Action

For more information, contact the U.S. Chamber of Commerce at 1615 H St. NW, Washington, DC 20062-2000, (202) 659-6000, fax: (202) 463-3190, www.us chamber.org.

Hire Power

If you decide to hire a consultant to help you prepare your plan, take care that you select the right person. Here are guidelines:

1. *Get referrals.* Ask colleagues, acquaintances, and professionals such as bankers, accountants, and lawyers for the names of business-plan consultants they recommend. A good referral goes a long way to easing concerns you may have. Few consultants advertise anyway, so referrals may be your only choice.
2. *Look for a fit.* Find a consultant who is expert in helping businesses like yours. Ideally, the consultant should have lots of experience with companies of similar size and age in similar industries. Avoid general business experts or those who lack experience in your field.
3. *Check references.* Get the names of at least three clients the consultant has helped to write plans. Call the former clients and ask about the consultant's performance. Was the consultant's final fee in line with the original estimate? Was the plan completed on time? Did it serve the intended purpose?
4. *Get it in writing.* Have a legal contract for the consultant's services. It should discuss in detail the fee, when it will be paid, and under what circumstances. And make sure you get a detailed, written description of what the consultant must do to earn the fee. Whether it's an hourly rate or a flat fee isn't as important as each party knowing exactly what's expected.

Business Plan Consultants

Businesspeople tend to fall into two camps when it comes to consultants. Some believe strongly in the utility and value of hiring outside experts to bring new perspective and broad knowledge to challenging tasks. Others feel consultants are overpaid yes-men brought in only to endorse plans already decided upon or to take the heat for unpopular but necessary decisions.

Who's right? Both are, depending on the consultant you hire and your purpose for hiring one. Most consultants are legitimate experts in specific or general business areas. And most consultants can be hired to help with all or part of the process of writing a business plan.

The downside is you have to spend a lot of time on communication before and during the process of working with a consultant. Be sure you have fully explained, and the consultant fully understands, the nature of your business, your concept and strategy, your financial needs, and other matters such as control, future plans, and so on. Refer to these important issues throughout the process—you don't want to pay for a beautifully done plan that fits somebody else's business, not yours. And when the work is done, debrief the consultant to find out if there's anything you can learn that wasn't included in the plan.

Business Plan Competitions

If you happen to be a business student, you may be able to enter your business plan in a college business plan competition. These competitions, of which there are more than three dozen in the United States, confer a measure of fame and even some money on the winners. A panel of plan experts including college professors, venture capitalists, and bankers usually judges entries.

Winners are the plans that best lay out a convincing case for a business's success. Judges can be tough; contestants can expect scathing criticism of poorly thought-out plans.

Moot Corporation is the name of the best known of the nation's business plan competitions. It's sponsored each May by the University of Texas at Austin. Moot Corporation calls itself the "Super Bowl of world business-plan competition" and is the oldest of the approximately three dozen business school-sponsored plan competitions. More than two dozen

From Schoolhouse to Penthouse

A fair number of business-plan competition winners go on to become real businesses that succeed in the real world, often helped by investors attracted by the competition. Here are a few:

1. WebLine Communications Corporation, an internet technology firm, won the Massachusetts Institute of Technology business plan competition. In addition to the $30,000 prize, founder Pasha Roberts eventually raised more than $8 million from investors impressed with his plan's finish.

2. Ampersand Art Supply, an art supply distributor, won the University of Texas plan competition. Ampersand CEO Elaine Salazar's presentation impressed one competition judge so much he threw in his own investment of $300,000.

3. 1-800 Contacts, a mail order contact lens firm, won the contest put on by Brigham Young University. Today the company has annual sales of nearly $169 million.

Not every contest-winning plan turns into a company. Entering could even be a negative. Some contestants say that if you don't win, investors consider it a strike against you, while even if you do, the academic connection may paint your plan as a mere ivory-tower exercise.

plan-writing teams from as far away as Australia participate in the contest, which began in 1983. The winner of the UT competition receives $15,000 and a significant publicity boost.

The most financially rewarding contest is the $50,000 competition sponsored by Massachusetts Institute of Technology. The MIT winner takes home $30,000, while the next two finishers take $10,000 each. Business schools such as Harvard University and the University of Chicago are among other prestigious business institutions sponsoring plan contests.

Sample Business Plans

T HE FOLLOWING FIVE SAMPLE PLANS WERE CHOSEN TO REPRESENT A cross section of companies and a variety of reasons for writing a plan. Please note that these companies are fictitious and that their concepts may or may not be applicable to your business. For the purposes of this book, they show how business owners can approach various issues relating to a business plan depending on the type of industry, size of the company, characteristics of the market, caliber of management, and other factors.

Read the sample plans with an eye toward seeing whether any of the approaches taken in them fits what you're trying to do.

Appendix A

Business Plan for a Retailer Seeking Start-Up Capital

WATER WORKS INC. IS A RETAIL FOOD-SERVICE OPERATION SEEKING start-up capital. Its business plan is succinct, carefully thought-out, and well-documented. Particular attention has been paid to studying the national sales trends for the beverages WaterWorks will serve. The plan provides adequate financial data, including a three-year income statement projection and a month-by-month cash flow projection for the first year.

The primary purpose of this plan is to facilitate a $30,000 bank loan so the two partners can launch their business and get through the first six months. From that point on, the business will be able to sustain itself on cash flow. When the partners need additional financing to open their second location in a couple of years, they should have little difficulty in obtaining a second loan for expansion.

There are several strengths to this business plan. First is the fact that management is experienced in the hospitality industry. Second, the partners are providing a significant portion of the start-up capital themselves, which delights bankers. Third is that demand for WaterWorks' products appears to be growing, with little or no direct competition in its market. Most important from a financier's point of view is that the plan shows enough cash generated from sales to pay off the loan in 12 months.

Among the weaknesses revealed by this business plan are that the idea is unproven, at least in its geographic market. Second, the partners are paying themselves salaries. Some lenders would prefer to see borrowers do without salaries, at least in the beginning. This is somewhat offset by the facts that the partners are not taking a draw—a dividend paid from profits in addition to salary—and that the salaries will be modest.

Business Plan
for
WaterWorks Inc.

WaterWorks Inc.

12709 Enfield Terrace

Austin, TX 78704

(512) 555-1212

Albert Walter, President

Matthew Strang, CEO

September 1, 2003

Contents

I. Executive Summary

Market

According to *Beverage Digest* (April 2005), still, or noncarbonated, water beverages are the trendiest new drinks since gourmet coffee. The market for still-water drinks has been building steadily for three years and now appears ready to enter an accelerated period of growth.

Still-water drinks are different from the mass-produced carbonated beverages sold by the soft-drink giants like Coca-Cola. They are usually produced in small quantities by small operations, product quality is high, and they often include functional additives, such as nutriceuticals, that differentiate them from mass-market soft drinks and appeal to health-conscious consumers.

Business Description

WaterWorks will sell still-water beverages through a retail outlet in Austin, Texas. The store will have a bar and seating area as well as a service counter and will serve beverages prepared on the premises for consumption there or off-site, along with prepackaged products like baked goods.

The store, which will also include a drive-through window, will be located in an existing facility near the intersection of Loop 1 and Enfield Road in central Austin.

Products

The product line, all purchased from outside vendors, will consist of approximately 20 different still-water and functional beverages, in addition to a selection of freshly baked breads, muffins, cookies, and other locally produced foods.

Management

WaterWorks is registered as a partnership owned in equal shares by Albert Walter and Matthew Strang. Mr. Walter will serve as President and Mr. Strang as Chief Executive Officer. Mr. Walter and Mr. Strang are both experienced in food-service operations. (See "Management" for more information.)

Financing Needs

WaterWorks needs $30,000 in short-term financing to cover start-up costs, purchase necessary equipment, and provide working capital until the business can support itself from cash flow. The owners will invest $20,000 of their own cash and would like to borrow $20,000 initially, with the remaining $10,000 available as a line of credit over the next 180 days. Interest payments will begin after the first month. After 10 months, operations will generate sufficient cash to pay down the balance of the loan in two balloon payments, which will result in the loan being paid off by the end of the first year. The owners are prepared to pledge personal assets as collateral for this loan.

II. Business Mission and Strategy

Mission Statement

WaterWorks will sell still-water and functional beverages to health-conscious consumers in Austin, Texas. Customers will include students, faculty, and staff from the nearby University of Texas, the nation's largest institution of higher education, and residents of the well-educated, affluent surrounding neighborhoods.

Strategic Elements

The WaterWorks strategy embodies several key elements:

- ▶ The store will be the first of its kind in Austin, a major metropolitan area of more than one million people.
- ▶ The location is near Sixth Street and Lamar Boulevard, one of the city's busiest intersections and hottest retail environments.
- ▶ Only products of the highest quality will be offered.
- ▶ Austin has one of the country's highest per-capita rates of consumption of natural foods and beverages.

Strategic Objectives

- ▶ To repay initial bank loans by the end of the first year of operation.
- ▶ To produce a net profit of at least $75,000 by the third year of operation.
- ▶ To expand to three additional retail locations by the end of the fifth year of operation.
- ▶ To explore additional expansion through the creation of more company-owned or possibly franchised outlets after year five.

III. Sources and Uses of Funds

Start-Up Costs Summary

Start-up costs will be approximately $55,000, which includes initial lease payments, leasehold improvements, inventory, permits, and other expenses. Start-up costs will be financed primarily through a combination of bank borrowing and investment by the partners.

Sources and Uses of Funds

USE OF FUNDS

Capital Expenditures

Leasehold Improvements	$10,000
Equipment	10,000
Total Capital Expenditures	**$20,000**

Working Capital

Legal	$1,000
Permits and Licenses	1,500
Printing	1,000
Graphic Design	1,000
Insurance	2,500
Rent (three months)	10,000
Salaries	10,000
Start-Up Inventory	5,000
Other Business Activities	3,000
Total Working Capital	**$35,000**

TOTAL USE OF FUNDS	**$55,000**

SOURCES OF FUNDS

Partner Investments	$20,000
Trade Credit	5,000
Bank Loan	30,000
Total Sources of Funds	**$55,000**

IV. Products

WaterWorks will sell still-water drinks and baked goods to customers in Austin, Texas.

Company Locations and Facilities

WaterWorks will be located near the intersection of Loop 1 and Enfield Road in Austin, Texas, an attractive retail location near desirable residential areas, the state capitol complex, and the University of Texas main campus.

An existing 900-square-foot facility with seating and a drive-up window will be leased. Improvements will include additions to the seating area, a water bar, and landscaping.

A second location is planned for the third year of operation at a site to be determined.

Products

The primary products sold through WaterWorks will be functional still-water drinks in three categories:

1. *Nutriceuticals*
   Nutriceutical waters include still waters to which minerals such as potassium and calcium, vitamins including C or D, or other substances such as caffeine have been added.
2. *Bacteria-Free Still Water*
   Bacteria-free still waters are processed using techniques that eliminate microorganisms, including associated flavors and particles, from the water.
3. *Exotic Waters*
   Exotic waters are bottled and imported from locations such as Alaska, Canada, France, Hawaii, Sweden, and Russia.

V. Markets and Competition

Still Water Sales Trends

Still water is the fastest-growing segment of the alternative beverage industry. Sales for 2004, the most recent year available, were up 25 percent, almost double the industry average of 13 percent. Other alternative beverages include juices, teas, sport drinks, sparkling waters, and natural sodas.

Still-water sales totaled 731 million cases, making the category the dominant one in alternative beverages, whose total sales neared 1.9 billion cases. Still water's share of the alternative beverage market exceeded 39 percent, up 3.7 percent from the previous year, when 585 million cases of still waters were sold. Other strong categories included sport drinks and teas.

Source: *Beverage Digest,* February 2005.

Industry Analysis

Alternative beverage producers include some of the beverage industry's largest companies. The graph on the following page shows the top alternative beverage producers and their respective market shares.

Suppliers

The following products will be supplied by various vendors:

Aqua Health, Water for Life, H2Ah!, Nutri-Water, Hydration Technologies, Guava Cool, and Soft Beverages. Vendors supply a variety of beverages with features such as nutriceutical content, bacteria-free processing, and a number of organic flavorings including berries, other fruits, and spices.

Suppliers are for the most part located in the continental United States. While they are not currently available for wholesale distribution in Austin, which partially explains the lack of local retail distribution, all operate existing distribution systems with representatives in other Texas cities, including Houston, San Antonio, and Dallas. No problems in obtaining adequate supplies of important products are anticipated.

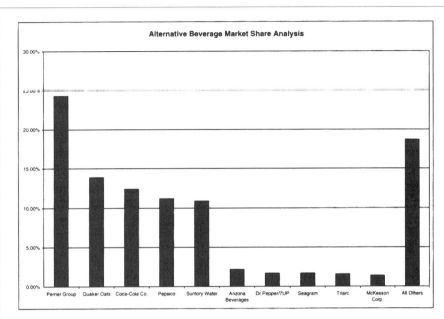

Source: *Beverage Week*

Market Analysis Summary

Austin, the capital of Texas, is located near the center of the state, approximately 70 miles north of San Antonio and 200 miles south of Dallas. The city has a population of approximately 500,000 and is the hub of a metropolitan area of more than 1 million people. Austin is home to the nation's largest university, many offices related to the state government, and a booming business community that includes the headquarters of Dell Computer Corporation and Whole Foods Market, the nation's largest retailer of natural foods.

Austin has one of the highest percentages of adults with college degrees of any American city and is generally regarded as a center of progressive lifestyles in the Southwest.

WaterWorks is an ideal business for Austin given a market of this size and demographics. Based on average individual transactions of approximately $2.25, including still-water drinks and related products, the business has the potential to gross more than $400,000 in sales by the third year of operation.

Competitive Analysis

No other business in Austin focuses exclusively on the still-water market. This opportunity provides considerable flexibility in pricing and allows WaterWorks to create a great deal of customer awareness and brand loyalty.

While no retail businesses devoted exclusively to water beverages exist in Austin, water beverages are sold at Whole Foods, Whole Earth Provision, Randall's Markets, and other grocery retailers.

Research in San Francisco reveals information on six still-water beverage retail locations. The oldest has been in operation for slightly more than two years. These businesses are thriving, selling still-water drink units at prices ranging from $1.25 for small, counter-prepared beverages to be consumed on the premises to $24 for larger bottles to be installed off-premises in water coolers.

The owner of one of the older San Francisco businesses indicated that first-year sales in his market, which, like the WaterWorks location, is near a university and an affluent residential district, were 200 units per day, yielding a first-year revenue potential of $117,000, assuming minimal average transaction value of $1.75. Considerable price flexibility is likely to exist in markets where competition is lower or non-existent. Research conducted in Ann Arbor, Michigan, a city comparable to Austin in size, showed that in the two existing still-water retailers, counter-prepared drinks sold for as high as $5 each.

Competition and Buying Patterns

Still-water retailing will be new to Austin. Competitors primarily sell mass-market waters through grocery store-type locations and do not focus on the still-water beverage market. There are no retail providers of counter-prepared still-water beverages for consumption on the premises—so-called water bars.

WaterWorks' success will come from educating consumers about the appeal and benefits of still-water beverages and from providing high-quality products not available in grocery stores. Price competition will be a minimal concern given current market conditions.

VI. Marketing

Marketing Strategy

WaterWorks' overall marketing strategy will be to educate consumers about the benefits of still-water beverages and to promote the availability of these products through WaterWorks. Customers will be reached through fliers, newspaper advertisements, and special events.

Location also plays an important role in marketing and promotion, with the business being located near a high-traffic retail area in central Austin.

Target Markets and Market Segments

WaterWorks will target health-conscious and generally well-educated and affluent consumers who are interested in trying new products and dissatisfied with the limited selection and lack of personal service found in grocery store-type water retailers.

Pricing Strategy

Still-water fountain drinks will be offered at the following prices:

Small: $1.50
Medium: $2.25
Large: $3.75

In addition, larger sizes of water will be sold for customer carryout or delivery. They will range in size from one-liter bottles to 20-liter plastic jugs at prices from $3.75 to $35.00.

Products will be sold on a cash basis to retail customers. Corporate customers, expected to represent an insignificant proportion of sales at the beginning, will be invoiced and given 30 days to pay.

Promotion Strategy

WaterWorks will promote its still-water drinks to customers through:

- ► Regular newspaper advertisements focusing on the benefits of still-water beverages.

- ▶ A publicity campaign that will spotlight company owners on health-related TV and radio broadcasts and position them as experts in print publications.
- ▶ Educational and promotional fliers that are distributed to residences within a one-mile radius
- ▶ Discounts offered to groups such as health-food cooperatives, organic gardening clubs, and cultural associations.

Distribution Strategy

- ▶ Primary distribution of still-water drinks will be through the retail facility.
- ▶ Secondary distribution will consist of deliveries of bottled water to restaurants, retailers, and corporate locations.
- ▶ Additional distribution will be through temporary booths set up at athletic and cultural events such as bicycle races and concerts.

Sales Projections

Sales will start in January 2006. Sales forecasts are based on experiences of similar start-ups in San Francisco. Forecasts include retail sales consistent with similar markets with significant competition and may be considered conservative. Corporate sales include sales of bottles for office water coolers and beverages for corporate parties. Special-events sales include products sold through booths set up at concerts, races, and other events. Third-year sales are projected to include partial results from opening a new retail location.

Sales Forecast

Year	2006	2007	2008
Retail walk-in	$147,000	$183,000	$390,000
Corporate	0	6,000	12,000
Special events	15,000	18,000	30,000
Total	$162,000	$207,000	$432,000

VII. Management

Albert Walter has five years' experience in the retail restaurant industry. He served for three years as manager of the Java Coffee Beanery and for two years as assistant manager of the Travis Bagel Shop. He is a 1994 graduate of the University of Texas at Austin business school, where he earned an MBA.

Matthew Strang has seven years of experience in the hospitality industry. He served as assistant general manager of the Hill Country Bed & Breakfast in Fredericksburg, Texas, for five years and as manager of Bee Cave Bar & Grill in Austin for two years.

WaterWorks will hire one part-time employee to assist with the business. The partners will perform the bulk of the duties required to operate the initial store.

VIII. Financial Data

Financial Plan

WaterWorks will finance growth through cash flow. Expansion will begin in year three and will include the opening of a second location, an increase in corporate sales, and added emphasis on special-event promotions.

Seasonal Data

As a result of Austin being a "college town," seasonal variations will be most pronounced in June, July, and August. During these months, many between-term college students leave the city, causing a significant—but temporary—reduction in the size of Austin's market.

Break-Even Analysis

The following table and chart show break-even analysis for year one. The owners have determined that the business will require sales of approximately $12,591 per month to break even during the first year of operation. Assumptions include average monthly fixed expenses of $9,443 (general and administrative expenses less depreciation divided by 12) and a gross profit margin of 75 percent.

Break-Even Analysis

$$\frac{\$9,443}{75\%} = \$12,591$$

Projected Profit and Loss

Profits for the next three years are projected to equal:

2006: $1,581
2007: $24,086
2008: $78,022

Projected Income Statement

	2006	2007	2008
INCOME			
Gross Sales	**$157,500**	**$207,000**	**$432,000**
Less Returns and Allowances	0	0	0
Net Sales	157,500	207,000	432,000
Cost of Sales	40,500	49,653	99,360
Gross Profit	**$117,000**	**$157,347**	**$332,640**
Gross Profit Margin	74%	76%	77%
OPERATING EXPENSES			
General & Administrative Expenses			
Salaries and Wages	$45,360	$54,750	$121,500
Employee Benefits	2,721	3,285	7,290
Payroll Taxes	2,268	2,738	6,075
Sales Commissions	0	0	0
Professional Services	1,725	1,725	2,400
Rent	29,400	29,400	58,800
Maintenance	1,350	1,350	2,250
Equipment Rental	1,650	2,250	3,375
Furniture and Equipment Purchase	1,875	2,400	3,375
Insurance	2,820	3,000	6,300
Interest Expenses	2,025	2,025	3,000
Utilities	3,225	3,375	3,840
Office Supplies	1,350	1,425	1,800
Postage	1,125	1,388	1,575
Marketing and Advertising	15,225	19,875	26,138
Travel	825	1,125	1,500
Entertainment	375	450	600
Bad Debt	0	0	0
Depreciation and Amortization	2,100	2,700	4,800
TOTAL OPERATING EXPENSES	**$115,419**	**$133,261**	**$254,618**
Net Income before Taxes	$1,581	$24,086	$78,022
Provision for Taxes on Income	608	2,406	7,802
NET INCOME AFTER TAXES	**$973**	**$21,680**	**$70,220**

Notes to projected income statement:
1. Figures for 2006 include added income and operating expenses from second location.
2. Cost of Sales reflects slight but steady increase in gross profit margins.
3. Salaries and Wages include one part-time employee the first two years of operation, three part-time employees the third year of operation (when two locations will be staffed), and the following annual salaries for each partner in lieu of draw:

>   2006: $18,000
>   2007: $22,500
>   2008: $45,000

Projected Cash Flow

Projected cash flow for the next three years is estimated as follows:

>   2006: $6,750
>   2007: $22,300
>   2008: $93,000

Projected Cash Flow Statement for 2006

	Jan.	Feb.	Mar.	Apr.	May	Jun.	Jul.	Aug.	Sep.	Oct.	Nov.	Dec.	TOTAL
CASH RECEIPTS													
Income from Sales													
Cash Sales	$3,000	$7,500	$10,500	$10,500	$16,500	$15,000	$15,000	$15,000	$16,500	$16,500	$18,000	$18,000	$162,000
Collections	0	0	0	0	0	0	0	0	0	0	0	0	$0
Total Cash from Sales	**$3,000**	**$7,500**	**$10,500**	**$10,500**	**$16,500**	**$15,000**	**$15,000**	**$15,000**	**$16,500**	**$16,500**	**$18,000**	**$18,000**	**$162,000**
Income from Financing													
Interest Income	0	0	0	0	0	0	0	0	0	0	0	0	$0
Loan Proceeds	15,000	0	0	3,750	0	0	3,750	0	0	0	0	0	$22,500
Total Cash from Financing	**15,000**	**0**	**0**	**3,750**	**0**	**0**	**3,750**	**0**	**0**	**0**	**0**	**0**	**$22,500**
Other Cash Receipts	15,000	0	0	0	0	0	0	0	0	0	0	0	$15,000
Total Cash Receipts	**33,000**	**$7,500**	**$10,500**	**$14,250**	**$16,500**	**$15,000**	**$18,750**	**$15,000**	**$16,500**	**$16,500**	**$18,000**	**$18,000**	**$199,500**
CASH DISBURSEMENTS													
Expenses													
Cost of Goods	750	1,875	2,625	2,625	4,125	3,750	3,750	3,750	4,125	4,125	4,500	4,500	$40,500
Operating Expenses	18,750	6,225	6,600	7,200	7,538	9,488	7,875	8,587	9,825	9,975	10,087	10,050	$112,500
Loan Payments	0	225	225	225	225	225	225	225	225	225	11,362	11,563	$24,750
Income Tax Payments	0	0	0	0	0	0	0	0	0	0	0	0	$0
Equipment Purchase	7,500	0	0	3,750	0	0	0	0	0	0	0	0	$11,250
Contingency	0	0	0	0	0	0	0	0	0	0	0	3,750	$3,750
Owners Draw	0	0	0	0	0	0	0	0	0	0	0	0	$0
Total Cash Disbursements	**27,000**	**$8,325**	**$9,450**	**$13,800**	**$11,888**	**$13,463**	**$11,850**	**$12,562**	**$14,175**	**$14,325**	**$25,959**	**$29,563**	**$192,750**
Net Cash Flow	**6,000**	**-825**	**1,050**	**450**	**4,612**	**1,537**	**6,900**	**2,438**	**2,325**	**2,175**	**-7,950**	**-11,563**	**$6,750**
Opening Cash Balance	0	6,000	5,175	6,225	6,675	11,288	12,825	19,725	22,163	24,488	26,663	18,713	$0
Cash Receipts	33,000	7,500	10,500	14,250	16,500	15,000	18,750	15,000	16,500	16,500	18,000	18,000	$199,500
Cash Disbursements	−27,000	−8,325	−9,450	−13,800	−11,887	−13,463	−11,850	−12,562	−14,175	−14,325	−25,950	−29,563	−$192,750
Ending Cash Balance	**$6,000**	**$5,175**	**$6,225**	**$6,675**	**$11,288**	**$12,825**	**$19,725**	**$22,163**	**$24,488**	**$26,663**	**$18,713**	**$6,750**	

Notes to projected cash flow statement:

1. Cash sales reflect summer slowdown due to college students being out of town.
2. Other Cash Receipts consist of investment by partners.
3. Contingency fund set up at year-end to provide cash reserves.
4. Owners receive nominal salaries instead of draws.
5. Loan Payments cover interest at 10 percent on $30,000 loan until balance of principal and interest are repaid in two third-quarter balloon payments.
6. April equipment purchase is for trailer, portable equipment, and booth, to prepare for promotions at outdoor events.

Balance Sheet Projection

Projected shareholders' equity and net worth after one year of operation is $29,250.

Projected Balance Sheet
for Year ending
December 31, 2006

ASSETS

Current Assets

Cash	$6,750
Accounts Receivable	0
Inventory	4,125
Prepaid Expenses	3,750
Total Current Assets	**$14,625**

Fixed Assets

Land	$0
Buildings	0
Equipment	3,000
Furniture	7,500
Fixtures	7,500
Less Accumulated Depreciation	3,375
Total Fixed Assets	**$21,375**
Other Assets	**0**
TOTAL ASSETS	**$36,000**

LIABILITIES

Current Liabilities

Accounts Payable	$4,125
Accrued Payroll	2,250
Taxes Payable	375
Short-Term Notes Payable	0
Total Current Liabilities	**$6,750**
Long-Term Liabilities	
Long-Term Notes Payable	$0
Total Long-Term Liabilities	**$0**
Net Worth	**$29,250**
Retained Earnings	0
Total Net Worth	**$29,250**
TOTAL LIABILITIES & NET WORTH	**$36,000**

Note to projected balance sheet:

1. Accounts receivable will be minimal in the first year, since all business will be conducted on a cash basis.

Appendix B

Business Plan for a High-Tech Company Seeking Financing for Growth

THE FOLLOWING BUSINESS PLAN IS FOR A HIGH-TECH COMPANY LOOK-ing for a second round of financing to enable it to market and distribute its product nationwide. The strongest parts of this plan are the industry analysis and management sections. Management is clearly experienced enough to achieve the objectives set in its plan. Two other positive indicators are the industry's strong growth and trends favoring the introduction of this company's product.

The plan's weakness relates to the amount of money being requested. The $750,000 that the owners are asking for reduces the expected return, based purely on net income projections, to a rate below that at which most venture capitalists are likely to be interested.

It's possible that another company might be interested in buying out Software Solutions or that the company may go public after a few more years. For now, the owners need to make a stronger case for an enticing cash-out or to ask for less money.

Software Solutions

*Helping to Make
Automobile Dealerships More Productive*

26209 Fairfax Ave.

Cincinnati, OH 45207

513-555-7272

Bradley Regent, CEO

Table of Contents

Executive Summary

Software Solutions is a one-year-old software manufacturer. Our initial product is an inventory management system for automobile dealers to use with portable handheld computers.

Many automobile dealers complain about the lack of good inventory management systems. Current methods involve paper stock cards, sales slips, and invoice books. However, these are frequently out-of-date and inaccurate and always time-consuming to maintain.

Additional problems with existing inventory management systems include employees' inability to access inventory records while on the showroom floor or away from the office. This can result in missed sales opportunities, as employees must return to the office or call a prospect later to provide information about the availability of a particular model.

Software Solutions' DriversSeat inventory management system runs on PalmPilot portable computers. These pocket-sized machines have become the best-selling product in the history of the computer industry, producing sales of more than 3 million units since they were introduced in 1996. Many successful industry-specific programs have been written for the PalmPilot.

Software Solutions was created specifically to produce Pilot-based applications for automobile dealers. The founder and CEO, Bradley Regent, spent 10 years as an information systems manager for automobile dealerships in Ohio and Pennsylvania. Mr. Regent understands dealership information issues and has many contacts with those responsible for purchasing information technology for dealerships. Other members of his team include a marketing manager, a programmer, and an office assistant.

Nine months were spent developing the DriversSeat product, including market research, programming, and testing. Initial sales of the product have been encouraging. Several of the largest dealers in the Cincinnati area have tested the programs, and at least two regional chains are also trying them out.

Software Solutions was launched with $80,000 provided by the founder and is now seeking an additional $750,000 to market and distribute DriversSeat nationwide. The company anticipates no difficulty raising this sum through a private equity placement of preferred stock, based on strong initial acceptance of the product and numerous pending sales.

Software Solutions' Management Team

One of Software Solutions' strengths is its management team's industry experience.

Bradley Regent, CEO

Prior to founding Software Solutions, Mr. Regent worked for several large automobile dealerships as a programmer, systems analyst, and information systems manager. A native of Cincinnati, Mr. Regent graduated from Ohio State University with a degree in computer science. After two years with a large systems integrator in Cincinnati, Mr. Regent began working in the automobile dealership industry.

Mr. Regent has extensive experience in analyzing, developing, and maintaining inventory management systems for automobile dealerships. He's received professional training and certification as a developer in Oracle, SAP, Microsoft SQL, and DB2 database environments and has managed information systems departments of up to seven people.

Mr. Regent's primary responsibilities at Software Solutions will be long-term planning, participating in product development, managing company growth, and meeting with investors, customers, and suppliers. Mr. Regent is now the primary owner of Software Solutions and holds 80 percent of the corporation's stock.

Wanda McIntire, Vice President of Marketing

Ms. McIntire has worked for five years as a marketing specialist for two companies serving automobile dealerships' information-systems needs in Kentucky and Indiana. Ms. McIntire has experience positioning and marketing new information systems products geared to automobile dealers. She developed the initial marketing plan for Parts Perfect, a parts inventory management system created by Autosoft Systems that is now used by more than 500 dealerships nationwide. Ms. McIntire graduated from Tulsa University in 1992 with a degree in business.

Ms. McIntire's responsibilities at Software Solutions are formulating and implementing marketing strategy, participating in product development, and working with customers and prospects. She holds 5 percent of the corporation's shares.

Perry Honeywell, Program Developer

Mr. Honeywell was one of the first 20 employees of Helping Hand Systems, a Palo Alto, California, company that is now the largest third-party supplier of software for the PalmPilot computer system. He led the team that designed and produced Third Hand, a data collection system running on the PalmPilot that is now used in ISO 9000 quality-control programs around the world. He received computer science degrees from San Francisco University and the University of California at Berkeley.

Mr. Honeywell's responsibilities at Software Solutions are overseeing program operation and interface design, and creating and testing code. He holds 10 percent of the corporation's shares.

Steven Wise, Human Resources and Administrative Manager

Mr. Wise has expertise in interviewing, screening, and hiring applicants for positions with information-systems firms. For the past three years, he has been in charge of staffing and administration for Staple Systems, a Cincinnati electronic commerce software firm that grew from three to more than 40 employees during the time that the leading-edge software became well received in the marketplace.

Mr. Wise's responsibilities at Software Solutions are managing office operations, including bookkeeping and accounts receivables and payables, as well as dealing with outside suppliers. As the company grows, he'll be responsible for recruiting and hiring program designers, programmers, testers, and other employees. Mr. Wise holds 5 percent of the corporation's shares.

The DriversSeat Product

DriversSeat is a compact, rugged, flexible, and cost-effective solution to the inventory-management needs of automobile dealerships. The program was created in the Palm OS environment, the operating system of the computing industry's most popular handheld computing device. The following table summarizes DriversSeat features and benefits to customers.

DriversSeat Features and Benefits

Features	Benefits
• Thoroughly tested software housed in a shock-resistant device that is pocket-sized and battery-operated	• Ready supply of inventory data in a portable, rugged, and inexpensive package
• Customized application for quickly and easily transferring inventory information and updates both to and from desktop systems to a PalmPilot	• Ability of salespeople, whether they're offsite or away from their desk, to quickly and easily provide customers with accurate information on the availability of specific automobile models
• Ability to interface with desktop inventory management systems from EDS, Dealer Solutions, ATP, Reynolds & Reynolds, and others	• Design reflects thorough understanding of the needs of automobile dealerships

Software Solutions believes that competing products, all of which are based on older laptop designs or outdated paper systems, cannot match the DriversSeat's combination of flexibility, convenience, and integration with other inventory-management systems.

DriversSeat Marketing Strategy

Software Solutions' marketing strategy takes advantage of two trends: the rapid growth of handheld computing systems for industrial and commercial applications, and the increasing need for more sophisticated and flexible inventory management as the automobile dealership industry consolidates and grows in size.

Recent figures from the National Automobile Dealers Association show:

▶ Total sales for auto dealerships are almost $700 billion annually and growing.

▶ More than 21,650 new-car dealerships exist, a number that has dropped approximately 50 units annually for the past several years.

▶ The industry has consolidated, with the number of smaller dealerships selling fewer than 150 vehicles annually, shrinking from 13,100 in 1991 to 3,460 in 2003.

▶ Information systems have become increasingly important to the remaining dealerships, with special concern being paid to the need for open systems for information interchange and dealer purchase of hardware.

▶ The PalmPilot computing platform has become the fastest-selling computer in the history of the industry. Pertinent facts include:

   – More than ten million units have been sold in approximately six years.

   – Thousands of software developers have written applications for a variety of uses.

   – The PalmPilot's ruggedness, versatility, and portability make it the most popular choice for industrial software developers.

Software Solutions has priced its product to compete with both off-the-shelf, general-purpose database and inventory-management systems for the Pilot and with existing laptop-based inventory-management systems specific to the auto dealership industry.

A price of approximately $10,000 for a five-unit site license, including five PalmPilot III computers, training, and an annual maintenance contract, has proved acceptable to dealerships and is far below what competing products based on larger systems sell for.

Software Solutions is using direct-mail marketing to auto dealership information systems managers, followed up with telemarketing and personal sales calls as its primary marketing method. This approach takes maximum advantage of the company principals' reputations and visibility in the Ohio automobile dealership community.

As marketing for the DriversSeat is rolled out nationwide to all 21,650 prospective auto dealer customers, additional marketing dollars will be required to produce direct-mail marketing materials, conduct telemarketing follow-up calls, arrange for personal sales calls to prospects, and staff these functions with appropriately skilled personnel.

Software Solutions believes it can achieve a 9 percent market share within four years. Sales of systems to approximately 2,000 dealerships, at an average purchase price of $10,000, indicates total sales through 2008 of approximately $2 million, with more than half that amount occurring in the final year as the effect of prior marketing efforts begins to be felt.

Program Development and Operations

One of Software Solution's biggest advantages is the expertise of its principals in the design, development, and maintenance of software for portable applications, particularly those in the automobile dealer industry.

The principal technologists, Bradley Regent and Perry Honeywell, combine years of experience in, respectively, auto dealership information systems and portable platform software development. In addition to extensive training in industry-standard database management systems, which allows Mr. Regent to effectively interface DriversSeat data with existing dealership computer systems, he maintains a network of beta testers, consisting primarily of auto dealership IS managers, sales managers, salespeople, and inventory management personnel, to help with testing, product development, feature refinement, and other tasks.

Mr. Honeywell is recognized as an expert in third-party PalmPilot software development. He serves on the advisory board for developing and maintaining standards for industrial software applications for the PalmPilot. His contacts and experience ensure that Software Solutions will have ongoing access to the latest and best technology for developing its products.

Management believes its combination of industry-specific and technical expertise make it unique among companies addressing the inventory management needs of automobile dealerships. Other competitors include EDS, Digital Dealership, Microsoft, and SAP. All these companies are much larger than Software Solutions and capable of bringing much greater resources to bear on the market. However, Software Solutions' management believes that its lead time in developing applications for this market, plus the market segment's small size relative to those its competitors are primarily interested in, will provide the company with an opportunity to secure a solid foothold.

Software Solutions operates out of offices at 26209 Fairfax Avenue in Cincinnati, Ohio. The offices measure approximately 5,000 square feet and offer adequate room for expansion over the next five years. Leasing terms are flexible, and management believes rent is competitive with comparable office space in the city.

In addition to office furniture and fixtures, Software Solution's primary physical assets consist of five computer workstations used for application development. The company also maintains a varying number of PalmPilots used for application testing and development.

Software Solution's inventory is limited to prepackaged versions of its software and a small number of PalmPilots that are ready for installation. While PalmPilots are typically ordered from Palm Computing on an as-needed basis, our practice minimizes inventory carrying costs and allows us to provide our customers with a rapid turnaround when they place an order.

Historical Financial Statements and Projections

Software Solution's start-up was financed by $80,000 from Bradley Regent. The current financial plan anticipates raising an additional $750,000 to market and distribute DriversSeat nationwide. Following this financing, equity ownership would be distributed as shown below.

Pro Forma Statement of Equity Ownership

Owner	Stock Class	Shares	Amount
Mr. Regent	Common	350,000	$660,000
Ms. McIntire	Common	2,000	44,000
Mr. Honeywell	Common	4,000	88,000
Mr. Wise	Common	2,000	44,000
Investors	Preferred	100,000	500,000
Total		**458,000**	**$1,336,000**

The proceeds of this financing will allow Software Solutions to distribute and market DriversSeat nationwide.

Software Solutions Income Statement

	2006	2007
Net Sales	$0	$83,400
COGS	0	48,713
Gross Margin	$0	$34,687
Operating Costs		
Development	$41,799	$20,831
SG&A	7,253	26,478
Other	1,985	2,694
Total Operating Costs	$51,037	$50,003
Operating Earnings	−51,039	−15,315
Interest Expense	−1,479	−2,138
Pretax Earnings	−52,518	−17,453
Income Tax	0	0
Net Income	**−$52,518**	**−$17,453**

Notes to income statement: Software Solution's income statement for the first two years of operation reflects no sales revenues the first year, when the founder's efforts were devoted to developing the product. Development costs that year were correspondingly high. Sales the second year took off nicely, and gross margin was also in line. However, heavy marketing expenses took their toll, and the company has produced a net loss of more than $66,000 for its first two years in operation.

Software Solutions Balance Sheet
December 31, 2006

ASSETS

Cash	$54,000
Accounts Receivable	17,780
Inventory	1,181
Prepaid Expenses	4,194
Other Current Assets	1,674
Total Current Assets	**$78,829**
Fixed Assets	$26,346
Intangibles	1
Other Noncurrent Assets	0
Total Assets	**$105,175**

LIABILITIES

Notes Payable	$11,435
Accounts Payable	3,411
Interest Payable	1,175
Taxes Payable	978
Other Current Liabilities	2,376
Total Current Liabilities	**$19,375**
Long-Term Debt	0
Other Noncurrent Liabilities	3,182
Total Liabilities	**$22,557**
Net Worth	**$82,618**
Total Liabilities & Net Worth	**$105,175**

Note to balance sheet: Assets included $54,000 in cash from the founder's $80,000 initial capitalization.

Software Solutions Cash Flow Statement

Sources of Cash

Sales	$83,400
Total Cash In	**$83,400**

Uses of Cash

COGS	$48,713
SG&A	26,478
Other	2,694
Interest	2,138
Taxes	0
Equipment Purchase	6,480
Total Cash Out	**$86,503**
NET CHANGE IN CASH	**−$3,103**
Beginning Cash on Hand	**$55,801**
Ending Cash on Hand	**$52,698**

Software Solutions Pro Forma Income Statement

INCOME PROJECTION

INCOME	2006	2007	2008	2009
Net Sales	**$191,250**	**$286,875**	**$788,907**	**$1,577,814**
Cost of Sales	95,625	137,700	362,897	788,907
Gross Profit	**$95,625**	**$149,175**	**$426,010**	**$788,907**
OPERATING EXPENSES				
General & Administrative Expenses				
Salaries and Wages	$116,288	$143,438	$236,672	$263,063
Sales Commissions	9,562	14,344	39,445	78,891
Rent	4,800	5,040	5,292	5,556
Maintenance	1,913	2,009	2,109	2,214
Equipment Rental	1,687	1,771	1,860	1,953
Furniture and				
Equipment Purchase	9,000	3,333	2,343	3,960
Insurance	2,280	2,394	2,514	2,998
Interest Expenses	1,875	1,970	2,068	3,909
Utilities	1,650	1,732	1,819	1,911
Office Supplies	975	1,239	3,266	1,466
Marketing				
and Advertising	150,225	98,250	120,000	135,000
Travel	15,750	18,750	22,500	26,250
Entertainment	900	450	640	830
Bad Debt	750	287	789	485
Depreciation				
and Amortization	2,700	4,050	6,075	9,113
TOTAL OPERATING				
EXPENSES	**$320,355**	**$299,057**	**$447,392**	**$537,599**
Net Income				
before Taxes	−$224,730	−$149,882	−$21,382	$251,308
Provision for				
Taxes on Income	0	0	0	37,697
NET INCOME				
AFTER TAXES	**−$224,730**	**−$149,882**	**−$21,382**	**$213,610**

Notes to income projections: Sales projections reflect assumptions of progressively greater rollout into the national market, with accordingly higher levels of sales. Heavy first-year marketing expenses level off as national distribution is achieved. Sales increase in subsequent years as the effect of initial marketing efforts is felt. Wage and salary increases reflect need to hire additional programmers, salespeople, and administrative personnel to cope with higher sales.

Sustained profitability is achieved in 2006. Projected income tax reflects effects of applying net operating loss from prior years to 2006 profits.

Software Solutions Pro Forma Balance Sheet

	2006	% Sales	2007 (projected)
Sales	**$83,400**		**$191,250**
ASSETS			
Cash	$54,000	64.7%	$123,739
Accounts Receivable	17,780	21.3%	40,736
Inventory	1,181	1.4%	2,678
Prepaid Expenses	4,194	5.0%	9,563
Other Current Assets	1,674	2.0%	3,825
Total Current Assets	**$78,829**	**94.5%**	**$180,541**
Fixed Assets	26,346	31.6%	60,435
Intangibles	1	0.0%	0
Other Noncurrent Assets	0		0
Total Assets	**$105,175**		**$240,976**
LIABILITIES			
Notes Payable	$11,435	13.7%	$26,201
Accounts Payable	3,411	4.1%	7,841
Interest Payable	1,175	1.4%	2,678
Taxes Payable	978	1.2%	2,295
Other Current Liabilities	2,376		2,506
Total Current Liabilities	**$19,375**		**$41,521**
Long-Term Debt	0		0
Other Noncurrent Liabilities	3,182		4,833
Total Liabilities	**$22,557**		**$46,354**
Net Worth	**$82,619**		**$194,622**
Total Liabilities & Net Worth	**$105,176**		**$240,976**

Note to balance sheet projection: Balance sheet projections were based on relationships among various items reflected in 2005 actual results. Intangibles include goodwill, proprietary technology, and long-term service and maintenance contracts.

Software Solutions Pro Forma Cash Flow Statement

Projected Cash Flow for 2006

	Jan.	Feb.	Mar.	Apr.	May	Jun.	Jul.	Aug.	Sep.	Oct.	Nov.	Dec.	TOTAL
CASH RECEIPTS													
Income from Sales													
Sales	$11,475	$11,475	$13,387	$13,388	$15,300	$15,300	$17,212	$17,213	$17,213	$19,125	$19,125	$21,037	$191,250
Total Cash from Sales	**11,475**	**11,475**	**13,387**	**13,388**	**15,300**	**15,300**	**17,212**	**17,213**	**17,213**	**19,125**	**19,125**	**21,037**	**$191,250**
Financing Income													
Net Offering Proceeds	649,500	0	0	3,750	0	0	0	0	0	0	0		$653,250
Interest Income	5,250	5,250	3,750	3,750	3,000	3,000	2,625	2,625	2,250	2,250	1,875	1,875	$37,500
Total Cash Receipts	**666,225**	**$16,725**	**$17,137**	**$20,888**	**$18,300**	**$18,300**	**$19,837**	**$19,838**	**$19,463**	**$21,375**	**$21,000**	**$22,912**	**$882,000**
CASH DISBURSEMENTS													
Expenses													
COGS	5,738	5,737	6,693	6,693	7,648	7,649	8,605	8,606	8,605	9,561	9,561	10,518	$95,614
SG&A	18,150	15,832	13,842	9,037	13,125	12,333	14,336	14,287	12,333	15,750	13,125	14,258	$168,178
Taxes	0	0	0	0	0	0	0	0	0	0	0	0	$0
Equipment Purchase	12,000	0	0	0	0	0	6,000	0	0	0	0	0	$18,000
Dividends	0	0	0	0	0	0	0	0	0	0	0	0	$0
Total Cash Disbursements	**35,888**	**21,569**	**20,535**	**15,730**	**20,773**	**19,982**	**28,941**	**22,893**	**20,938**	**25,311**	**22,686**	**24,776**	**$281,792**
Net Cash Flow	**$630,337**	**-$4,844**	**-$3,398**	**$5,158**	**-$2,473**	**-$1,682**	**-$9,104**	**-$3,055**	**-$1,475**	**-$3,936**	**-$1,686**	**-$1,864**	**$600,208**
Opening Cash Balance	54,000	684,337	679,493	676,095	681,253	678,780	677,098	667,994	664,939	663,464	659,528	657,842	$0
Cash Receipts	666,225	16,725	17,137	20,888	18,300	18,300	19,837	19,838	19,463	21,375	21,000	22,912	$882,000
Cash Disbursements	-35,888	-21,569	-20,535	-15,730	-20,773	-19,982	-28,941	-22,893	-20,938	-25,311	-22,686	-24,776	-$281,792
Ending Cash Balance	**$684,337**	**$679,493**	**$676,095**	**$681,253**	**$678,780**	**$677,098**	**$677,994**	**$664,939**	**$663,464**	**$659,528**	**$657,842**	**$655,378**	

Note to cash flow projection: Cash flow projections for 2006 reflect offering proceeds, net of fees, of $649,500. Interest income is generated from investing excess proceeds of offering.

Appendix C

Business Plan for a Service Firm Seeking Working Capital

THE FOLLOWING BUSINESS PLAN IS FOR AN ESTABLISHED COMPANY IN need of working capital. Draper Rains Associates, a public relations and marketing firm, has grown steadily for 15 years—it employs 109 people and has a solid base of customers and billings. Recently, the company began expanding its operations to other cities in order to attract new and larger clients. The result has been an increase in expenses and a clear need for working capital, which the company is looking for in the form of a bank loan.

The company is forward-thinking and prudent to seek this type of loan now. Its cash flow is positive, and its expenses will increase as its geographic expansion efforts gather steam.

Confidential Business Plan

Draper Rains Associates

14479 Jackson St.
San Francisco, CA 94115
415-555-6968

Alice Draper, Chairman, President, and CEO

Executive Summary

Draper Rains Associates is a 15-year-old public relations and marketing firm serving the health-care industry in the San Francisco Bay area.

Draper Rains offers integrated public relations and marketing consulting services to its clients, who consist of large hospitals, clinics, and health maintenance organizations. While the majority of the services Draper Rains offers are available from other firms, the company believes its execution is superior. This is evidenced by the fact that the majority of its clients have been active with the firm for more than five years, some have been active more than 10 years, and one client has been with the firm since its founding.

After several years of steady growth as a regional services provider, the company is now poised to break out into the national scene. In pursuit of this strategy, the company has expended a substantial proportion of its capital reserves in opening new offices, increasing staff, and acquiring necessary equipment and technology.

The strategy has been successful so far, and the firm has acquired several national accounts whose billings are much larger than the average client the firm has worked with in the past. These larger clients, many of whom are also slower in cycling invoices than other clients, are causing increases in accounts payable and accounts receivable. As a result, the company is now seeking additional funding to provide working capital during this period of expansion.

Bank financing of $525,000 is currently being sought. The objective is a line of credit in that amount, with approximately $262,500 paid out immediately and the balance paid out in equal installments for the next five quarters. At the end of two years, payments against principal will begin, and the entire principal amount will be paid off after four years.

Product

Draper Rains provides integrated public relations and marketing services to large hospitals, clinics, and health maintenance organizations.

The company's services consist of planning marketing strategy, writing and editing marketing materials and press releases, conducting publicity and media placement campaigns, media training for key executives, and related services. The company arranges for production of videotapes and printed materials, conducts on-premises briefings and seminars, and participates in high-level strategy sessions with its clients' executives.

The mission of the company is to provide its clients with positive, integrated public images in the marketplace, with the ultimate goal of increasing client sales and profits.

Draper Rains competes with numerous other companies for customers. Many of these competitors provide similar services. However, the company believes that its reputation for quality service and its long-established relationships with existing clients will allow it to maintain and expand its current level of sales in this competitive environment.

Industry

The health-care industry is undergoing monumental shifts as changes in payer policies, declining bed utilization rates, and increasingly expensive new medical technology combine to make marketing more important than it has been previously.

The marketing and public relations industry is also undergoing a period of consolidation as numerous global advertising and marketing firms establish large, United States-based public relations divisions. These same competitors are targeting health care for much the same reasons as is Draper Rains.

If current trends play out as expected, the business of providing marketing and public relations services to large health-care clients will become increasingly consolidated among a few sizable firms. To remain competitive in this market, Draper Rains must develop a national presence to attract large, new clients.

In pursuit of this goal, Draper Rains has opened new offices on the East and West coasts as well as in the Midwest and the Southeast. It has also increased employees by approximately 25 percent, or 16 people, to staff these offices.

Marketing

Draper Rains obtains clients almost exclusively through word-of-mouth. Because of the large size of its typical client—average clients are billed approximately $30,000 annually—and the long-standing conservatism of health-care institutions in matters of marketing, personal referrals, informal testimonials, and an excellent reputation among hospital administrators and professionals in the health-care marketing field continue to be the best marketing tools available.

Draper Rains has a formal program for generating and disseminating positive word-of-mouth, informal testimonials, and referrals in the marketplace. While this program is difficult to track for effectiveness, the company believes its program is working and will continue to use it.

For the company to compete effectively in new geographic markets, it must establish and maintain a physical presence in those markets. To that end, the company has in the past year opened new offices in several cities, each of which serves as a hub for its region of the United States. New offices are located in Miami, Chicago, New York, and Los Angeles.

The company's headquarters in San Francisco consist of approximately 8,000 square feet of leased space in a modern office building, with a staff of 80. In each of the new cities, the firm has begun with small facilities and small staffs. Offices average approximately 600 square feet and have staffs of five people in order to control expenses while providing a marketing foothold in the new markets. Each of the new offices has adjoining space suitable for expansion. Draper Rains has acquired formal options to lease adjoining space in New York, Miami, and Los Angeles and has an informal understanding with its landlord in Chicago.

In addition to establishing a physical presence in the new cities, Draper Rains is mounting a modest advertising campaign. The effort includes placing advertisements in the printed programs for meetings of local health-care marketing organizations, advertising groups, and the like. The firm has purchased outdoor advertising space on one or more billboards in each of the cities for a term of approximately one year to build name recognition among its target group.

Another key element of the company's marketing campaign consists of personal sales calls by the principal and other personnel. These sales calls are scheduled with hospital administrators, hospital marketing directors, HMO chief executives and marketing vice presidents, and similar individuals. The initial intent of these sales calls is to introduce our firm to potential clients and to begin a dialogue. We anticipate that these sales calls, the increased frequency of which is indicated in the growing travel budget, will yield significant numbers of new clients and increased billings over time.

Management

Alice Draper
Chairman, CEO, and President

Ms. Draper, a resident of San Rafael, California, since 1976, is one of the best-known figures in the field of public relations and marketing in the Bay area. She is past president of Northern California Media Relations Professionals, was a delegate from the Public Relations Society of America to a global conference in London, England, in 1996, and has taught marketing at San Jose State University as an adjunct professor since 1994. Ms. Draper founded the firm as a home-based business in 1988 in San Francisco. During the next 15 years, she grew the firm to its present size of 109 employees. She is a graduate of San Jose State University.

Charles Allen
Vice President, Marketing

Mr. Allen is the firm's chief marketing officer and handles many of the marketing duties that are beyond the scope of the president's duties. He and his staff are responsible for developing marketing strategy and preparing and executing the marketing plan. Mr. Allen has been employed by Draper Rains for seven years and is a graduate of the University of Colorado.

Cheryl Plant
Vice President, Technology

Ms. Plant is Draper Rains' chief information officer. She is responsible for developing technology strategies; selecting hardware, software, and vendors; staffing the information office; and preparing a budget for information technology expenditures. Her role has become more important as information management becomes essential to providing the firm's services and as remote offices are incorporated into the firm's technology network. Ms. Plant joined the firm last year from Intel Corporation, where she served as assistant director of information services for a major division. She is a graduate of Carnegie Mellon University.

Facilities

Draper Rains' headquarters are at 14479 Jackson Street in San Francisco, with additional offices in New York, Miami, Chicago, and Los Angeles. Until 2001, the firm's only office was in San Francisco. The additional offices were opened as part of the long-range expansion plan.

One of the company's key operational resources is the integrated communications and computing network that links all personnel in its headquarters, as well as those in the remote offices. This network allows the company to quickly and effectively compose, edit, reproduce, and disseminate client marketing materials. The investment in technology provides the company with a significant edge over competitors in terms of increased quality and reduced turnaround time to complete assignments.

The company's physical assets consist primarily of the computers, modems, cabling and other equipment required to construct this network. Other assets are furniture, equipment, and fixtures in its headquarters office. Most fixtures and furnishings in the new offices are leased rather than purchased.

Financial Statements

Income Statement 2006

Sales Receipts	$8,176,635
Interest Income	16,068
COGS	5,396,579
Gross Margin	2,796,124
Expenses	2,044,160
Depreciation	38,528
Operating Earnings	713,436
Interest Expense	113,487
Pretax Earnings	599,949
Income Tax	179,985
Net Income	**$419,964**

Balance Sheet

June 30, 2006

ASSETS

Cash	$267,798
Accounts Receivable	651,678
Prepaid Expenses	204,858
Other Current Assets	113,741
Total Current Assets	**$1,238,075**
Fixed Assets	385,281
Total Assets	**$1,623,356**

LIABILITIES

Notes Payable	$215,784
Accounts Payable	170,346
Interest Payable	9,458
Taxes Payable	44,997
Other Current Liabilities	1,479
Total Current Liabilities	**$442,064**
Long-Term Debt	380,334
Other Noncurrent Liabilities	1,734
Total Liabilities	**$824,132**
Net Worth	**$799,224**
Total Liabilities & Net Worth	**$1,623,356**

Note to balance sheet: The company operates on a June 30 fiscal year.

Cash Flow Statement

Sources of Cash

Sales	$7,767,804
Other Sources	
Interest	16,068
Short-Term Borrowings	150,000
Total Cash In	**$7,933,872**

Uses of Cash

COGS	$5,126,750
SG&A	2,044,160
Interest	113,487
Taxes	179,985
Equipment Purchase	80,313
Debt Principal Payments	38,763
Dividends	0
Total Cash Out	**$7,583,458**
NET CHANGE IN CASH	**$350,414**
Beginning Cash on Hand	**$81,581**
Ending Cash on Hand	**$431,995**

Note to cash flow statement: The company intends to reduce short-term borrowings in favor of less costly long-term debt.

Pro Forma Income Statement

INCOME PROJECTION

	2004	2005	2006	2007 (projected)
INCOME				
Net Sales	$7,379,414	$7,767,804	$8,176,635	$8,994,299
Interest Income	9,528	12,813	16,068	17,286
Cost of Sales	4,796,619	5,049,072	5,396,579	5,846,294
Gross Profit	$2,592,323	$2,731,545	$2,796,124	$3,165,291
OPERATING EXPENSES				
General and Administrative Expenses				
Salaries and Wages	$969,656	$1,020,690	$1,058,466	$1,181,851
Sales Commissions	368,970	388,391	490,598	449,715
Rent	33,816	35,506	37,283	62,634
Maintenance	73,794	77,484	82,133	137,982
Equipment Rental	5,773	6,062	6,424	10,792
Furniture and Equipment Purchase	4,848	5,091	5,346	8,982
Insurance	10,467	13,083	16,353	19,623
Interest	54,375	57,237	113,487	214,491
Utilities	73,794	77,677	81,767	128,782
Office Supplies	47,966	50,490	53,966	52,617
Marketing and Advertising	125,450	132,052	139,004	10,806
Travel	26,164	32,706	40,883	1,500
Entertainment	22,139	23,304	24,529	831
Bad Debt	8,193	8,622	9,078	486
Depreciation and Amortization	24,657	30,822	57,792	57,792
TOTAL OPERATING EXPENSES	$1,850,062	$1,959,217	$2,217,109	$2,338,884
Net Income before Taxes	$742,261	$772,328	$579,015	$826,407
Provision for Taxes on Income	222,680	231,699	179,985	247,021
NET INCOME AFTER TAXES	$519,581	$540,629	$399,030	$579,386

Pro Forma Balance Sheet

	2006	% Sales	2007 (projected)
Sales	**$8,176,635**		**$8,994,299**
ASSETS			
Cash	$267,798	3.3%	$296,812
Accounts Receivable	651,678	8.0%	719,544
Prepaid Expenses	204,858	2.5%	224,857
Other Current Assets	113,741	1.4%	125,920
Total Current Assets	**$1,238,075**	**15.1%**	**$1,367,133**
Fixed Assets	385,281	4.7%	422,732
Total Assets	**$1,623,356**		**$1,789,865**
LIABILITIES			
Notes Payable	$215,784	2.6%	$233,852
Accounts Payable	170,346	2.1%	188,880
Interest Payable	9,458	0.1%	8,994
Taxes Payable	44,997	0.6%	53,966
Other Current Liabilities	1,479	0.0%	0
Total Current Liabilities	**$442,064**	**5.4%**	**$485,692**
Long-Term Debt	380,334	4.7%	422,732
Other Noncurrent Liabilities	1,734		2,202
Total Liabilities	**$824,132**		**$910,626**
Net Worth	**$799,224**		**$879,211**
Total Liabilities & Net Worth	**$1,623,356**		**$1,789,837**

Note to pro forma balance sheet: Long-term debt projected includes $262,500 in loan proceeds.

Pro Forma Cash Flow Statement

Projected Cash Flow: 2007

	Jan.	Feb.	Mar.	Apr.	May	Jun.	Jul.	Aug.	Sep.	Oct.	Nov.	Dec.	TOTAL
CASH RECEIPTS													
Income from Sales													
Cash Sales	$719,544	$656,585	$728,538	$800,493	$683,567	$764,516	$674,573	$791,499	$746,528	$818,481	$800,493	$818,481	$9,003,298
Total Cash from Sales	$719,544	$656,585	$728,538	$800,493	$683,567	$764,516	$674,573	$791,499	$746,528	$818,481	$800,493	$818,481	$9,003,298
Income from Financing													
Loan Proceeds	262,500	0	0	0	0	0	0	0	0	0	0	0	$262,500
Other Cash Receipts	1,440	1,440	1,440	1,440	1,440	1,440	1,440	1,440	1,440	1,440	1,440	1,440	$17,280
Total Cash Receipts	$983,484	$658,025	$729,978	$801,933	$685,007	$765,956	$676,013	$792,939	$747,968	$819,921	$801,933	$819,921	$9,283,078
CASH DISBURSEMENTS													
Expenses													
COGS	$474,899	$433,345	$480,835	$528,325	$451,018	$504,580	$404,718	$522,390	$492,708	$540,198	$528,325	$540,198	$5,901,539
SG&A	179,886	164,146	182,134	200,124	170,892	191,128	168,643	197,875	186,631	204,621	200,124	204,621	$2,250,825
Interest	17,874	17,874	17,874	17,874	17,874	17,874	17,874	17,874	17,874	17,874	17,874	17,874	$214,488
Taxes	20,585	20,585	20,585	20,585	20,585	20,585	20,585	20,585	20,585	20,585	20,585	20,585	$247,014
Equipment Purchase	8,250	0	8,250	0	8,250	0	8,250	0	8,250	0	8,250	0	$49,500
Debt Principal Payments	3,000	3,000	3,000	3,000	3,000	3,000	3,000	3,000	3,000	3,000	3,000	3,000	$36,000
Dividends	0	0	0	0	0	0	0	0	0	0	0	0	$0
Total Cash Disbursements	$704,494	$638,950	$712,678	$769,908	$671,619	$737,167	$623,070	$761,724	$729,048	$786,278	$778,158	$786,278	$8,699,366
Net Cash Flow	278,990	19,075	17,300	32,025	13,388	28,789	52,943	31,215	18,920	33,643	23,775	33,643	$583,712
Opening Cash Balance	267,798	546,788	565,863	583,163	615,188	628,576	657,365	710,308	741,523	760,443	794,086	817,861	$0
Cash Receipts	983,484	658,025	729,978	801,933	685,007	765,956	676,013	792,939	747,968	819,921	801,933	819,921	$9,283,078
Cash Disbursements	−704,494	−638,950	−712,678	−769,908	−671,619	−737,167	−623,070	−761,724	−729,048	−786,278	−778,158	−786,278	$8,699,366
Ending Cash Balance	$546,788	$565,863	$583,163	$615,188	$628,576	$657,365	$710,308	$741,523	$760,443	$794,086	$817,861	$851,504	$851,504

Appendix D

Business Plan for a Manufacturer Seeking a Partner

THE COMPANY IN THE FOLLOWING BUSINESS PLAN IS A MANUFACTURER courting a strategic partner. The plan writer hopes to persuade a larger company to join in a strategic alliance to manufacture and distribute its patented quick-connect device for coaxial cables. CableNexus' basic business strategy is sound. The company sees a terrific opportunity in the growth of the internet and projected demand for cable modems and other devices requiring large numbers of coaxial cable connectors.

The existing coaxial connectors on the market are cumbersome and inefficient compared with this company's improved design, and the company has hopes of snaring a significant market share amid rapidly growing demand.

The problem is that the opportunity is bigger than CableNexus. The company has only 24 employees and, while it's generating profits and cash flow sufficient for moderate growth, there's no way it can fund a big rollout of product from operations. In addition, it is carrying a fairly heavy debt load—its debt-to-equity ratio is approximately 4.3:1. That amount of leverage has apparently given CableNexus' bankers pause, so the company is looking at other options for funding its expansion.

CableNexus is proposing a modest degree of alliance—not a formal and long-term joint venture but rather a manufacturing license and distribution agreement. The company hopes that it will dramatically increase its market share while giving up to its partner only a portion of profits it would make if it were able to conduct the expansion on its own.

Confidential Business Plan for
CableNexus Inc.
Manufacturers of Cable Connectors for All Purposes

16901 Rising Sun Avenue
Philadelphia, PA 19111
215-555-7227

Contact: Paula Bench, President

Executive Summary

CableNexus Inc. designs and manufactures coaxial cable connectors for the cable TV, internet access, broadcasting, security, and data transmission industries. The company's proprietary designs for quick-connect coaxial cable connectors have proved superior to existing products. Since their introduction in 1995, they have gained approximately 1 percent of the market.

Management feels that much larger sales gains and market share could be obtained, given CableNexus' edge relative to its competition. However, the company's current production and distribution capacity is limited.

Management is seeking a partner to license manufacture of the patented CableNexus connector line and assist in providing or arranging distribution to a larger market. It is anticipated that the partner will not need to invest any funds in the company, with the exception of licensing fees.

CableNexus's 24-employee team includes people with expertise in connector design, light manufacturing operations, and industrial marketing.

Industry

This opportunity for CableNexus to expand is being fueled by one of the most sweeping industrial and commercial revolutions in history—the rapid growth in the use and number of connections to the internet. An increasing number of internet users use coaxial cable to access the network, and each one of these connections, plus many more between the user and the infrastructure, is a prospective customer for a CableNexus connector.

The following statistics are relevant to CableNexus' business plan:

- World Wide Web users, estimated to number approximately 300 million at the end of 2003, will grow to approximately 500 million by the year 2006.
- The number of web users is currently increasing at a rate of more than one million per month.
- Content is growing rapidly as well. The number of internet hosts grew from approximately 10 million in 1996 to more than 100 million in 2006.
- The complexity of internet content has increased to include real-time video, CD-quality audio, and high-resolution graphics.
- Cable-delivery systems are capable of delivering information to millions of internet users at rates up to 1,000 times as fast as traditional modems operating over telephone networks.
- Cable companies plan to invest more than $20 billion in equipment upgrades through 2006.
- Set-top boxes that will bring cable-delivered internet services as well as movies on demand, on-screen program guides, and other services are expected to cost between $300 and $400 per subscriber.
- Cable infrastructure is already available to 97 percent of American homes, giving the cable industry an edge in becoming the internet access provider.

As a well-established supplier of connectors to the cable-TV and data-transmission industry, CableNexus is positioned to take maximum advantage of the explosive growth potential in coaxial cable connector supply.

Management Team

Paula Bench, President

Paula Bench has served as president of CableNexus since 1993. Her responsibilities include overseeing new-product development, setting long-range strategy, and building and maintaining relationships with key customers and suppliers. She previously was employed at a company then known as Pennsylvania Connectors in a variety of capacities until the founder's retirement in 1993. Working as general manager, Ms. Bench purchased the company from the founder and has served as sole owner and president since that time. Ms. Bench is past president of the Pennsylvania Small Business Group. She is a 1985 graduate of Pennsylvania State University with a degree in engineering.

David Stone, Vice President, Operations

David Stone has served as vice president, operations of CableNexus since 1994. His responsibilities include overseeing the manufacture of new CableNexus products, setting up and running manufacturing operations, specifying new-equipment purchases and installation, overseeing maintenance of the company's fleet of vehicles, and other duties relating to the manufacture and delivery of the company's products. Prior to joining CableNexus, he was employed as manufacturing supervisor for Cable Manufacturing in Blue Bell, Pennsylvania. He is a 1983 graduate of Rensselaer Polytechnic Institute.

Peter August, Chief Financial Officer

Peter August has served as chief financial officer of CableNexus since 1996. Prior to that time he served in various capacities as treasurer, controller, and bookkeeper. He is a 1990 graduate of the University of Indiana.

Diane Paterson, Vice President, Marketing

Diane Paterson has served as vice president, marketing of CableNexus since 1992. Her duties include determining marketing strategy, pricing, product design, customer communications, sales staffing, and other marketing-related duties.

Product Description

Cable modems connect TVs to the cable TV coaxial wiring and may also attach a personal computer via a standard Ethernet connection to the cable infrastructure. Internet appliances and similar devices, a few of which are already on the market, may provide access to many users in the near future. Cable modems are sold by a number of vendors, including Hewlett-Packard, Motorola, and several smaller manufacturers.

CableNexus' patented easy-on connectors provide cable modem companies, cable installers, and cable TV and data service access providers with a rapid, secure method for completing the numerous connections associated with a typical installation of cable service to a home or business. These connectors use a proprietary, patented serrated-tooth locking mechanism to achieve a solid, radiation-secure attachment that can nevertheless be completed with one hand, a significant convenience to installation personnel.

To be most effective, the company's cable connections must be installed on both the coaxial cable and the device being connected to. For that reason, the company has negotiated supply contracts with several smaller cable modem manufacturers. It is hoped that the presence of a larger partner will allow the negotiation of similar arrangements with a number of the larger device manufacturers.

In addition to offering significant improvement in functionality compared with traditional threaded connectors, CableNexus' connectors are competitive in price. When purchased in volume, the company's connectors are priced in the range of five to seven cents per connection. Competing designs are priced at four to six cents. The price difference, when compared with the increase in usability and efficiency, has not proved sufficient to inhibit customer purchases to date, and the company sees no reason why it should in the future.

Marketing

CableNexus' marketing plan focuses on presenting the advantages of its fastening system to large cable operators, cable system installers, and equipment manufacturers.

The goal for equipment manufacturers is to obtain the specifications of CableNexus connectors for new devices to be connected to the cable infrastructure. Installers are approached in the same fashion, with the goal being to have CableNexus connectors specified for new installations and retrofit projects. Cable system operators are invited to use CableNexus connectors in their back-office operations as well as to specify them for use by installers and end-user device manufacturers.

In all cases, CableNexus' primary marketing method consists of personal sales calls to engineers, network architects, designers, maintenance managers, and others responsible for specifying the use of coaxial connectors in cable systems and devices.

The company has experienced considerable success with this approach. It has exclusive supplier agreements with four of the top six cable system operators in Pennsylvania and three of the top five installation companies. In addition, the company has made good progress in presenting the advantages of the CableNexus system to manufacturers of end-user devices, including set-top boxes and cable modems, and anticipates announcing a major new contract in this area shortly.

For example, the company recently agreed to be the exclusive supplier of cable connectors to NetCable, a Philadelphia provider of cable modem internet access. NetCable has grown rapidly and promises to become one of the industry's premier providers. After less than two years of commercial availability, NetCable now serves approximately 127,000 cable modem subscribers across the Northeast, an increase of 53 percent from late 2002. NetCable's cable modem subscriber base has nearly tripled since the beginning of 2001. The base of homes with access to two-way upgraded systems increased to 11 million on December 31, 2002, from 7.7 million on March 31, 2003.

Given that the cable industry is moving toward standardization of all aspects of plant, equipment, and operation, many other service providers can be expected to follow NetCable's lead. As a result, CableNexus anticipates further agreements with other leading operators will be concluded during the coming year.

Operations

CableNexus operates out of a 10,000-square-foot manufacturing and office space in Philadelphia. The company owns the building and land. Various machines, including drill presses, metal stampers, extruding machines, and packing equipment, are also owned or leased by the company.

The company uses industry-standard production machinery in all processes. Its materials are obtained from vendors who supply its competitors—no unusual materials are used in their construction. Likewise, the company employs no proprietary processes or technologies in the manufacture of its products.

The primary value-added feature of the company's products is the design, which applies to coaxial cable connection technology proven in other uses. This technology, on which the company holds patents for application in coaxial cable connections, requires only moderate retooling of machinery used by the majority of manufacturers to make industry-standard coaxial cable connectors.

The company's current monthly production capacity amounts to approximately 1.5 million connectors. While current production capacity is adequate to meet the existing level of orders, management believes additional sales could be procured if service, especially the turnaround time on orders, were improved.

Achieving a significant improvement in service, including reducing turnaround, would require substantial investments in new, higher-capacity production equipment plus the addition of an improved distribution center and, likely, geographically dispersed distribution centers to serve clients in far-off regions. Management believes that the company's financial structure will not support the added debt burden that would be necessary to accomplish these operational improvements. Therefore, the decision has been made to pursue a strategic alliance with an existing manufacturer who can license CableNexus' designs and provide appropriately located distribution centers.

Financial Data

Income Statement

Sales Receipts	$1,795,500
Interest Income	5,370
COGS	1,185,030
Gross Margin	615,840
Expenses	466,830
Depreciation	30,402
Operating Earnings	118,608
Interest Expense	30,858
Pretax Earnings	87,750
Income Tax	26,325
Net Income	**$61,425**

Balance Sheet

June 30, 2004

ASSETS

Cash	$89,463
Accounts Receivable	143,100
Prepaid Expenses	38,904
Other Current Assets	38,739
Total Current Assets	**$310,206**
Fixed Assets	304,026
Total Assets	**$614,232**

LIABILITIES

Notes Payable	$185,376
Accounts Payable	38,904
Interest Payable	2,571
Taxes Payable	6,582
Other Current Liabilities	3,534
Total Current Liabilities	**$236,967**
Long-Term Debt	230,349
Other Noncurrent Liabilities	3,447
Total Liabilities	**$470,763**
Net Worth	**$143,369**
Total Liabilities & Net Worth	**$614,132**

Cash Flow Statement

Sources of Cash	
Sales	$1,705,725
Other Sources	
Interest	5,367
Short-Term Borrowings	24,366
Total Cash In	**$1,735,458**
Uses of Cash	
COGS	$1,125,777
SG&A	466,830
Interest	30,857
Taxes	26,325
Equipment Purchase	52,818
Debt Principal Payments	16,236
Dividends	0
Total Cash Out	$1,718,843
NET CHANGE IN CASH	**$16,615**
Beginning Cash on Hand	**$89,463**
Ending Cash on Hand	**$106,078**

Income Projection

	2004	2005	2006	2007 (projected)
INCOME				
Net Sales	$1,637,496	$1,723,680	$1,795,500	$2,082,780
Interest Income	2,688	3,622	5,370	4,506
Cost of Sales	1,064,373	1,120,392	1,125,777	1,353,807
Gross Profit	**$575,811**	**$606,910**	**$675,093**	**$733,479**
OPERATING EXPENSES				
General & Administrative Expenses				
Salaries and Wages	$215,169	$226,491	$232,428	$273,678
Sales Commissions	81,896	86,184	107,730	104,139
Maintenance	16,374	17,193	18,225	30,621
Equipment Rental	5,775	6,060	6,423	10,794
Furniture and Equipment Purchase	4,848	5,091	5,346	8,982
Insurance	2,298	2,874	3,591	4,308
Interest Expenses	12,066	12,570	30,855	58,320
Utilities	16,377	17,235	17,955	28,278
Office Supplies	10,644	11,205	11,850	12,183
Marketing and Advertising	27,837	29,304	30,524	13,806
Travel	5,745	7,182	8,979	1,500
Bad Debt	1,818	1,914	1,994	483
Depreciation and Amortization	19,455	24,321	30,402	45,603
TOTAL OPERATING EXPENSES	**$420,302**	**$447,624**	**$506,302**	**$592,695**
Net Income Before Taxes	155,509	159,286	168,791	140,784
Provision for Taxes on Income	23,328	23,895	26,325	21,117
NET INCOME AFTER TAXES	**$132,181**	**$135,391**	**$142,466**	**$119,667**

Note: Sales projections include an estimated $150,000 from licensing fees.

Balance Sheet Projection

	2006	% Sales	2007 (projected)
Sales	**$1,705,725**		**$2,082,780**
ASSETS			
Cash	$89,463	5.2%	$108,305
Accounts Receivable	143,100	8.4%	174,954
Prepaid Expenses	38,904	2.3%	47,904
Other Current Assets	38,739	2.3%	47,904
Total Current Assets	**$310,206**	**18.2%**	**$379,066**
Fixed Assets	304,026	17.8%	370,735
Total Assets	**$614,232**		**$1,128,868**
LIABILITIES			
Notes Payable	$185,376	10.9%	$227,023
Accounts Payable	38,904	2.3%	47,904
Interest Payable	2,571	0.2%	4,166
Taxes Payable	6,582	0.4%	8,331
Other Current Liabilities	3,534	0.2%	4,166
Total Current Liabilities	**$236,967**	**13.9%**	**$291,590**
Long-term Debt	230,349	13.5%	281,175
Other Noncurrent Liabilities	3,447		2,844
Total Liabilities	**$470,763**		**$575,609**
Net Worth	**$143,469**		**$553,259**
Total Liabilities & Net Worth	**$614,232**		**$1,128,868**

Cash Flow Projection

Projected Cash Flow for 2007

	Jan.	Feb.	Mar.	Apr.	May	Jun.	Jul.	Aug.	Sep.	Oct.	Nov.	Dec.	TOTAL
CASH RECEIPTS													
Income from Sales													
Sales & Licensing Fees	$166,623	$164,945	$174,954	$177,036	$199,947	$149,960	$193,698	$168,671	$158,292	$197,864	$170,789	$149,958	$2,012,737
Total Cash from Sales	166,623	164,945	174,954	177,036	199,947	149,960	193,698	168,671	158,292	197,864	170,789	149,958	$2,012,737
Income from Financing													
Loan Proceeds	7,500	0	0	7,500	0	0	7,500	0	0	7,500	0	0	$30,000
Other Cash Receipts	0	0	0	0	0	0	0	0	0	0	0	0	$0
Total Cash Receipts	$174,123	164,945	174,954	$184,536	$199,947	$149,960	$201,198	$168,671	$158,292	$205,364	$170,789	$149,958	$2,042,737
CASH DISBURSEMENTS													
Expenses													
COGS	$110,011	$108,596	$115,470	$116,844	$134,967	$98,973	$127,841	$111,345	$104,472	$130,590	$112,722	$98,973	$1,370,804
SG&A	41,658	41,136	43,740	44,259	49,989	37,491	48,426	42,177	39,573	49,467	42,699	37,491	$518,106
Interest	4,860	4,860	4,860	4,860	4,860	4,860	4,860	4,860	4,860	4,860	4,860	4,860	$58,320
Taxes	1,761	1,761	1,761	1,761	1,761	1,761	1,761	1,761	1,761	1,761	1,761	1,761	$21,132
Equipment Purchase	2,246	0	0	2,246	0	0	2,246	0	0	0	2,246	0	$8,982
Debt Principal Payments	1,848	1,848	1,848	1,848	1,848	1,848	1,848	1,848	1,848	1,848	1,848	1,848	$22,176
Dividends	0	0	0	0	0	0	0	0	0	0	0	0	$0
Total Cash Disbursements	$162,384	$158,201	$167,679	$171,818	$193,425	$144,933	$186,982	$161,991	$152,514	$188,526	$166,136	$144,933	$1,999,520
Net Cash Flow	11,739	6,744	7,275	12,718	6,522	5,027	14,216	6,680	5,778	16,838	4,653	5,025	$43,217
Opening Cash Balance	89,463	101,202	107,946	115,221	127,939	134,461	139,488	153,704	160,384	166,162	183,001	187,654	$0
Cash Receipts	174,123	164,945	174,954	184,536	199,947	149,960	201,198	168,671	158,292	205,364	170,789	149,958	$2,042,737
Cash Disbursements	−162,384	−158,201	−167,679	−171,818	−193,425	−144,933	−186,982	−161,991	−152,514	−188,525	−166,136	−144,933	−$1,999,520
Ending Cash Balance	$101,202	$107,946	$115,221	$127,939	$134,461	$139,488	$153,704	$160,384	$166,162	$183,001	$187,654	$192,679	

Appendix E

Business Plan for a Start-Up Needing an Equipment Loan

THE PRIMARY PURPOSE OF THIS BUSINESS PLAN IS TO SECURE A LOAN for equipment, which the business needs to begin operation. Although the idea for this type of business is new in this particular market, it has been successful in other, similar markets. The owner and his partners are helping to fund the business's working-capital needs with their equity stake, which helps bolster the business's debt-to-equity ratio, strengthens its balance sheet, and makes the business more attractive to prospective lenders. Other funding comes from two low-interest, three-year loans—one from a state development agency to help bring jobs to the area and another from a vendor to fund initial marketing expenses.

The strengths of this plan include the business's solid balance sheet and the owner's years of experience in the food industry. He's also done lots of market research, which helps him make a strong case for starting this business.

The primary weakness of this plan is that it assumes cash flow will be strong through the first year, enabling the business to begin paying the owner a salary in the second year and retiring the two short-term loans the following year.

Confidential Business Plan

for

JAVANET

Eugene's First Internet Café

Cale Bruckner

President

1435 10th Street

Eugene, Oregon 97403

(541) 555-7654

EXECUTIVE SUMMARY

JavaNet, Eugene's first internet café, will provide a unique forum for communication and entertainment as well as respond to increasing demand in its market. According to market research conducted by JavaNet president Cale Bruckner, the public wants access to the internet at an affordable cost in a social setting. JavaNet's goal is to provide the community with a social, educational, and entertaining atmosphere for worldwide communication.

This business plan was prepared to request a $21,000 equipment loan that the business projects repaying in four years. Additional financing has already been secured for $20,000 from the Oregon Economic Development Fund to support our efforts to create new jobs, $19,000 from majority owner Cale Bruckner, $36,000 from three investors, and $5,000 from Microsoft to help fund start-up marketing expenses.

JavaNet will be incorporated as a limited-liability corporation, which offers the business all the benefits of a corporation but allows Mr. Bruckner and his partners to be taxed as if they were in a partnership. The partners—Luke Walsh, Doug Wilson, and John Underwood—will not be involved in the day-to-day management of JavaNet.

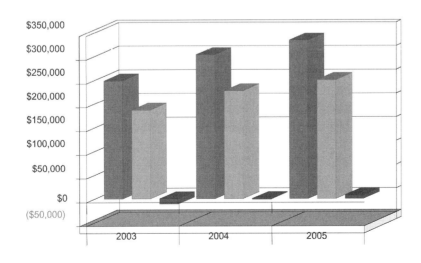

Projected Sales for JavaNet

As shown in the financial statements, this financial arrangement allows JavaNet to launch the business, provide customers with a full-featured internet café, and maintain operations through 2003. Mr. Bruckner believes that successful operation in the first year will provide JavaNet with a sufficient and loyal customer base so that the company can sustain itself on income from operations in the second year.

JavaNet's Mission

JavaNet's goal is to create a unique, upscale, comfortable, innovative environment that will promote what the internet has to offer to the community, provide affordable access to the internet and other online services, bring people with diverse interests and backgrounds together in a common forum, and offer high-quality coffee and baked goods at reasonable prices.

Keys to Success

In order to succeed, JavaNet must create a unique space and differentiate itself from other local coffee shops and future internet cafés. It must also encourage customer loyalty by promoting itself as a hub for socializing and entertainment. At the same time, JavaNet must position itself as an educational resource for novice users while also providing resources for more experienced users. Finally, JavaNet needs to provide outstanding coffee and bakery items.

Risks

Three questions are raised concerning the success of JavaNet. First, what will the level of demand be for the services offered by JavaNet in Eugene? Second, will people be willing to pay for the services JavaNet offers? And third, will the cost of internet access from home drop so significantly that there will not be a market for internet cafés such as JavaNet?

COMPANY SUMMARY

JavaNet will be located in downtown Eugene on 10th and Oak Streets and will provide full access to e-mail, the Web, FTP, Usenet, and other internet applications such as Telnet and Gopher. JavaNet will also provide customers with a pleasant environment in which to enjoy great coffee, specialty beverages, and baked goods.

JavaNet will offer instructional internet classes and a helpful staff on duty at all times to appeal to those who are not computer-savvy. This educational aspect will attract both young and elderly members of the community, while the downtown location will draw businesspeople, who can do their work in a pleasant environment and enjoy their morning coffee at the same time.

Company Ownership

JavaNet is a privately held limited liability corporation registered in Oregon. Cale Bruckner, the founder of JavaNet, is the majority owner (70 percent), and Luke Walsh, Doug Wilson, and John Underwood are minority shareholders (10 percent each).

Start-Up Expenses

JavaNet's start-up costs include coffee-making equipment; site modification; funds to cover first-year operations; and the hardware, software, and other equipment necessary to get its customers online. The equipment necessary to provide JavaNet customers with a high-speed internet connection makes up a large portion of the start-up costs. These costs include computers and their set-up, along with two laser printers and a scanner.

Coffee-making equipment includes one espresso machine, an automatic coffee grinder, and minor additional equipment that will be purchased from Allann Brothers.

Sources and Uses of Funds at Start-Up

START-UP EXPENSES

Legal	$ 3,000
Letterhead, business cards	2,000
Brochures	1,000
Consultants	2,000
Advertising	5,000
Insurance	2,400
Rent	6,000
Automatic coffee machine	1,700
Bean grinder	795
Computer systems (x11)	22,000
Communication lines	840
Furniture, other equipment	11,695
Remodeling, decorator fee	9,605
Inventory	5,000
Working capital for payroll	18,750
Total Start-Up Expenses	**$91,785**

Sources of Start-Up Funds

Investors

Cale Bruckner	$19,000
Luke Walsh	12,000
Doug Wilson	12,000
John Underwood	12,000
Total Investment	**$55,000**

Short-Term Liabilities

Oregon Development Fund	$20,000
Microsoft	5,000
Total Short-Term Liabilities	25,000
Long-Term Liabilities	21,000
Total Liabilities	**$46,000**
Total Funds Available at Start-Up	**$101,000**
Profit/(Loss) at Start-Up	**$9,215**

Location and Facilities

The site at 10th and Oak in downtown Eugene was chosen for its:

▶ Proximity to the downtown business community.

▶ Proximity to trendy, upscale restaurants, such as West Brothers and Allegra.

▶ Abundance of parking.

▶ Low-cost rent.

▶ High visibility.

JAVANET'S SERVICES

JavaNet customers will have full access to external POP3 e-mail accounts, or they can sign up for a JavaNet e-mail account. These accounts will be managed by JavaNet servers and be accessible from computer systems outside the JavaNet network. FTP, Telnet, Gopher, and other popular internet utilities will be available to customers, who will be able to choose either Netscape or Internet Explorer browser for surfing. Other services available to customers will include laser and color printing, scanning, access to popular software applications like Adobe Photoshop and Microsoft Word, and introductory courses on how to use the internet. For the customers' convenience, these classes will be held in the afternoon and early evening. This way, JavaNet can cultivate a loyal client base that feels at home in its comfortable surroundings.

In keeping with the trend of other internet cafés to offer customers state-of-the-art equipment, JavaNet will invest in high-speed computers to provide its customers with a fast and efficient connection to the internet. The computers will be new, reliable, and fun to work on. JavaNet will continue to upgrade and modify the systems to stay current with communications technology.

Technical Support

Bellevue Computers in Eugene will provide JavaNet with internet access, network consulting, and the hardware required to run the JavaNetwork. Allann Brothers will provide JavaNet with coffee equipment, bulk coffee, and paper supplies. Baked goods will be provided by Morningstar Bakery and Le Patisserie.

Future Services

As JavaNet grows, more communications systems will be added. The possibility of additional units has been accounted for in the current floor plan. As the demand for internet connectivity increases (along with competition in the market), JavaNet will continue to add new services to keep up with customer demand.

THE MARKET

JavaNet is faced with the exciting opportunity of being the first cyber-café in the Eugene market.

Market Segmentation

JavaNet's customers can be divided into two groups. The first is familiar with the internet and wants an inviting atmosphere where they can get out of their offices or living rooms and enjoy a great cup of coffee. The second group is not familiar with the internet yet but is waiting for the right opportunity to join the online community. JavaNet's target market falls anywhere between the ages of 18 and 50. Within these two broad categories, JavaNet's target market can be further divided into specific market segments, the majority of whom are students and businesspeople. See the Market Analysis table below for more specifics.

Potential Customers	Growth	2003	2004	2005	2006	2007
University Students	4%	$15,000	$15,600	$16,224	$16,873	$17,548
Office Workers	3%	25,000	25,750	26,523	27,319	28,139
Seniors	5%	18,500	19,425	20,396	21,416	22,487
Teenagers	2%	12,500	12,750	13,005	13,265	13,530
Others	0%	25,000	25,000	25,000	25,000	25,000
Total	**2.68%**	**$96,000**	**$98,525**	**$101,148**	**$103,873**	**$106,704**

Strategy for Reaching Our Target Market

JavaNet will cater to novices who want a guided tour on their first spin around the internet to experienced users eager to indulge their passion for computers in a social setting. Furthermore, JavaNet will be a magnet for local and traveling professionals who want to work or check their e-mail messages in a friendly atmosphere. These professionals will either use JavaNet's PCs or plug their notebooks in to internet connections.

Factors such as current trends and historical sales data ensure that the demand for coffee will remain constant over the next five years. The rapid growth of the internet and online services that has been witnessed worldwide is only the tip of the iceberg. The potential growth of the internet is enormous, to the point where in ten years, according to *PC Week* (September 2002, page 46), a computer terminal with an online connection will be as common and necessary as a telephone. Despite the fact that competitors will enter the market over the next five years, JavaNet has set a goal to maintain at least a 50 percent market share.

Mr. Bruckner hired Rumblefish Marketing to conduct a market survey in Eugene 2001. Key findings include:

- More than 70 percent said they'd be willing to pay for access to the internet.
- Five dollars an hour was the most popular hourly internet fee.
- More than 50 percent already use the internet on a regular basis.

Rumblefish also provided data for cybercafés in comparable markets like Cambridge, Massachusetts, Seattle, and San Francisco, and found that JavaNet's services, fees, environment, and equipment were in line with this young industry's standards.

The retail coffee industry in Eugene experienced rapid growth in the early 1990s and is now moving into the mature stage of its life cycle. Many factors contribute to the still-healthy demand for good coffee in Eugene. The biggest is university students and staff. To differentiate itself from other providers of coffee, specialty drinks, and baked goods, JavaNet will offer internet service in a café setting.

Business Vendors

There are approximately 16 coffee wholesalers in Lane County. These wholesalers distribute coffee and espresso beans to more than 20 retailers in the Eugene area. Competition in both channels creates an even amount of bargaining power between buyers and suppliers, resulting in extremely competitive pricing for coffee beans and related products.

In Eugene there is a positive relationship between price and quality of coffee. Some coffees retail at $8/pound while other, more exotic beans may sell for as high as $16/pound. Wholesalers sell beans to retailers at an average of a 50 percent discount. For example, a pound of Sumatran beans wholesales for $6.95 and retails for $13.95. As in most industries, price decreases as volume increases.

There are currently eight online service providers in Eugene. These small, regional service providers use a number of different pricing strategies. Some charge a monthly fee, while others charge hourly and/or phone fees. Regardless of the pricing method used, obtaining internet access through one of these firms can be expensive. Larger internet service providers such as America Online (AOL), Prodigy, and CompuServe are also fighting for market share in this rapidly growing industry. But they can still be rather costly for some people. Consumers who may use the internet only intermittently may not be willing to lock into paying these prices.

The main competitors in the retail coffee segment are Cafe Paradisio, Full City, Coffee Corner, and Cuppa Joe. These businesses are located in or near the downtown area and target a market segment similar to JavaNet's (students and businesspeople). However, none of these competitors has made the investment in equipment, facility, and fixtures that JavaNet will make to enable customers to use the internet.

Marketing Strategies

JavaNet's plans on attracting new internet users by:

- ▶ Providing knowledgeable employees focused on serving the customer's needs and helping them navigate the internet.
- ▶ Staffing the customer service desk during business hours. If a customer has any type of question or concern, a JavaNet employee will always be available to assist.
- ▶ Offering introductory classes designed to help new users familiarize themselves with e-mail, the internet, and the JavaNet computer system.

To attract seasoned internet users, JavaNet will provide:

- ▶ The latest in computing technology.
- ▶ Scanning and printing services.
- ▶ Access to powerful software applications.
- ▶ A social environment that enhances the entertainment value the internet can provide.

JavaNet will position itself as an upscale coffeehouse and internet service provider that serves high-quality coffee and espresso specialty drinks at a competitive price. JavaNet will place print ads in *The Register Guard*, *The Eugene Weekly*, and *The Emerald* to help build customer awareness. A coupon for a free hour of internet use will accompany these ads. Furthermore, JavaNet will give away three free hours of internet use to beginners who sign up for a JavaNet workshop.

Pricing Strategy

JavaNet bases its prices for coffee and specialty drinks on the "retail profit analysis" provided by our supplier, Allann Brothers Coffee Co. Inc. Allann Brothers has been in the coffee business for 22 years and has developed a solid pricing strategy.

Determining a fair-market hourly price for online use is more difficult because there is no direct competition from another cybercafé in Eugene. Therefore, JavaNet considered three sources to determine the hourly charge rate. First, we considered the cost to use other internet servers, whether it is a local networking firm or a provider such as

America Online. Some charge a monthly fee, while others charge an hourly fee. Second, JavaNet looked at how cybercafés in other markets such as Portland and Ashland went about pricing internet access. Third, JavaNet used the market survey conducted in 2001. Evaluating these three factors resulted in JavaNet's hourly price of $5.

Promotion Strategy

Initially, JavaNet will budget $5,000 for promotional efforts, which will include advertising with coupons for a free hour of internet time in local publications and in-house promotions such as offering customers free internet time if they pay for an introduction to the internet workshop taught by JavaNet's computer technician. JavaNet realizes that in the future, when competition enters the market, additional revenues must be allocated for promotion in order to maintain market share.

Sales Strategy

Computer literacy is a requirement for all JavaNet employees. If an employee does not have basic computer skills when hired, he or she can be trained by our full-time technician.

Sales Forecast

Sales forecast data is presented in the table below.

UNIT SALES	2003	2004	2005
Coffee (based on average)	$12,015	$14,068	$15,475
Specialty Drinks (based on average)	6,654	7,913	8,705
E-mail Memberships	8,704	10,505	11,556
Hourly Internet Fees	38,270	46,365	51,002
Baked Goods (based on average)	32,673	42,150	46,365
Other	0	0	0
Total Unit Sales	**$98,316**	**$121,001**	**$133,103**

UNIT PRICES	2003	2004	2005
Coffee (based on average)	$1.00	$1.00	$1.00
Specialty Drinks (based on average)	2.00	2.00	2.00
E-mail Memberships	10.00	10.00	10.00
Hourly Internet Fees	2.50	2.50	2.50
Baked Goods (based on average)	1.25	1.25	1.25
Other	0.00	0.00	0.00

SALES	2003	2004	2005
Coffee (based on average)	$12,015	$14,068	$15,475
Specialty Drinks (based on average)	13,308	15,826	17,409
E-mail Memberships	87,038	105,053	115,558
Hourly Internet Fees	95,676	115,913	127,505
Baked Goods (based on average)	40,841	52,688	57,957
Other	0	0	0
Total Sales	**$248,878**	**$303,548**	**$333,904**

DIRECT UNIT COSTS	2003	2004	2005
Coffee (based on average)	$0.25	$0.25	$0.25
Specialty Drinks (based on average)	0.50	0.50	0.50
E-mail Memberships	2.50	2.50	2.50
Hourly Internet Fees	0.63	0.63	0.63
Baked Goods (based on average)	0.31	0.31	0.31
Other	0.00	0.00	0.00

DIRECT COST OF SALES	2003	2004	2005
Coffee (based on average)	$3,004	$3,517	$3,869
Specialty Drinks (based on average)	3,327	3,957	4,352
E-mail Memberships	21,759	26,263	28,890
Hourly Internet Fees	23,919	28,978	31,876
Baked Goods (based on average)	10,210	13,172	14,489
Other	0	0	0
Subtotal Direct Cost of Sales	**$62,219**	**$75,887**	**$83,476**

Milestones

The JavaNet management team has established milestones to keep the business-planning process on target. Mr. Bruckner is responsible for meeting the following deadlines, which will be revised as needed.

Milestone	Start Date	End Date
Business Plan	1/1/2003	2/1/2003
Secure Start-Up Funding	2/15/2003	3/1/2003
Site Selection	3/1/2003	3/15/2003
Architect Designs	4/1/2003	5/1/2003
Designer Proposal	4/1/2003	4/15/2003
Technology Design	4/1/2003	4/15/2003
Year 1 Plan	6/1/2003	6/5/2003
Personnel Plan	7/1/2003	7/10/2003
Accounting Plan	7/1/2003	7/5/2003
Licensing	9/1/2003	9/15/2003

Milestones

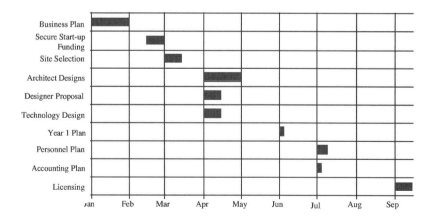

MANAGEMENT SUMMARY

JavaNet is 70 percent owned and 100 percent operated by Mr. Cale Bruckner, who makes all major management decisions. Mr. Bruckner's three partners—Luke Walsh, Doug Wilson, and John Underwood—each own 10 percent of the corporation, and none are involved in the day-to-day management of JavaNet.

After earning his MBA at the University of Oregon, Mr. Bruckner went to work for ten years at Peet's, a worldwide distributor of fine teas based in San Francisco. He worked his way up to vice president, marketing (a position he held for five years), and was responsible for all market-planning efforts, including the company's successful foray into the e-business arena.

JavaNet's Personnel Plan

JavaNet's staff will consist of six part-time employees, each working 20 hours a week at $7.50 per hour for the first two years. In 2005, raises will be given to $8 per hour. One full-time technician (who can handle minor terminal repairs/inquiries) will be on duty 40 hours a week at $15 per hour for 2003, $16.50 per hour for 2004, and $18.15 per hour in 2005.

Personnel	2003	2004	2005
Owner	$0	$15,000	$30,000
Part Time 1	7,500	7,500	8,000
Part Time 2	7,500	7,500	8,000
Part Time 3	7,500	7,500	8,000
Part Time 4	7,500	7,500	8,000
Part Time 5	7,500	7,500	8,000
Part Time 6	7,500	7,500	8,000
Technician	30,000	33,000	36,300
Total Payroll	75,000	93,000	114,300
JavaNet share of FICA and Medicare	5,738	7,115	8,744
TOTAL PAYROLL EXPENSE	**$80,738**	**$100,115**	**$123,044**

FINANCIAL PLAN

Sales

JavaNet is basing its projected coffee and espresso sales on information from Allann Bros. Coffee Co. Internet sales were estimated by calculating the total number of hours each terminal will be active each day and then generating a conservative estimate as to how many hours will be purchased by consumers.

Cost of Goods Sold

The cost of goods sold for coffee-related products was determined by the "retail profit analysis" obtained from Allann Bros. Coffee Co. The cost of bakery items is 20 percent of the selling price. The cost of internet access is $990 per month, paid to Bellevue Computers for networking fees. The cost of e-mail accounts is 25 percent of the selling price.

Fixture Costs

Fixture costs associated with starting JavaNet are: 11 computers = $22,000, two printers = $2,000, one scanner = $500, one espresso machine = $1,700, one automatic espresso grinder = $795, two coffee/food preparation counters = $1,000, one information display counter = $1,000, one drinking/eating counter = $500, 16 stools = $1,600, six computer desks w/chairs = $2,400, two telephones = $200, decoration expense = $9,605 for a total fixture cost of $43,300 (including the computers).

Payroll Expense

Mr. Bruckner will receive no salary in year one, $15,000 in year two, and $30,000 in year three. JavaNet's six part-time employees will be paid $7.50 an hour in the first two years and $8 in the third year. The full-time technician will start at $15/hour in the first year, and his/her salary will increase 10 percent each subsequent year. The total cost of employing seven people at these rates for the first year is $6,250/month.

Rent

JavaNet is leasing a 1,700-square-foot facility for $2,000/month for a total of 36 months. At the end of the third year, the lease is open for negotiation, and JavaNet may or may not re-sign the lease depending on the demands of the lessor.

Utilities

As stated in the lease, JavaNet's landlord is responsible for paying the heating, air conditioning, gas, garbage disposal, and real-estate tax expenses. JavaNet is responsible for its 15 phone lines (13 dedicated to modems and two for business purposes). The monthly charge for each line provided by US West is $23.58. The 13 lines used to connect the modems will make local calls to the network provided by Bellevue, resulting in a monthly charge of $306.54. The two additional lines used for business communication will cost $47.16/month plus long-distance fees. JavaNet assumes that it will not make more than $60/month in long-distance calls. Therefore, the total cost associated with the two business lines is estimated at $107.16/month and the total phone expense at $413.70/month. There is an additional utility expense estimated at $1,200 for electric bills.

Marketing

JavaNet has allocated $5,000 for advertising expenses at start-up, to be used to run advertisements in local newspapers in order to build consumer awareness.

Insurance

JavaNet has allocated $9,600 for insurance for the first year. As revenue increases in the second and third year of business, JavaNet intends to spend more money for additional insurance coverage.

Legal and Accounting

The one-time cost for our attorney to draft the agreement and other paperwork for our LLC is $2,000.

Depreciation

To depreciate our capital equipment, JavaNet used the modified accelerated cost recovery method. We depreciated our computers over a five-year period and our fixtures over seven years.

Loans Payable

JavaNet acquired a $21,000 loan from a bank at a 10 prcent interest rate. It will be paid back at $750/month over the next four years. The $5,000 loan from Microsoft and the $20,000 from the Oregon Economic Development Fund will be paid back over three years at an interest rate of 4 percent.

Financial Projections

Profit and Loss (Income Statement)

	2003	2004	2005
Sales	$273,317	$355,323	$500,856
Direct Cost of Sales	93,330	113,830	125,214
Other	$0	$0	$0
Total Cost of Sales	$93,330	$113,830	$125,214
Gross Margin	179,987	241,493	375,642
Gross Margin %	66%	68%	75%
Operating Expenses			
Advertising/Promotion	$20,000	$24,000	$28,800
Travel	1,125	0	0
Office, Inventory	18,000	20,000	22,000
Payroll Expense	80,738	100,115	123,044
Utilities	19,200	21,120	23,230
Insurance	9,600	11,520	13,820
Rent	24,000	24,000	24,000
Legal & Accounting	4,000	3,000	3,000
Total Operating Expenses	$176,663`	$203,755	$237,894
Profit Before Interest and Taxes	(3,324)	(37,738)	137,748
Interest Expense Short-Term	660	0	0
Interest Expense Long-Term	2,820	1,785	1,050
Taxes Incurred	($5,511)	($609)	$3,782
Net Profit	**$5,355**	**$30,895**	**132,916**

Pro Forma Cash Flow

	2003	2004	2005
Sources of Cash			
Sales	$273,317	$355,323	$500,856
Loan Proceeds	46,000	0	0
Total Cash In	$319,317	$355,323	$500,856
Uses of Cash			
Cost of Goods Sold	$93,300	$113,830	$125,214
Overhead	176,663	203,755	237,894
Interest	3,480	1,785	1,050
Taxes	0	0	3,782
Equipment Purchase	36,190	0	3,000
Debt, Principal Payments	17,975	16,853	16,011
Total Cash Out	$327,608	$336,223	$386,951
Net Change in Cash	(8,291)	(19,100)	113,905
Plus Beginning Cash on Hand	55,000	46,709	19,100
Ending Cash on Hand	$46,709	$27,609	$133,005

Pro Forma Balance Sheet

	2003	2004	2005
ASSETS			
Short-Term Assets			
Cash	$55,000	$46,709	$19,100
Inventory	2,500	2,900	3,100
Accounts Receivable	$0	$0	$0
Total Short-Term Assets	$57,500	$49,609	$22,200
Long-Term Assets			
Fixed Assets	36,190	30,000	35,200
Total Long-Term Assets	36,190	30,000	35,200
TOTAL ASSETS	**$93,690**	**$79,609**	**$57,400**
LIABILITIES			
Short-Term Liabilities			
Accounts Payable	12,348	12,453	13,542
Interest Payable	3,480	1,785	1,050
Taxes Payable	0	0	3,782
Total Short-Term Liabilities	$15,828	$14,238	$18,374
Long-Term Liabilities	46,000	29,850	16,011
Total Liabilities	**$61,828**	**$44,088**	**$34,385**
NET WORTH	**$31,862**	**$35,521**	**$23,015**
LIABILITIES AND NET WORTH	**$93,690**	**$79,609**	**$57,400**

Appendix F

Business Plan for a Freelance Artisan/Contractor

THIS BUSINESS PLAN WAS WRITTEN WHILE GEOFF CROSBY, THE OWNER of Construct Design, was making the decision to leave an executive job with a high-tech company and go into business for himself. He has since rented and fitted out appropriate industrial space, and is in business full-time. Pay particular note to his careful and thorough analysis of both the industry and the competition, and to the composition of his advisory board. While he doesn't need additional capital (the business became cash-flow positive and self financing within ten months of startup), he would have no problem finding investors.

His financial statements are confidential. However, his projections clearly justified his decision to go out on his own, and experience has shown the decision to be a good one.

Construct Design, LLC
Business Plan

Geoffrey K. Crosby

Revised March 3, 2004

Table of Contents

Executive Summary

Construct Design is transitioning from a part-time to a full-time business. The purpose of this plan is provide a framework to (a) evaluate the business potential of Construct Design and (b) project a series of financial scenarios to determine the amount of capital needed to get Construct Design up and running. At this time no additional funds are sought.

Section One: The Business

What We Do

We build high quality custom concrete counters and tables. We work with customers and designers to create counters not available anywhere else, and we do so with passion, good design sense, and fun. We want to be a pleasure to do business with, and we want to create high quality, highly functional concrete art.

Construct Design—bringing highly functional concrete art into home and office.

Location

We are located in Portsmouth, NH, and plan to offer products and services within a 20 mile radius of Portsmouth, but focused on the Seacoast corridor up into Maine. However, we will accept jobs within a 50 mile radius.

Products and Services

We will start initially with our strength—custom residential countertops, which require custom samples, custom templates, custom molds, and installation. As we grow, we will add additional products and services.

Initial Products and Services

- Custom concrete counters for residential customers and contractors
- Custom pieces for small commercial installations
- Refinishing/sealing services

Future Products and Concepts

- Production tables supplied to furniture stores
- Outdoor tables, benches, etc.
- Cabinet pulls and interior doorknobs
- Large commercial installations
- Production sinks for local supply, (i.e., Sonoma Cast Stone)
- Other countertop materials, (i.e., copper, zinc, or soapstone)
- Alignment with bigger firm, (i.e., Cheng or Stone Soup, to produce products for them in this area or perform installations)

The Market

Our primary market is high end, art and design focused local architects, kitchen designers, interior designers, and high end contractors, who are executing kitchen or bath remodels or new construction. Our secondary market is the actual end user: high income, art and design focused home or business owners.

The U.S. Market for residential kitchen and bath countertops in 2000 was $11.7 billion (460 million square feet, average price equals $25.43 per square foot). Annual growth from 1995 to 2000 was nearly 10 percent. Demand is expected to increase at 3.9 percent between 2000 and 2005.

"Industry advances will be fueled by a trend toward higher value added styles of laminates and tiles, as well as a shift in the overall product mix toward more expensive countertops such as solid surface and natural and engineered stone." (*Source*: Freedonia Focus on Countertops, July 2002.)

"Natural stone (primary competitor) is composed of granite, marble, slate, limestone, soapstone, lavastone, and bluestone. Granite accounts for 92 percent of natural stone countertop demand. While each stone has unique characteristics, these countertops are in general high maintenance and expensive. Demand stems from growing consumer interest in the luxurious appearance of natural materials. Sales of natural stone countertops reached $1.2 billion, or 11 percent of total demand (3.5 percent by volume, Average Price = $74.53/square foot), in 2000." (*Source*: Freedonia Focus on Countertops, July 2002.)

"Other: Other types of countertops include stainless steel, wood butcher block, engineered stone, concrete, miscellaneous cast polymers, copper and zinc. Stainless steel has been the largest of this group, due to the popularity of the professional kitchen look and its heat and stain resistance. Engineered stone, introduced to the United States in the late 1990s, by far the fastest growing, is durable, requiring low maintenance, and mimics the look and feel of natural stone. These materials had a combined market share of 9 percent in 2000 ($1.05 billion) (6 percent in volume terms, average price equals $38.15 per square foot), growing at just over 6 percent annually between 1995 and 2000." (*Source*: Freedonia Focus on Countertops, July 2002.)

Eighty percent of the $11.7 billion market is in remodeling, 20 percent in new construction.

Business SIC Code 3281 Cut Stone and Stone Products

Marketing Plan: Awareness, Interest, Desire, Action

We plan to focus our business within a 20 mile radius of Portsmouth on the Seacoast corridor up into Maine, but we will accept jobs within a 50 mile radius. We could also explore south to Boston, but this market already has some formidable competition.

Why We Will Win

- We provide a high quality, highly personalized product
- We have good design sense
- It will be a pleasure to do business with us
- We have good experience
- We will deliver on schedule, and we are reliable
- We will continually learn and improve and explore
- We will network with the design and contractor communities
- We are expensive, but justified by all the above

Target Audience: All High End Businesses

- Kitchen designers
- Architects
- Interior designers
- Contractors
- High-end artsy furniture stores

Initial Goals of Customer Contact

- Find out what their wants and needs are
- Create awareness of Construct Design capabilities
- Create interest in concrete as a medium

Initial Marketing Tactics

- Direct mailings and phone follow up
- Personal visits with samples and portfolio

- ▶ Web site
- ▶ Yellow Pages listing

Pricing Strategy

- ▶ We will start at $100 per square foot for direct business
- ▶ We will evaluate 10-15% discounts for contractors
- ▶ We will evaluate kitchen design businesses as dealers
- ▶ We will position ourselves against quality granite and soapstone surfaces
- ▶ The web site, concretenetwork.com, states prices range from $65 to $125 per square foot.
- ▶ We will undertake a new pricing study for installed price per square foot.

Options to Increase Credibility and Publicize Contact Information

- ▶ Join chamber of commerce
- ▶ Become a member of the Concrete Exchange?
- ▶ Become a member of the Concrete Network?
- ▶ Become a member of the Decorative Concrete Council?
- ▶ Become a member of the American Society of Concrete Contractors?
- ▶ PR through local magazines and newspapers
- ▶ Create pieces and retail displays for display showrooms

Competition

Competition here comes primarily from other countertop material manufacturers, such as granite and soapstone. I need to do pricing research on local suppliers for these products as installed. There are a limited quantity of concrete counter suppliers in the area, with limited experience and capabilities. The national concrete counter suppliers can ship nationally, but this seriously hampers the personal and creative touch.

Local Concrete Countertop Suppliers

▶ Form/Function, Rowley, MA, Ray Iacobacci, (978) 432-1093 $65-75 per square foot, www.formfunctionconcrete.com. Good article in Globe, looks like good quality stuff, On Concretenet work.com.

▶ Marathon Concrete, Bellingham, MA, Mark Brunelle, (508) 509-5247, On Concrete Exchange.

▶ Distinctive Concrete of New England, Rowley, MA, Bill Guthro, (978) 948-2970, www.distinctiveconcrete.com. Counters look rough, looks primarily like stamping business. On Concretenet work.com.

▶ Stone Soup Concrete, Florence, MA, (413) 582-0783, www.stone soupconcrete.com. Very sharp, excellent design and quality look. Counters, sinks, tubs. On Concrete Exchange and concretenet work.com

▶ Dimensional Creations, Dover, NH, Owen Whisnant, (603) 750-0055. On Concrete Exchange.

▶ Stonecraft, Portland, ME, Scott Chasse, (207) 699-2422 $60 per square foot, www.astonecraft.com. Not many examples, looks very new, not great quality. On concretenetwork.com.

▶ Ocho Furniture, Kittery, ME, Bradlee Hall Kirkpatrick. Concrete-topped tables, available through Nahcotta and Lekkers in Boston.

▶ Custom Concrete Design/Precision Flatwork, North Berwick, ME, Michael Littlefield (207) 459-7700, www.precisionflat work.com. Not many examples, looks like very new product. Could have new web site www.concretecountertopdesigns.com. This site has good shots.

▶ Reye Studio, Eliot, ME, Richard Webber, (207) 748-1084 $55 to $75 per square foot, plus $11 per square foot for installation, www.reye-studio.com. Concrete counters and sinks; on display at Lifestyles. Looks decent, but also looks new. From concretenet-work, prices range from $65 to $125 per square foot.

Local Granite and Soapstone Countertop Suppliers

- ▶ W.S. Goodrich, Epping, NH
- ▶ Home Depot, Newington, NH
- ▶ Arens Stoneworks, Greenland, NH
- ▶ Eno Building Supply, Hampton, NH
- ▶ Stoneyard, Eliot, ME. Just outdoor products?

National Concrete Countertop Suppliers

- ▶ Buddy Rhodes, San Francisco, CA
- ▶ Cheng Design, Berkeley, CA
- ▶ Soupcan Inc., Chicago, IL

Management

Geoff Crosby is the owner of Construct Design. Geoff first started building concrete countertops in 1998 as a result of a lack of local supply, and has been experimenting and building counters on a part time basis since. He has completed projects for Portsmouth area kitchen designers, contractors, architects, and individual home owners.

Geoff has an extensive background in sales and marketing, having worked in retail sporting goods, consumer products, industrial capital equipment, and laboratory equipment sales and marketing positions over the past 15 years.

He also has experience in the operations and construction side, having supervised commercial renovations and industrial equipment installation, as well as having two years' experience remodeling homes professionally.

Geoff has a Bachelor of Science degree in Molecular Biology with a Management minor, and has continuing education credits in Project Management, Product Management, and Services Selling. He has also worked with P&L statements and other financial business models and controls for 15 years.

Advisory Board/Board of Directors – Wish List

Chairman	Geoff Crosby
Human Resources/Personnel	Amanda Telford
General Business	David H. Bangs, Jr.
Finance/M&A	Aaron Gowell
Engineering	Chris Dundorf
Production	Ric Hayes
Construction/Industry	Ben Auger, Lisa DeStefano
Marketing/Sales	Deb Ludington, Tim LeFebvre
Customer Member	Laura Ludes, Jeannie Ryan? Mehalls?
Options	Jay Prewitt, Stewart Johnson, Penny Stevens, Drew Wilson

Personnel

Initially, Geoff will perform all work, but as volume increases, will add on labor for production purposes. Construct Design will use the legal services of George Venci Law PLLC, and the accounting services of Edward R. Caito, CPA.

For installation purposes, which typically require two to three additional people to transport slabs, we will reach agreements with individual contractors, set up barter agreements with contractor friends, and rely on friends.

Production Capabilities

At start up, we will have 370 square feet of production space, broken down into 190 square feet of heated space, and 180 square feet of unheated space. These spaces contain five pouring tables, four heated, one unheated. As we currently estimate 17 hours of labor per average slab, we are limited by pouring tables, able to produce roughly 70 slabs per year on our tables at full capacity, which is roughly 30 weeks of labor.

Quoted lead times on custom counters will be five to six weeks from receipt of deposit. This includes time to template, build custom molds, pour, cure, finish, and schedule installation.

Future capabilities should consider larger space for material and tool storage, mold production, pouring tables, and a gallery/office space. Production space should consider heating capabilities, air handling/filtration capabilities, and material handling (i.e., overhead crane) for pallets of supplies and large slabs.

Estimated production space should require roughly 1,000 square feet for nine pouring tables capacity, which could produce 156 counter slabs per year, or $240,000 of revenue. Office space requirements are flexible, but should be around 200 to 300 square feet for an office and customer meeting area, and bathroom.

Suitable commercial space in the Portsmouth area is typically available at $8 to $12 per square foot per year. This would result in a yearly lease of $8,000 to $18,000 for the space. We have looked at space in Newington, NH, and $10 per square feet per year in Greenland, NH. (Note: Deb is paying $1,025/month in Greenland for 1,200 square feet of space).

Cost for labor for production is currently $11 to 15 per hour in Portsmouth, and similar in surrounding towns. Additional benefits/costs?

Summary

Construct Design will offer high quality, design oriented concrete countertops to a focused, local audience of high-end customers. We will use our existing network of architects, designers, and contractors to continue to build our reputation, and we will market to new architects, designers and contractors. We will rely upon our reliability, quality, timeliness, fair pricing, and personalized service to win business.

Section Two: Financials

Sources and Applications of Funding

Capital Equipment List

Existing Capital Equipment

1994 Ford F-150	$4,500
Four pouring tables	1,200
Concrete mixer	200
Miscellaneous tools	1,600
Computer and software	2,000
Office supplies and phones	350
Total existing capital equipment	**$9,850**

Future Purchases

Trailer and hitch	$3,000
Color laser printer	700
Phones	200
Miscellaneous tools	200
Accounting software	400
Air filtration/dust collection	500
Total future purchases	**$5,000**

Balance Sheet {confidential}

Break Even Analysis {confidential}

Projected Income Statement {confidential}

Cash Flow Projection {confidential}

Deviation Analysis {confidential}

Historical Financial Information

This will be a summary of previous jobs, their prices, material costs, and labor estimates.

Appendix

A. Freedonia Countertop Study, 2002

B. Exit Strategies

- ▸ Sell to local contractor
- ▸ Sell to local concrete supplier
- ▸ Sell to local counter supplier
- ▸ License to established national supplier such as Cheng or Sonoma Stone.
- ▸ Sell out to employees
- ▸ Close up shop

Appendix G

Government Listings

Government Agencies

Copyright Clearance Center
222 Rosewood Dr.
Danvers, MA 01923
(978) 750-8400
Fax: (978) 750-4470
www.copyright.com

U.S. Copyright Office
Library of Congress
101 Independence Ave., SE
Washington, DC 20559-6000
(202) 707-3000
Fax: (202) 707-6859
www.loc.gov/copyright

Department of Agriculture
1400 Independence Ave., SW
Washington, DC 20250

(202) 720-7420
www.fas.usda.gov

Department of Commerce
1401 Constitution Ave., NW
Washington, DC 20230
(202) 482-2000
Fax: (202) 482-5270
www.doc.gov

Department of Energy
1000 Independence Ave., SW
Washington, DC 20585
(202) 586-5000, (800) 342-5363
Fax: (202) 586-4403
www.energy.gov

Department of the Interior
1849 C Street, NW
Washington, DC 20240

(202) 208-3100
www.doi.gov

Department of Labor
200 Constitution Ave., NW
Room S-1004
Washington, DC 20210
(202) 219-6666, (866) 487-2365
www.dol.gov

Department of the Treasury
Main Treasury Building
1500 Pennsylvania Ave., NW
Washington, DC 20220
(202) 622-1502
Fax: (202) 622-6415
www.ustreas.gov

Export-Import Bank of the United States
811 Vermont Ave., NW, #911
Washington, DC 20571
(202) 565-3940,
(800) 565-3946, ext. 3908
Fax: (202) 565-3932
www.exim.gov

Internal Revenue Service
1111 Constitution Ave., NW
Washington, DC 20224
(202) 622-5000
www.irs.ustreas.gov

U.S. Patent & Trademark Office
Crystal Plaza 3, Room 2C02
Washington, DC 20231
(800) 786-9199
www.uspto.gov

U.S. Government Printing Office
Superintendent of Documents
Washington, DC 20402

(202) 512-1800
Fax: (202) 512-2250
www.access.gpo.gov

Securities & Exchange Commission
450 Fifth Street, NW
Washington, DC 20549
(202) 942-8088
Fax: (202) 942-7040
www.sec.gov

Small Business Administration
409 Third Street, SW
Washington, DC 20416
(800) 827-5722
www.sba.gov

SBA District Offices

Alabama
801 Tom Martin Dr.
Birmingham, AL 35211
(205) 290-7101
Fax: (205-290-7404

Alaska
510 L Street, #310
Anchorage, AK 99501
(907) 271-4022
Fax: (907) 271-4545

Arizona
2828 N. Central Ave., #800
Phoenix, AZ 85004-1093
(602) 745-7200
Fax: (602) 745-7210

Arkansas
2120 Riverfront Dr., #100
Little Rock, AR 72202
(501) 324-5871
Fax: (501) 324-5491

California
2719 Air Fresno Dr., #200
Fresno, CA 93727-1547
(559) 487-5791
Fax: (559) 487-5636

330 N. Brand Blvd., #1200
Glendale, CA 91203-2304
(818) 552-3210
Fax: (818) 552-3286

550 W. C Street, # 550
San Diego, CA 92101
(619) 557-7250
Fax: (619) 557-5894

455 Market St., 6th floor
San Francisco, CA 94105-1988
(415) 744-6820
Fax: (415) 744-6812

650 Capitol Mall, #7-500
Sacramento, CA 95814-2413
(916) 930-3700
Fax: (916) 930-3737

200 W. Santa Ana Blvd., #700
Santa Ana, CA 92701-4134
(714) 550-7420
Fax: (714) 550 0191

Colorado
721 19th Street, #426
Denver, CO 80202-2517
(303) 844-2607
Fax: (303) 844-6468

Connecticut
330 Main Street, 2nd floor
Hartford, CT 06106-1800
(860) 240-4700
Fax: (860) 240-4659

Delaware
824 N. Market St., #610
Wilmington, DE 19801-3011
(302) 573-6294

District of Columbia
1110 Vermont Ave. NW, #900
Washington, DC 20005
(202) 606-4000
Fax: (202) 606-4225

Florida
100 S. Biscayne Blvd., 7th floor
Miami, FL 3313-2011
(305) 536-5521
Fax: (305) 536-5058

7825 Baymeadows Way, #100-B
Jacksonville, FL 32256-7504
(904) 443-1900
Fax: (904) 443-1980

Georgia
233 Peachtree St., NE, #1900
Atlanta, GA 30303
(404) 331-0100
Fax: (404) 347-0694

Hawaii
300 Ala Moana Blvd.
Room 2-235, Box 50207
Honolulu, HI 96850-4981
(808) 541-2990
Fax: (808) 541-2976

Idaho
1020 Main St., #290
Boise, ID 83702-5745
(208) 334-1696
Fax: (208) 334-9353

Illinois
500 W. Madison St., #1250
Chicago, IL 60661-2511
(312) 353-4528
Fax: (312) 866-5688

511 W. Capitol Ave., #302
Springfield, IL 62704
(217) 492-4416

Indiana
429 N. Pennsylvania St., #100
Indianapolis, IN 46204-1873
(317) 226-7272
Fax: (317) 226-7264

Iowa
Mail Code 0736
The Lattner Building
215 Fourth Ave., SE, #200
Cedar Rapids, IA 52401-1806
(319) 362-6405
Fax: (319) 362-7861

210 Walnut St., Room 749
Des Moines, IA 50309-2186
(515) 284-4422
Fax: (515) 284-4572

Kansas
271 W. 3rd Street N. #2500
Wichita, KS 67202-1212
(316) 269-6616
Fax: (316) 269-6499

Kentucky
600 Dr. Martin Luther
King Jr. Pl. #188
Louisville, KY 40202
(502) 582-5761
Fax: (502) 582-5009

Louisiana
365 Canal St., #2820
New Orleans, LA 70130
(504) 589-6685
Fax: (504) 589-2339

Maine
Edward S. Muskie Federal Bldg.
68 Sewall Street, Room 512
Augusta, ME 04330
(207) 622-8274
Fax: (207) 622-8277

Maryland
10 S. Howard St., #6220
Baltimore, MD 21201-2525
(410) 962-4392
Fax: (410) 962-1805

Massachusetts
10 Causeway St. Room 265
Boston, MA 02222-1093
(617) 565-5590
Fax: (617) 565-5597

Michigan
McNamara Building
477 Michigan Ave., Room 515
Detroit, MI 48226
(313) 226-6075
Fax: (313) 226-4769

Minnesota
Butler Square 210-C
100 N. 6th Street
Minneapolis, MN 55403
(612) 370-2324
Fax: (612) 370-2303

Mississippi
Am South Bank Plaza
210 E. Capitol St., #900

Jackson, MS 39201
(601) 965-4378
Fax: (601) 965-5629

Missouri
323 W. 8th St., #501
Kansas City, MO 64105
(816) 374-6708
Fax: (816) 374-6759

815 Olive St., Room 242
St. Louis, MO 63101
(314) 539-6600
Fax: (314) 539-3785

Montana
Federal Building
10 W. 15th St., #1100
Helena, MT 59626
(406) 441-1081, (800) 776-9144 ext. 2
Fax: (406) 441-1090

Nebraska
11145 Mill Valley Rd.
Omaha, NE 68154
(402) 221-4691
Fax: (402) 221-3680

Nevada
300 S. Las Vegas Blvd., #1100
Las Vegas, NV 89101
(702) 388-6611
Fax: (702) 388-6469

New Hampshire
143 N. Main St., #202
Concord, NH 03301-1248
(603) 225-1400
Fax: (603) 225-1409

New Jersey
2 Gateway Center, 15th floor

Newark, NJ 07102
(973) 645-2434
Fax: (973) 645-6265

New Mexico
625 Silver Ave., SW #320
Albuquerque, NM 87102
(505) 346-7909
Fax: (505) 346-6711

New York
111 W. Huron St., #1311
Buffalo, NY 14202
(716) 551-4301
Fax: (716) 551-4418

26 Federal Plaza, #3100
New York, NY 10278
(212) 264-4354
Fax: (212) 264-4963

401 S. Salina St., 5th floor
Syracuse, NY 13202-2415
(315) 471-9393
Fax: (315) 471-9288

North Carolina
6302 Fairview Rd., #300
Charlotte, NC 28210-2227
(704) 344-6563
Fax: (704) 344-6769

North Dakota
657 2nd Ave., N, Room 219
Fargo, ND 58108
(701) 239-5131
Fax: (701) 239-5645

Ohio
1111 Superior Ave., #630
Cleveland, OH 44114-2507
(216) 522-4180
Fax: (216) 522-2038

2 Nationwide Plaza, #1400
Columbus, OH 43215-2542
(614) 469-6860
Fax: (614) 469-2391

Oklahoma
210 Park Ave., #1300
Oklahoma City, OK 73102
(405) 231-5521
Fax: (405) 231-4876

Oregon
1515 SW 5th Ave., #1050
Portland, OR 97201-5494
(503) 326-2682
Fax: (503) 326-2808

Pennsylvania
Robert N.C. Nix Federal Bldg.
900 Market St., 5th floor
Philadelphia, PA 19107
(215) 580-2722
Fax: (215) 580-2762

Federal Building, Room 1128
1000 Liberty Avenue
Pittsburgh, PA 15222-4004
(412) 395-6560
Fax: (412) 395-6562

Puerto Rico
Citibank Tower
252 Ponce de Leon Blvd., #201
Hato Rey, PR 00918
(787) 766-5572
Fax: (787) 766-5309

Rhode Island
380 Westminster St., 5th floor
Providence, RI 02903
(401) 528-4561
Fax: (401) 528-4539

South Carolina
1835 Assembly St., Room 358
Columbia, SC 29201
(803) 765-5377
Fax: (803) 765-5962

South Dakota
110 S. Phillips Ave., #200
Sioux Falls, SD 57102-1109
(605) 330-4231
Fax: (605) 330-4215

Tennessee
50 Vantage Way, #201
Nashville, TN 37228-1500
(615) 736-5881
Fax: (615) 736-7232

Texas
4300 Amon Carter Blvd., #114
Fort Worth, TX 75155
(817) 885-5500
Fax: (817) 684-5516

8701 S. Gessner Dr., #1200
Houston, TX 77074
(713) 773-6500
Fax: (713) 773-6550

222 E. Van Buren St., Room 500
Harlingen, TX 78550-6855
(956) 427-8533
Fax: (956) 427-8537

1205 Texas Ave., Room 408
Lubbock, TX 79401-2693
(806) 472-7462
Fax: (806) 472-7487

Federal Building—5th Floor
727 E. Durango Blvd., Room A-527
San Antonio, TX 78206-1204

(210) 472-5900
Fax: (210) 472-5935

Utah
125 S. State St., Room 2231
Salt Lake City, UT 84138-1195
(801) 524-3209
Fax: (801) 524-4160

Vermont
87 State St., Room 205, Box 605
Montpelier, VT 05601
(802) 828-4422
Fax: (802) 828-4485

Virginia
Federal Building
400 N. 8th Street, #1150
Richmond, VA 23240
(804) 771-2400
Fax: (804) 771-8018

Washington
1200 Sixth Ave., #1700
Seattle, WA 98101-1128
(206) 553-7310
Fax: (206) 553-7099

Spokane Regional Business Center
801 W. Riverside Ave., #200
Spokane, WA 99201
(509) 353-2800
Fax: (509) 353-2829

West Virginia
320 West Pike St., #330
Clarksburg, WV 26301
(304) 623-5631
Fax: (304) 623-0023

Wisconsin
740 Regent St., #100

Madison, WI 53715
(608) 441-5263
Fax: (608) 441-5541

Wyoming
100 E. B Street, Room 4001
P.O Box 2839
Casper, WY 82602-2839
(307) 261-6500
Fax: (307) 261-6535

Small Business Development Centers

Alabama
University of Alabama
Box 870223
Tuscaloosa, AL 35487
(205) 348-7443
Fax: (205) 348-5308
www.fbf.cba.ua.edu

Alaska
University of Alaska at Anchorage
430 W. Seventh Ave., #110
Anchorage, AK 99501
(907) 274-7232
Fax: (907) 274-9524
www.businessnation.com/local
info/index.html

Arizona
2411 W. 14th Street, #132
Tempe, AZ 85281
(480) 731-8720
Fax: (480) 731-8729
www.dist.maricopa.edu/sdbdc

Arkansas
2801 S. University Ave.
Little Rock, AR 72204

(501) 324-9043
Fax: (501) 324-9049
www.ualr.edu/~sbdcdept

California
Office of Small Business
1102 Q Street, #6000
Sacramento, CA 95814
(916) 324-5068, (800) 303-6600
Fax: (916) 322-5084
www.dgs.ca.gov

Colorado
Colorado Business Assistance Center
2413 Washington Street
Denver, CO 80205
(303) 592-5920, (800) 333-7798
Fax: (303) 592-8107
www.state.co.us/oed/sbdc/bac.html

Connecticut
University of Connecticut
2100 Hillside Rd., #1041
Storrs, CT 06269-1041
(860) 486-4135
Fax: (860) 486-0889
www.sba.uconn.edu

Delaware
University of Delaware
One Innovation Way, #301
Newark, DE 19711
(302) 831-1555
Fax: (302) 831-1423
www.delawaresbdc.org/locations.html

District of Columbia
Howard University
School of Business
2600 6th Street, NW, Room 128
Washington, DC 20059
(202) 806-1550

Fax: (202) 806-1777
husbdc@cldc.howard.edu

Florida
19 W. Garden Street, #300
Pensacola, FL 32501
(850) 470-4980, (850) 595-6060
Fax: (850) 595-6070
www.floridasbdc.com

Georgia
University of Georgia
Chicopee Complex
1180 E. Broad Street
Athens, GA 30602-5412
(706) 542-7436
Fax: (706) 542-6803
www.sbdc.uga.edu/athens_people. html

Guam
Pacific Islands
UOG Station
Mangilao, Guam 96923
(671) 735-2590
Fax: (671) 734-2002
www.uog.edu/sbdc/contact.html

Hawaii
University of Hawaii at Hilo
200 W. Kawili Street
Hilo, HI 96720-4091
(808) 974-7515
Fax: (808) 974-7683
www.hawaii-sbdc.org

Idaho
Boise State University
1910 University Dr.
Boise, ID 83725-1655
(208) 426-1640
Fax: (208) 426-3877
www.idahosbdc.org

Illinois
Greater North Pulaski
4054 W. North Ave.
Chicago, IL 60639
(773) 384-2262, (800) 252-2923
Fax: (773) 384-3850
www.gnpdc.org/sbdc.html

Indiana
1 N. Capitol Ave., #900
Indianapolis, IN 46204
(317) 234-2082
Fax: (317) 232-8872
www.isbdcorp.org/contact/contact.htm

Iowa
137 Lynn Ave., #5
Ames, IA 50014
(515) 292-6351
Fax: (515) 292-0020
www.iowasbdc.org

Kansas
137 Skirk Hall
1501 S. Joplin St.
Pittsburg, KS 66762
(620) 235-4920
Fax: (620) 235-4919
go.pittstate.edu/directory/dept.info#D

Kentucky
225 Gatton
College of Business and Economics
Lexington, KY 40506-0034
(859) 257-7668
Fax: (859) 323-1907
www.ksbdc.org/

Louisiana
University of Louisiana at Monroe
Administration 2-57
Monroe, LA 71209-6435

(318) 342-5506
Fax: (318) 342-5510
lsbdc.netl.nlu.edu

Maine
University of Southern Maine
96 Falmouth St., P.O Box 9300
Portland, ME 04104-9300
(207) 780-4420
Fax: (207) 780-4810
www.mainesbdc.org

Maryland
7100 E. Baltimore Ave., #402
College Park, MD 20740-3627
(301) 403-8300
www.dbed.state.md.us

Massachusetts
University of Massachusetts
205 School of Management
P.O. Box 34935
Amherst, MA 01003
(413) 545-6301
Fax: (413) 545-1272
msbdc.som.umass.edu

Michigan
Grand Valley State University
Seidman School of Business
510 W. Fulton Street
Grand Rapids, MI 49504
(616) 336-7480
Fax: (616) 336-7485
www.mi-sbdc.org/

Minnesota
Department of Trade and Economic
Development
100 Metro Square
121 7th Place, East
St. Paul, MN 55101-2146

(651) 296-5205
Fax: (651) 296-7095
www.dted.state.mn.us

Mississippi
University of Mississippi
P.O Box 1848
B 19 Jeanette Phillips Dr.
University, MS 38677-1848
(662) 915-5001
Fax: (662) 915-5650
www.olemiss.edu/depts/mssbdc

Missouri
1205 University Place, #1800
Columbia, MO 65211
(573) 882-7096
Fax: (573) 882-9931
www.business.missouri.edu/sbdc/
index.htm

Montana
1424 Ninth Avenue
Helena, MT 59620
(406) 444-4780
Fax: (406) 444-1872
www.businessnation.com/localinfo/
index.html

Nebraska
College of Business Administration
60th & Dodge St., Room 407
Omaha, NE 68182-0248
(402) 554-2521
Fax: (402) 554-3473
www.unomaha.edu

Nevada
University of Nevada at Reno
CBA, MS 32
Reno, NV 89557-0100

(702) 784-1717
Fax: (702) 784-4337
www.coba.unr.edu/

New Hampshire
670 N. Commercial St.,
4th floor, #25
Manchester, NH 03101
(603) 624-2000
Fax: (603) 647-4410
www.nhsbdc.org/manchest.htm

New Jersey
49 Bleeker St.
Newark, NJ 07102-1913
(973) 353-1927
Fax: (973) 353-1110
www.nj.com/njsbdc_new/

New Mexico
Santa Fe Community College
Lead Center
6401 S. Richards Avenue
Santa Fe, NM 87508
(505) 428-1362, (800) 281-7232
Fax: (505) 428-1469
www.nmsbdc.org

New York
University at Albany
One Pinnacle Plaza, #218
Albany, NY 12203
(518) 453-9567
Fax: (518) 453-9572
www.nys-sbdc.suny.edu

North Carolina
SB & TDC
5 W. Hargett St., #600
Raleigh, NC 27601-1348
(919) 715-7272, (800) 258-0862

Fax: (919) 715-7777
www.sbtdc.org

North Dakota
University of North Dakota
118 Gamble Hall, P.O. Box 7308
Grand Forks, ND 58202
(701) 777-3700, (800) 445-7232
Fax: (701) 777-3225
www.und.nodak.edu/dept/ndsbdc

Ohio
37 N. High St.
Columbus, OH 43215
(614) 221-1321, (614) 225-6910
Fax: (614) 221-9360
www.columbus-chamber.org/
sbdc.html
www.ohiosbdc.org

Oklahoma
Southeastern OK State University
517 W. University Blvd.
Durant, OK 74701
(580) 745-7577
Fax: (580) 745-7471
www.osbdc.org

Oregon
44 W. Broadway, #501
Eugene, OR 97401-3021
(541) 726-2250
Fax: (541) 345-6006
www.bizcenter.org

Pennsylvania
University of Pennsylvania
Vance Hall, 3733 Spruce St., 4th floor
Philadelphia, PA 19104
(215) 898-1219
Fax: (215) 573-2135

www.pasbdc.org

Rhode Island
Bryant College
1150 Douglas Pike
Smithfield, RI 02917
(401) 232-6111
Fax: (401) 232-6933
www.risbdc.org

South Carolina
University of South Carolina
The Darla Moore School of Business
Columbia, SC 29208
(803) 777-4907
Fax: (803) 777-4403
http://sbdcweb.badm.sc.edu

South Dakota
University of South Dakota
School of Business
414 E. Clark St.
Vermillion, SD 57069-2390
(605) 677-5011
Fax: (605) 677-5427
www.usd.edu/brbinfo/sbdc

Tennessee
University of Memphis
South Campus-Bldg. 1, Box 526324
Memphis, TN 38152
(901) 678-2500, 901-678-2000
Fax: (901) 678-4072
www.memphis.edu

Texas
2302 Fannin St., #200
Houston, TX 77002
(713) 752-8444
Fax: (713) 756-1500
smbizsolutions.uh.edu

Utah
125 S. State St., Room 2231
Salt Lake City, UT 84111
(801) 957-3840, (801) 524-3209
Fax: (801) 524-4160
www.sbaonline.sba.gov

Vermont
P.O. Box 188
Randolph Center, VT 05061-0188
(802) 728-9101, (800) 464-7232
Fax: (802) 728-3026
www.vtsbdc.org/contact.htm

Virginia
116 E. Franklin St., #100
Richmond, VA 23219
(804) 783-9314
Fax: (804) 648-7849
www.dba.state.va.us
www.grsbdc.com/

Washington
Washington State University
P.O. Box 644851
Pullman, WA 99164-4851
(509) 335-1576
Fax: (509) 335-0949
www.wsbdc.org/
www.sbdc.wsu.edu

West Virginia
State Capitol Complex
Building 6, Room 652
1900 Kanawha Blvd., E
Charleston, WV 25305
(304) 558-2960, (888) 982-7732
Fax: (304) 558-0127
www.wvsbdc.org

Wisconsin
University of Wisconsin at
Whitewater
2000 Carlson Hall
Whitewater, WI 53190
(262) 472-3217, (800) 621-7235
Fax: (262) 472-5692
www.uww.edu/sbdc/

Wyoming
111 W. Second St., #502
Casper, WY 82601
(307) 234-6683
Fax: (307) 577-7014
www.businessnation.com/localinfo/
index.html

State Commerce and Economic Development Departments

Alabama
401 Adams Ave., #670
Montgomery, AL 36130
(334) 242-0400, (800) 248-0033
Fax: (334) 242-2414
www.ado.state.al.us

Alaska
P.O. Box 110800
Juneau, AK 99811-0801
(907) 465-2500
Fax: (907) 465-5442
www.dced.state.ak.us

Arizona
Business Assistance Center
3800 N. Central Ave., #1500
Phoenix, AZ 85012
(602) 280-1480, 602) 280-1300

(800) 542-5684
Fax: (602) 280-1339
www.commerce.state.az.us/
smallbus.htm

Arkansas
Advocacy and Business Services
One Capitol Mall
Little Rock, AR 72201
(501) 682-1060, or 501) 682-1121
Fax: (501) 682-7394
www.aedc.state.ar.us/home.htm

California
Trade and Commerce Agency
Office of Secretary/Legal
1102 Q Street, # 6000
Sacramento, CA 95814
(916) 322-1394
Fax: (916) 323-2887
www.commerce.ca.gov

Colorado
1625 Broadway, #1710
Denver, CO 80202
(303) 892-3864
Fax: (303) 892-3848
www.state.co.us/oed/sbdc

Connecticut
Economic Resource Center
805 Brook St., Bldg. 4
Rocky Hill, CT 06067
(860) 571-7136, (800) 392-2122
Fax: (860) 571-7150
www.cerc.com

Delaware
Economic Development Office
99 Kings Highway

Dover, DE 19901
(302) 739-4271
Fax: (302) 739-2028
www.state.de.us/dedo

District of Columbia
1350 Pennsylvania Ave., NW, #317
Washington, DC 20004
(202) 727-6365
Fax: (202) 727-6703
www.dc.gov/agencies/index.asp

Florida
Enterprise Florida
390 N. Orange Ave., #1300
Orlando, FL 32801
(407) 316-4600, (407) 316-4700
Fax: (407) 316-4599
www.eflorida.com/all_about.html

Georgia
Department of Community Affairs
60 Executive Park S., NE
Atlanta, GA 30329-2231
(404) 679-4940
Fax: (404) 679-4940
www.dca.state.ga.us

Hawaii
Business Action Center, 2nd Level
1130 N. Nimitz Hwy., Room A-254
Honolulu, HI 96817
(808) 586-2545
Fax: (808) 586-2544
www.hawaii.gov/dbedt/

Idaho
700 W. State Street
P.O. Box 83720
Boise, ID 83720-0093

(208) 334-2470, (800) 842-5858
Fax: (208) 334-2631
www.idoc.state.id.us

Illinois
Dept. of Commerce and
Community Affairs
Springfield-Bressmer Bldg.
3rd floor, S-3
620 E. Adams Street
Springfield, IL 62701
(217) 524-6293, (217) 524-1931
www.commerce.state.il.us

Indiana
1 N. Capitol Ave., #700
Indianapolis, IN 46204-2288
(317) 232-8800
Fax: (317) 232-4146
www.state.in.us/doc

Iowa
200 E. Grand Ave.
Des Moines, IA 50309
(515) 242-4700, (800) 532-1216
Fax: (515) 242-4809
www.state.ia.us/ided/

Kansas
Dept. of Commerce and Housing
Business Development Division
1000 SW Jackson St., #100
Topeka, KS 66612-1354
(785) 296-5298
Fax: (785) 296-3490
kdoch.state.ks.us/ProgramApp/home.jsp

Kentucky
Central Division, Hoge House
302 Wilkinson Blvd.
Frankfort, KY 40601

(502) 564-5891, (800) 847-4251
Fax: (502) 564-5932
www.edc.state.ky.us

Capitol Plaza Tower
500 Mero Street
Frankfort, KY 40601
(502) 564-7140
Fax: (502) 564-3256
www.thinkkentucky.com

Louisiana
P.O. Box 94185
Baton Rouge, LA 70804-9185
(225) 342-3000
Fax: (225) 342-5349
www.lded.state.la.us

Maine
Dept. of Economic and Community
Development
59 Statehouse Station
Augusta, ME 04333-0059
(207) 624-9804, (800) 872-3838
Fax: (207) 287-5701
www.econdevmaine.com/

Maryland
Division of Regional Development
217 E. Redwood St., 10th floor
Baltimore, MD 21202
(410) 762-3376
Fax: (410) 338-1836
www.mdbusiness.state.md.us/
business/offices.asp

Massachusetts
Office of Business Development
10 Park Plaza, #3720
Boston, MA 02116
(617) 973-8686, (617) 973-8600

Fax: (617) 973-8600
www.state.ma.us/mobd

Michigan
300 N. Washington Square
Lansing, MI 48913
(517) 373-9808
Fax: (517) 335-0198
www.michigan.gov

Minnesota
Small Business Assistance Office
121 7th Place, E., #500
St. Paul, MN 55101
(651) 282-2103, (800) 657-3858
Fax: (651) 296-1290
www.dted.state.mn.us

Mississippi
Division of Existing Industry and
Business
P.O. Box 849
Jackson, MS 39205-0849
(601) 359-3593
Fax: (601) 359-3458
www.mississippi.org

Missouri
P.O. Box 118
301 W. High St., Room 720
Jefferson City, MO 65101
(573) 751-2863
Fax: (573) 526-2416
www.ecodev.state.mo.us/mbac

Montana
1424 Ninth Ave.
Helena, MT 59601
(406) 444-3797
Fax: (406) 444-2903
www.montana.gov

www.commerce.state.mt.us

Nebraska
301 Centennial Mall S.
P.O. Box 94666
Lincoln, NE 68509-4666
(402) 471-3111, (800) 426-6505
Fax: (402) 471-3778
www.neded.org/

Nevada
Department of Business and
Industry
Center for Business Advocacy
555 E. Washington Ave., #4900
Las Vegas, NV 89101
(702) 486-2750
Fax: (702) 486-2758
www.dbi.state.nv.us/

New Hampshire
Office of Business and Industrial
Development
172 Pembroke Rd.
Concord, NH 03302-1856
(603) 271-2341
Fax: (603) 271-6784
www.dred.state.nh.us/
www.nheconomy.com

New Jersey
P.O. Box 820
20 State St.
Trenton, NJ 08625
(609) 292-2146, (888) 239-1288
Fax: (609) 292-9145
www.newjersey.gov/njbiz/y_small
bus_offsmbus.shtml

New Mexico
P.O. Box 20003

345

1100 St. Francis Dr.
Santa Fe, NM 87504
(505) 827-0300, (800) 374-3061
Fax: (505) 827-0407
www.edd.state.nm.us

New York
Empire State Development
30 South Pearl St.
Albany, NY 12245
(800) 782-8369
Fax: (518) 474-1515
www.empire.state.ny.us

North Carolina
SB and Technology Development
Center
5 West Hargett St., #600
Raleigh, NC 27601-1348
(919) 715-7272, (800) 258-0862
Fax: (919) 715-7777
www.sbtdc.org

North Dakota
University of North Dakota Center
for Innovation
Rural Technology Incubator
P.O. Box 8372
4300 Dartmouth Dr.
Grand Forks, ND 58202
(701) 777-3132
Fax: (701) 777-2339
www.innovators.net

Ohio
One-Stop Business Center
P.O. Box 1001
77 S. High St., 28th floor
Columbus, OH 43216-1001
(614) 644-4232

Fax: (614) 466-0829
www.ohio.gov
www.odod.state.oh.us/onestop/

Oklahoma
Dept. of Commerce
OKC Metro
P.O. Box 26980
900 N. Stiles Ave.
Oklahoma City, OK 73126-0980
(405) 815-6552, (800) 879-6552
Fax: (405) 815-5142
www.odoc.state.ok.us

Oregon
775 Summer St. NE, #200
Salem, OR 97301-1280
(503) 986-0123, (800) 233-3306
Fax: (503) 581-5115
www.econ.state.or.us

Pennsylvania
Small Business Resource Center
Commonwealth Keystone Bldg.
400 N Street, 4th floor
Harrisburg, PA 17120-0225
(717) 783-5700
Fax: (717) 234-4560
www.inventpa.com

Rhode Island
1 W. Exchange St.
Providence, RI 02903
(401) 222-2601
Fax: (401) 222-2102
www.riedc.com

South Carolina
Enterprise Inc.
P.O. Box 1149
Columbia, SC 29202

(803) 252-8806
Fax: (803) 252-0455
www.myscgov.com

South Dakota
711 E. Wells Ave.
Pierre, SD 57501-3369
(605) 773-5032, (800) 872-6190
Fax: (605) 773-3256
www.sdgreatprofits.com/

Tennessee
Small Business Service
William R. Snodgrass TN Tower
312 8th Ave. North, 11th floor
Nashville, TN 37243-0405
(615) 741-2626
Fax: (615) 532-8715
www.state.tn.us/ecd/con_bsv.htm

Texas
Office of Small Business Assistance
P.O. Box 12728
1700 N. Congress Ave
Austin, TX 78711-2728
(512) 936-0100
Fax: (512) 936-0435
www.tded.state.tx.us/SmallBusiness/

Utah
324 S. State Street, #500
Salt Lake City, UT 84111
(801) 538-8700
Fax: (801) 538-8888
www.dced.state.ut.us

Vermont
National Life Building
Drawer 20
Montpelier, VT 05620-0501
(802) 828-3211

Fax: (802) 828-3258
www.state.vt.us/dca/
www.thinkvermont.com

Virginia
Dept. of Business Assistance
Development Center Network
707 E. Main St., #300
Richmond, VA 23219 or
P.O. Box 446
Richmond, VA 23218-0446
(804) 371-8200
Fax: (804) 225-3384
www.dba.state.va.us/smdev/

Washington
Community Trade and Economic
Development
Business Assistance Division
210-11th Ave. SW, #101
Olympia, WA 98504-2500
(360) 725-5050
Fax: (360) 586-0873
www.busdev.wa.gov/

West Virginia
Capitol Complex, Bldg. 6
1900 Washington St. E.
Room 553
Charleston, WV 25305-0311
(304) 558-2234
Fax: (304) 558-0449
www.wvdo.org/

Wisconsin
201 W. Washington Ave.
Madison, WI 53717
(608) 266-1018
Fax: (608) 267-2829
www.commerce.state.wi.us

Wyoming
Wyoming Business Council
214 West 15th Street
Cheyenne, WY 82001
(307) 777-2800, (800) 262-3425
Fax: (307) 777-2838
www.wyomingbusiness.org

Glossary

balloon payment. A single, usually final, payment on a loan that is much greater than the payments preceding it; some business loans, for example, require interest-only payments the first year or two, followed by a single large payment that repays all the principal.

branding. The marketing practice of creating a name, symbol, or design that identifies and differentiates a product from other products; well-known brands include Tide, Dockers, and Twinkies.

business concept. The basic idea around which a business is built; for instance, FedEx is built on the idea of overnight delivery, while Amazon.com is built around the idea of selling books over the internet.

cash conversion cycle. The amount of time it takes to transform your cash outlays into cash income; for a manufacturer, the number of days or weeks required to purchase raw materials and turn them into inventory, then sales, and, finally, collections.

competitive advantage. Factor or factors that make one company, product or service different from and better than other offerings; lower price, higher quality, and better name recognition are examples.

co-op promotion. Arrangement between two or more businesses to cross-promote their enterprises to customers.

current assets. Assets likely to be turned into cash within a year.

current liabilities. Amounts you owe and are to pay in less than a year, such as accounts payable to suppliers and short-term loans.

349

due diligence. Actions an investor should do to check out an investment's worthiness; it has a legal definition when applied to the responsibilities of financial professionals, such as stockbrokers; in general, it includes such things as requiring audited financial statements and checking warehouses for claimed inventory stocks.

EBIT. Acronym for earnings before interest and taxes, an accounting term for a company's operational earnings separate from the effects of interest payments and taxation.

electronic commerce. Selling products and services through sites on the World Wide Web; also called e-commerce.

electronic data interchange. A computer-to-computer link-up of ordering and inventory systems between manufacturers and retailers; also called EDI.

executive summary. Section of a business plan that briefly describes what the rest of the plan contains.

factoring. The flip side of trade credit; what happens when a supplier sells its accounts receivables to a financial specialist called a factor; the factor immediately pays the amount of the receivables, less a discount, and receives the payments when they arrive from customers; an important form of finance in many industries.

goal. Short-term objective, usually incorporating firm time deadlines and quantifiable measures.

kaizen. Japanese term, popular in the 1980s and early 1990s that means continuous improvement that seeks to constantly obtain small gains in productivity and quality over a long period, producing greater long-term gains.

leverage. The use of borrowed funds to increase purchasing power.

lifestyle entrepreneur. Someone who starts a business for the sake of ownership or flexibility as opposed to the desire to build a large enterprise or become wealthy.

limited liability corporation. Business legal structure resembling an S corporation but allowing owners more flexibility in dividing up profits while still providing protection from liability; abbreviated LLC.

liquidity. A description of a company's ability to convert noncash assets, such as inventory and accounts receivable, into cash; essentially, the company's ability to pay its bills.

logistics. The science of moving objects, such as product inventory, from one location to another.

mission statement. A sentence describing a company's function, markets, and competitive advantages.

objectives. Long-term aims, frequently representing the ultimate level to which you aspire.

organization, functional. A company or other entity with a structure that divides authority along functions such as marketing, finance, etc.; these functions cross product lines and other boundaries.

organization, line and staff. A company or other entity with a structure calling for staff managers, like planners and accountants, to act as advisors supporting a line manager, such as the operations vice president.

organization, line. A company or other entity with a structure divided by product lines, means of production, industries served, etc.; each line may have its own support staff for the various functions.

outsourcing. Having a component or service performed or supplied by an outside firm such as a manufacturer, wholesaler, or broker; used to reduce time and money costs for support work and add flexibility in production staffing.

positioning. Marketing tool that describes a product or service in reference to its position in the marketplace; for example, the newest, smallest, cheapest, second-largest, etc.

psychographics. Market researchers' attempt to accurately measure lifestyle by classifying customers according to their activities, interest, and opinions.

rate of return. The income or profit earned by an investor on capital invested into a company; usually expressed as an annual percentage.

rich text format. Standard word-processing format in which most plan-writing software allows you to export your work; also called RTF.

strategy. The steps you plan to implement to achieve your business objectives.

subordinated. Term usually applied to a debt and meaning its claim on the debtor's assets comes second to another's claim; senior subordinated debt has a claim before junior subordinated debt; preferred debt is the opposite of subordinated—it gets first claim.

trade credit. Accounts payable representing bills owed to suppliers; typical trade credit terms allow payment in 30 days without penalty; an important source of financing for many companies.

turnaround. A reversal in a company's fortunes, taking it from near death to robust health; for example, in the 1970s, Chrysler had to be bailed out by the federal government, then in the 1980s, Chrysler turned around, and Daimler-Benz bought the revived company in what was then history's biggest industrial buyout.

unique selling proposition. The factor or consideration presented by a seller as the reason that one product or service is different from and better than the competition.

vision statement. A sentence or two describing a company's long-range aims, such as achieving dominant market share or attaining a reputation for world-class quality.

working capital. The amount of money a business has in cash, accounts receivable, inventory, and other current assets; normally refers to net working capital, which is current assets minus current liabilities.

Index

353

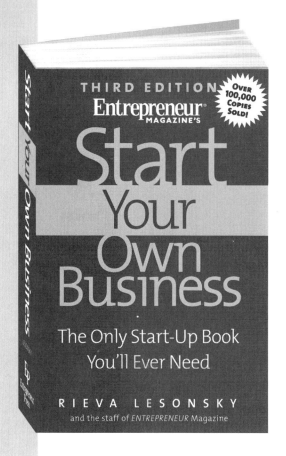